Reflexive mediation

– with a sustainable perspective

危

机

"The Chinese view of conflict or crisis is dialectic. A crisis has both a beginning and an end; it contains dangers as well as opportunities, and this is shown in the Chinese character for 'crisis', which is composed of the characters for both these concepts.
Our word 'crisis' is derived from the same word in Greek – crisis, meaning decision, judgement."

Vibeke Vindeløv

Reflexive mediation

– with a sustainable perspective

Translated by Steven Harris

DJØF Publishing
2012

Vibeke Vindeløv
Reflexive mediation
– with a sustainable perspective
Translated by Steven Harris

Print: Narayana Press, Gylling
Binding: Jysk Bogbind, Holstebro

Printed in Denmark 2011
ISBN 978-87-574-2086-9

Sold and distributed in Scandinavia by:
DJØF Publishing
Copenhagen, Denmark
Email: forlag@djoef.dk
www.djoef-forlag.dk

Sold and distributed in North America by:
International Specialized Book Services (ISBS)
Portland, USA
Email: orders@isbs.com
www.isbs.com

Sold in all other countries by:
The Oxford Publicity Partnership Ltd
Towcester, UK
Email: djof@oppuk.co.uk
www.oppuk.co.uk

Distributed in all other countries by:
Marston Book Services
Abingdon, Oxon, UK
Email: trade.orders@marston.co.uk
www.marston.co.uk

Table of contents

Foreword ... 13
Whom does this book address? ... 15
The structure of the book and how it should be used ... 16

Chapter 1. Conflict mediation with a reflexive approach – an introduction . 19

Chapter 2. Underlying values and assumptions ... 31
I. Values and assumptions ... 31
Individuality and relations ... 34
Mutual interdependence leads to shared responsibility ... 35
II. Paradigms ... 37
III. Short descriptions of the six well-known models ... 41
a. The problem-solving, settlement-focused model ... 41
b. The cognitive model ... 42
c. The transformative model ... 43
d. The narrative model ... 44
e. The humanistic model ... 44
f. The organic model ... 45
IV. The reflexive model ... 45

Part 1. Key concepts for mediation ... 49

Chapter 3. An overview ... 51
I. The basic principles of mediation ... 51
II. Definition of conflict mediation ... 52
III. Structure and flexibility ... 55
IV. The conduct of the meeting ... 56

Chapter 4. Conflicts and their escalation 57
Introduction 57
I. The concept of conflict 58
Conflicts in context 63
Reactions to conflict 63
II. The cycle of conflict and the ripe moment 65
III. The dimensions of a conflict 66
IV. Psychological factors in a conflict 71
V. Escalation 78
Step 1: Disagreement 79
The interface of conflict 79
Step 2: Personification 80
Step 3: The problem grows 80
Step 4: Dialogue is abandoned 80
Step 5: Images of hostility 81
Step 6: Open hostility 81
Step 7: Polarisation 81
VI. The language of escalation and de-escalation ('Me'-oriented language and seeing things from our own standpoint) 83

Chapter 5. Truth, dialogue and culture 87
I. Truth 87
II. Contact 93
III. Empathy 94
IV. Dialogue 96
V. Intercultural aspects 98

Chapter 6 Active listening and movement in communication 103
I. Positions, interests and needs 103
Interests 105
Needs 106
III. Facts and feelings 111
IV. Communication 112

Chapter 7. Negotiation 121
I. The negotiation 'minuet' 122
II. Different negotiating strategies 124
1. The competitive negotiator: meeting fire with fire 124
2. The co-operative negotiator: Who risks making concessions 125
3. The problem-solving negotiator: firm on the case and open to the person. . 127
4. The Tit-for-Tat Strategy 131
III. Effective negotiation requires preparation 132
IV. Negotiating strength 134
V. BATNA 137
VI. Causes of failed negotiations 138

Chapter 8. Voluntariness and confidentiality 143
I. Voluntariness 143
II. Confidentiality 144

Chapter 9. Neutrality and impartiality 149
I. Understanding the concepts 149
II. Neutrakty in international conflicts 153
III. The manager as mediator 155

Chapter 10. Power and justice 157
I. Introduction 157
II. Power 157
1. Distinations in power 158
III. Power in mediation 162
IV. Justice 163
1. The concept of justice 164
b. Justice in the courts and in mediation 167

Chapter 11. Reconciliation 171
I. Trust and reconciliation 171
II. When is reconciliation relevant? – an individual perspective 173
III. The basis for reconciliation 175
IV Reconciliation in a societal context 178

Chapter 12. Mediation in international conflicts and the link between major and minor conflicts ... 183
I. Introduction ... 183
II. The link between international conflicts and individual conflicts ... 184
III. Explanation of concepts ... 185
IV. Differencer between the micro and macro level ... 187
1. Escalation ... 187
2. Neutrality ... 189
3. Difficult negotiations ... 191
V. The solution of international conflicts ... 192
VI. Dilemmas over the choice of form of conflict resolution ... 198
VII. The traditional and the new paradigms in international conflicts ... 200

Chapter 13. Ethics and liability ... 205
I. The expert and the reflective practitioner ... 206
Discussion ... 213
The reflective practitioner ... 216
II. Ethics ... 219
a. Standards for the professional conduct of mediators ... 219
b. Professional ethics ... 221
c. The mediator's personal ethical standards ... 223
III. Mediators' liability ... 226

Part 2. A practical step by step description of mediation ... 229

Chapter 14. Before the meeting ... 231
I. The initiative for mediation ... 231
II. What kinds of conflict are suitable for mediation? ... 233
III. Consent to mediation ... 234
IV. What information should the mediator have? ... 234
V. Who should take part in mediation? ... 236
VI. Payment ... 237
VII. Where and when? ... 237
VIII. Physical preparations ... 239
IX. Mental preparations ... 240
X. One or more mediators? ... 241
XI. Mediation in groups – multiparty mediation ... 242

Chapter 15. Stage 1: Opening – The first joint meeting 245
I. Creating a good atmosphere 245
II. Welcome, seating and presentation 246
III. Information about the mediation process, rules of conduct 248

Chapter 16. Stage 2: The submissions of the parties and dialogue 253
I. How to reveal the underlying interests and needs of parties in conflict? 258
1. Power in mediation 261
2. How the mediator involves the question of justice 265
3. Separate meetings (Caucuses) 268
4. Often mentioned reasons for use of separate meetings: 269
II. Who, where and how 273
III. Confidentiality in separate meetings 275
IV. The transition from separate meetings to a joint meeting 278
V. Manipulation and separate meetings 278
VI. Aids for the mediator 279

Chapter 17. Stage 3: Defining the problem areas and setting the agenda 283

Chapter 18. Stage 4: Generating possible solutions 287
I. Brainstorming 287
II. How to help the parties on their way 291
III. Separate meetings 293

Chapter 19. Stage 5: Negotiating the agreement 295
I. Introduction 295
II. Aids for the mediator in the negotiating phase 297
a. Start with the easiest – and change 298
b. Look at the agreement as a whole 298
c. Distinguish between the person and the argument 299
d. Summarising, breaks, focus on the future 299
e. Help the parties consider the best alternative 299
f. Reality testing 300
g. 'Point of despair' 301
h. Moderating high expectations 302
i. Parties in deadlock 302

j. Single text procedure ... 303
k. Legal concerns ... 304

Chapter 20. Stage 6: The agreement must be checked and approved ... 307
I. Formalising the agreement ... 308
II. Writing down the agreement ... 311
III. The good agreement ... 312
IV. The conclusion of the mediation ... 314

Chapter 21. After the meeting ... 317
I. Implementation ... 317
II. The mediator's own post-mediation conduct ... 319

Chapter 22. The parties do not keep to the agreement ... 321

Chapter 23. Problematic mediations ... 325
I. Characteristics of mediations which do not result in agreement ... 325
a. Lack of motivation ... 326
b. The absence of the real decision-maker ... 327
c. Negative atmosphere ... 328
d. Unpopular agreements ... 328
II. Tips for tackling difficult situations ... 329

Chapter 24. Lawyers and other professional advisers in mediations ... 333
I. Clarification of roles ... 333
II. Conflicts of interest ... 337
III. 'Professional brotherhood' ... 338

Postscript. Mediation in the Nordic countries – past, present and future ... 339
Conflict as Property ... 343

Annexes 347
Annex A 347
Annex B 355
Annex C 359
Annex D 363

Litterature 367

Index 377

Figures

Figure 1. The metaphor of the iceberg 22
Figure 2. Paradigms 39
Figure 3. The circular process of escalation, with action and psychological reaction 72
Figure 4. The conflict ladder 82
Figure 5. The 'mountains' of positions 104
Figure 6. Hierarchy of interests and needs 105
Figure 7. The connection between facts and feelings 112
Figure 8. Double acknowledgement 118
Figure 9. Zero-sum negotiation 126
Figure 10. The problem-solving negotiation 127
Figure 11. ABC triangle 186
Figure 12. Expanded ABC triangle 186
Figure 13. Different settlements following wars and civil wars 204
Figure 14. Riskin's Grid 208
Figure 15. Seating for a mediation meeting 240

Foreword

Many mediators, maybe even most of us who work with mediation, started with a desire to contribute to a more peaceful and more just world – neither more nor less.

This is where mediators get their enthusiasm, the energy to be pioneers, to go against the stream and work for something they believe is better. There may have been personal sacrifices in terms of careers, and maybe also in terms of families, some may even have risked their lives, but what has kept many mediators going, no matter what kind of mediation they are dealing with is, that they believe in what they are doing.

However, we all meet challenges, no matter our field of mediation. Whether we work in the courts and feel under pressure to be efficient and to meet budgets and expectations from the system and our colleagues; whether we work at a political level and are challenged by political power games and misinterpretations or the public's unrealistic expectations; or whether we work at NGO level, where lack of resources and personal rivalries can become obstacles – even life-threatening – it all makes our work difficult at times.

How do we as mediators ensure that our beliefs are not distracted or obstructed by these challenges? How do we as mediators keep our enthusiasm and prevent our work from becoming dull and 'just a job' like any other job? How do we avoid falling into the trap of doing exactly the same as those we want to provide an alternative to? How do we maintain the qualities of mediation?

This author believes it is time for mediators to look further than merely discussing skills, techniques and models, and to take up the personal challenge and responsibility of being conscious of the deeper values and beliefs that drive us, and then constantly, during and after each mediation, to evaluate what we did and how we did it. Just as we, in mediation, believe that the ultimate responsibility for reaching a satisfactory outcome to a conflict belongs to the parties, so we must be willing to take the responsibility for preserving mediation as a unique process, as it was when we started.

If we consider the value of mediation to society, it must be compared with other methods for dealing with conflicts, including court litigation. Traditionally, the role of the courts has been to enforce important social rights and to ensure that important rights and obligations are respected. Courts should act as a bulwark against uncivilised and criminal behaviour, and maintain order. This function, the maintenance of order, is not a promise of paradise; it is the minimum required for establishing social harmony. The courts thus provide a formal framework and act as enforcers of civilised behaviour.

Society cannot get by without this enforcer, and mediation cannot be a substitute for conflict resolution via the courts. But if mediation and litigation are to retain their special qualities, this will require the protection of the basic values on which each of court proceedings and mediation are built, as expressed in the two paradigms described in Chapter 2.

In his book *Hvorfor Demokrati?(Why Democracy?)*, published in 1946 shortly after World War II, Alf Ross concluded his reflections by describing 'democracy's future as the fateful question of our time'.[1] Ross concluded that 'in the end, the outcome of this rests on the power of the democratic ideals over the minds of men, ideals which are ultimately based on respect for individuals and the inner sense of connectedness of each man with his fellow man.'[2]

It is now more than 60 years since the end of World War II, but this statement is no less relevant. The long dominance of the Western world is being challenged on all fronts by what was previously called the 'third world'; climate change and the exhaustion of fossil fuels are developing faster than we can foresee; the world's population is expanding; there is starvation and so on, and so on. Sometimes one can fear that, rather than improving the world, humankind is set on a course towards a more comprehensive global collapse than we have ever experienced. At the same time, everything indicates that we have the political, economic and technological tool to make it possible to implement the reforms that are necessary to deal with these changes. Why doesn't it happen – or perhaps more optimistically, where shall we find the key to the solution of the paradox that confronts us, that we know the problems, we have the solutions but we don't apply them?

As far as I can see, the outward and inward changes go together, and an inescapably necessary component of a comprehensive solution to the situation, which is both threatening and promising, in which the human race finds itself is the development of feelings of solidarity between peoples. This means that the connection must not merely be acknowledged outwardly; climate change and its associated problems, and the problems of international crime etc. cross borders. But these problems also cannot be solved unless we acknowledge inwardly their connectedness, and thus the feeling of responsibility for solving these problems. Thus,

1. Alf Ross 1946, p. 367. An English translation was published in 1952 under the title *Why Democracy?*
2. Ross, 1946, p. 368.

one can talk of the viability as well as sustainability of both outward and inward components, which are equally important, and on sustainability in a broad sense.

Mediation fits well into this context. Even though, naturally, mediation cannot 'save the world', an approach to conflicts in which one recognises the needs both of the individual and of society and the essential connection between them – in both major and minor conflicts – is a necessary development. The reflexive model thereby takes a longer view and has a sustainable perspective. As such, the motivation which was once the driving force behind my interest in mediation has developed to become a more deeply rooted conviction of its necessity. Thus, mediation remains the alternative to the legal treatment of conflicts that was intended from the start and which it should continue to be.

After training as a lawyer and as a psychotherapist, I have worked for many years in mediation and conflict resolution as a practitioner, researcher, teacher at the Faculty of Law at the University of Copenhagen, as a volunteer in various NGOs and as both an NGO and an official representative in several international contexts, most notably the Former Yugoslavia, and recently in Kenya, as well as a trainer of both UN and African Union representatives and participants in liberation movements. It seems obvious to me that mediation and conflict resolution are inseparable. It is equally obvious that theory and practice are inseparably linked in the treatment of these subjects. Finally, my international experience has shown me the undeniable connection between conflicts between individuals and international conflicts.

The mediation model which is the subject of this book largely refers to the same respect and sense of connectedness as was referred to earlier by Alf Ross. The model can therefore be interpreted as part of a democratic development, so one may hope that this model will have sufficiently favourable conditions to thrive in the future. However, with modesty, it must be added, with reference to Larry Fong, that this book does not claim the prize but is only a step in the right direction.[3]

Whom does this book address?

This book is a textbook. Many textbooks from many different parts of the world describe a process corresponding to the one described in this book. In this respect this book is not unusual. However, what distinguishes this book from most other books on mediation is the way it links together the now classical elements of the mediation process with the explicit values and attitudes of the mediator, and regardless of whether these concern technical matters, philosophical attitudes or

3. Haynes, Haynes & Fong, *Mediation*, 2004, p 21.

values, and regardless of the type of conflict which is the subject of mediation or who the parties to the mediation are, these must guide and motivate the mediator.

The book is not written as a heavyweight scientific thesis. There are two reasons for this: first it is hoped that the book will be reasonably accessible for as wide a readership as possible and second, and more important, the book should not have the appearance of being a narrowly focused objective presentation of mediation and conflict resolution, as is the custom with the more scientific literature. As is stated, mediation and conflict resolution are not subjects about which one can be 'neutral'. Values and concepts such as fairness, truth, power and neutrality etc. will always have a role to play, not just for the parties involved, but also for the mediator.

However, the book includes enough theory to give a reasonable basis for the training of a mediator. But theory alone is not enough – one only becomes a mediator through practice and yet more practice, so the teaching of theory must always be supported by practical exercises. The education of a mediator is a lifelong process – as one learns through the practice of mediation. Apart from acquiring the insight and knowledge that is offered here, mediators also have to find their own style – it is only in this way that they can be authentic.

The structure of the book and how it should be used

The aim of this book is to guide prospective mediators through the mediation process. Because of this educational aim, this book is structured as if the process is schematic, with each phase easily identifiable, but this is far from always being the case in practice.

After many years work as a mediator, including work with major international conflicts, the connection between these has become ever more clear, and it is important that this connection is recognised. For this reason, even though the main focus of this book is on direct conflicts between a few parties, discussion of conflicts between groups and conflicts at international level will often be referred to.

The first two chapters look at the values and assumptions which lie behind the practice of mediation. Part I deals with concepts of a more general nature, such as justice, power, neutrality etc., which are always actualised in the mediation process.

The practical step by step description of mediation in Part II, comes after the survey of the general concepts in Part I, so that their applicability can be illustrated in the practical review of the mediation process.

If, in the book, a mediator is sometimes referred to as 'he' and sometimes as 'she', this has no deep significance. Good mediators can be either male or female.

In the course of my work with mediation and conflict resolution I have received inspiration, knowledge and help from many quarters. The Faculty of Law at the University of Copenhagen, has encouraged me to develop this subject so that today it not only includes topics that are demanded by many law students, but for the last 10 years it has formed the basis for a successful government-approved interdisciplinary adult education programme for older professionals, the Master in Mediation and Conflict Resolution (MMCR). I am sincerely grateful for the support I have received and the flexibility shown by the Faculty.

Next, my association with the NGO, the Danish Center for Conflict Resolution since it was set up in 1994 has inspired me to work on the similarities between big conflicts and small conflicts, work which I have carried forward in cooperation with the Swedish Folke Bernadotte Academy (under the Swedish Foreign Ministry) which is committed to increasing understanding of the need for dialogue, also in the case of violent conflicts. Over the last couple of years, involvement in Kenya in connection with the Wangari Maathai Institute in Nairobi has given me the opportunity to work with both Danish and Kenyan colleagues.[4] Our joint project, Stabilizing Kenya by Solving Forest Related Conflicts, is a combination of cross-discipline, theory and practice, which is close to my heart.

Finally, a number of people have been important in the making of this book, in particular Lin Adrian, Ole Wæver and Melanie Helene Andersen. I thank them all. Steven Harris has undertaken the translation of the book, and in doing so he has not only translated but has contributed many helpful suggestions.

4. Wangari Maathai was former Professor of Agriculture at Nairobi University, was Minister for the Environment, founded the NGO Green Belt Movement, and in 2004 received the Nobel Peace Prize. Wangari Maathai sadly passed away in September 2011.

CHAPTER 1

Conflict mediation with a reflexive approach – an introduction

The reflexive model is characterised by being eclectic, though not in the sense that 'anything goes' as long as it works. It is eclectic because it allows for inspiration to be drawn from all the models described below and to use elements of them in practice, since what is of most importance to mediation is the values and assumptions that motivate the mediator and which are developed in the course of the mediation – neither more nor less. This means that the reflexive model is not something external, put on like a coat and taken off again after training; it is internal, concerned with mediator's world view and the values which are integrated in and which are part of the mediator, both in mediation and outside mediation. This is the second and most important reason for using the term 'the reflexive model'.

As it would be unreasonable to encourage reflection and to describe this form of conflict mediation in a book without at the same time being explicit about the values in relation to which there should be reflection, it is also necessary to make the underlying values clear here.

For some people these values and beliefs feel suitable right away, for others they are something which they come to experience over time as being significant and true, and for yet others they are just empty assertions, which are out of place in the real world. The reflexive model is not for people in this last group, and they must seek inspiration from one of the other well-known models.

It is not the intention, with this book, to impose on others the values described. But there can only be reflection if one is conscious of one's values and, at least as the basis for a book, if one is explicit about them. Once that is done, it is up to each to choose his or her own path.

At the same time, it is only fair to say that the values described here are derived from an understanding of the necessity of everyone acting more considerately than previously which means, among other things, that we must be aware of our mutual interdependence, both individually and globally, and we must be ready to take on our share of the responsibility for this.

The best known models in the schools of thought among mediators are the problem-solving model[1], the transformative model[2], the cognitive model[3], the narrative model[4], the humanistic model[5] and most recently the organic model[6]. All these models have been developed and described in the USA, Canada, the UK or New Zealand, and they are usually characterised by rejecting elements of other known models while introducing new elements, to which decisive importance is attached. For example, in the problem-solving model the emphasis is on interests and needs, but these are rejected in the narrative model, just as the transformative model attaches a lot of importance to the feelings

1. Formulated by the Harvard Negotiation Project and based on Fisher & Ury's best-selling book *Getting to Yes*, and for example demonstrated by Lawrence Susskind, 'Environmental Mediation and The Accountability Problem', *Vermont law Review* 1981B 6 (1) pp. 46-47; and L. Susskind & J. Cruikshank, *Breaking the Impasse*, Harvard 1987.
2. Formulated by Baruch Bush & Joe Folger, *The Promise of Mediation*, 1994 and 2005.
3. Formulated by Larry Fong in Haynes, Haynes & Fong, *Mediation* 2004.
4. Formulated by John Winslade & Gerald Monk, *Narrative Mediation; A New Approach to Conflict Resolution*, 2000.
5. Mark Umbreit, 'Humanistic Mediation: A Transformative Journey of Peacemaking', *Mediation Quarterly* 1997.
6. Formulated by, among others, Frederic Luskin, Director of the Stanford Forgiveness Projects.

of the parties, while in the cognitive model feelings are regarded as disturbing for the mediation process.

The reflexive model

The reflexive model was originally referred to as the 'Scandinavian model'. However, it would be remarkable if there were not many, other than Scandinavians, who perhaps prefer one of the well-known models but might nevertheless make use of some of the elements of one or more of the other models in practice. In other words, in reality they are eclectic. This view has been confirmed in exchanges of experiences with mediators from countries outside the Nordic region, so 'Scandinavian' has now been dropped from the name of the model. The name was later changed to the 'non-model', in an attempt to emphasise that a reflexive approach is difficult to place within a model which can easily become a straight-jacket in relation to reflection which is intended to designate dynamic movement. However, in recognition of the fact that many have found the reflexive approach both useful and liberating and, on that basis, have had a need for a simple way of referring to their mediation activity, the term 'the reflexive model' has come to be used as the name which best indicates the idea behind the model.

In several places there is criticism of the idea of drawing inspiration from other models, which is understandable to the extent that an eclectic approach allows mediation to be rootless. However, it cannot be emphasised enough that the rock on which this eclectic approach must be based is in clear and explicit underlying values and assumptions.

To be invited into other people's conflicts is both a privilege and a responsibility. It is a privilege because, by obtaining insight into others' conflicts as a mediator, one has a unique opportunity for acquiring an ever-increasing insight into both human and practical conditions. And it is a responsibility because of the trust shown by the parties inviting one into their conflict-filled and often vulnerable space, and they have a justifiable expectation that one will do one's utmost not to disappoint this trust. However, it is not enough to acquire the techniques and tools which may be consistent with certain values in the learning process, and thereby consider oneself ever after to be equipped to mediate in accordance with some specific model. All too soon, one's practice will develop in the direction of one's previous training, for example as a lawyer or therapist, and one may lose sight of the values underlying mediation. This is presumably why certain mediators, often lawyers, find it acceptable to put forward their views on the strengths and weaknesses of the parties' possible solutions or even, either with or without the encouragement of the parties, make suggestions for solutions. This approach pushes mediation in the direction of becoming arbitration, in spite of the fact that, as far as is known, no mediation training, and presumably not that which the mediator/lawyer has received, has suggested that it is acceptable for a mediator to put forward suggestions for solutions or included exercises for this. On the contrary, it is more likely that the training will have emphasised the importance of the mediator refraining from such actions.

The metaphor of the iceberg

The situation can be described by using the metaphor of the iceberg:

Figure 1. The metaphor of the iceberg

If one thinks of an iceberg which, as is well known, has 10% of its volume above the water and 90% below, and if one thinks of the wind coming from the west while the current comes from the east, it is clear that the iceberg will move with the current, in other words, against the wind.

The mediator's skills and techniques are comparable with the wind, and the mediator's ethic and underlying values are comparable with the current. Regardless of how much the mediator acquires skills and techniques during training which are consistent with the underlying values, it will be the mediator's deeper motivation which will come to the fore under pressure, whether that pressure is due to the parties being difficult, time being short or the mediator having a bad day. Mediators must therefore start by being sure of their view of humanity and society and must constantly challenge themselves to test the extent to which their practice is in accordance with this view.

Mediators must have respect for the trust which the parties show in asking for their help, respect for the mediation process and the lack of rigid formality which is its characteristic (and weakness), and respect for their own integrity which must be a mediator's strength and rock during difficult situations during the mediation process. To accept this description as a reflexive approach is the beginning of the integration of these values; it is to live them.

Explicit basis of values

For those who acknowledge the values in question, this has fundamental consequences for both mediation training and practice. First, it presumes that there is an explicit basis of values, and second it presumes that the mediator is constantly relating to the extent to which these values are expressed in mediation in practice.

Obviously one may not always live up to these values as a mediator. In this case it is important to acknowledge that it is not the values there is something wrong with, but that one has met challenges which, for one reason or another, one has not been able to deal with.

Regardless of how deeply we absorb the values in question, most of us have acquired some bad habits, even in relation to our own values, and from time to time these will raise their ugly heads. Apart from being attentive to the parties, mediators should also be aware of their own thoughts, feelings, prejudices and assumptions; this is important not just at the start of the mediation process, but as part of the continuing process which, in principle, never finishes.

This does not mean there is anything wrong, for example, in giving good advice to parties, or in saying anything about the strengths and weaknesses of their proposals for solutions. It merely means that such activity is not part of mediation. For example, the parties can indicate that they want a legal evaluation of their claims but that, for various reasons, they do not want to participate in court proceedings. Naturally, it must be respected that in most kinds of conflict the parties can do what they want with their conflict. It may be that the parties do not even want to take part in ordinary arbitration, as they want a speedier process. In this case, they can of course go to a lawyer whom they trust, and ask him or her to give a view on the case; and they can decide beforehand whether they will consider the assessment of the specialist to be binding or not. There can be no objection to this.

Since there will presumably be no presentation of evidence, one could call this kind of proceeding 'an early evaluation', 'rent-a-judge', 'superficial arbitration' or 'non-binding arbitration'. All this is quite in order.

Metatheory

But to call this 'mediation' would simply be to confuse the concept, and would lead to nothing but lack of clarity. If mediation is to retain its special characteristics and maintain the standard which makes it a respectable academic as well as practical discipline, it must be based on and practised in accordance with an explicit basis of values, on a metatheory. Just as it would be inappropriate for psychologists to annex mediation, so as to turn it into a form of therapy, it would be equally inappropriate for mediation to be annexed by lawyers, whatever the nature of those lawyers.

As a rule it is often emphasised that, regardless of the form of mediation in question, the parties themselves are free to determine the outcome of the mediation and thus they also have responsibility for arriving at a solution. But in addition to this, it is up to the individual mediator, or school of mediation, to determine the extent of the parties' freedom and the degree of dominance of the role of the mediator. There is also an overwhelming agreement that mediation should take place in a closed room, with the parties and the mediator respecting confidentiality about what takes place in the mediation. This means that in principle the mediator and the parties have a free space, without the risk of disturbing intrusions from outside. Since an agreement entered into under mediation cannot be brought before any appeal tribunal, and since the parties can have greater influence on their conflict than would be the case if the matter came before the courts, the parties also surrender the protection against abuse of power which would be given by access to the courts or the possibility of an appeal. For this reason, the *framework* for the mediation process described here is not sufficient to be a substitute for the protection against abuse of power given by the court system (public proceedings, always joint meetings, evaluation of evidence, an appeals system etc.).

It is clear that mediators, who do not have formal procedural rules to rely on, as would a judge, must to a high degree confront their own assumptions about what is right and what is morally justified. Everyone who acts as a mediator expresses a certain view of life, whether openly or not, which is present in the form of attitudes, reactions, questions or conclusions about what is put before them.

Mediators cannot avoid examining what comes before them in the course of mediation in relation to the values and beliefs which they consider important, without necessarily speaking openly about it. Thus, values and beliefs have a special importance as they influence the direction of the mediation process. It is therefore important that the irrational and the subjective are also acknowledged by and for mediators, to the extent that this is possible, of course.[7]

7. Rachel M. Goldberg, 'How Our Worldview Shape our Practice', *Conflict Resolution Quarterly*, Vol. 26, No 4, 2009 p. 409 et seq., writes: 'If conflicts are shaped and changed by parties' frames, it is possible that practitioners' frames affect conflict as well.' Thus

Some readers may know that, in philosophy, it is possible to divide people into two broad categories: those who believe that people are basically good, and consider that the wrongs of the world are caused by social inequality, a repressive society, etc.; and those who emphasise that people in general are born, to use Freud's definition, with three, and only three, instincts – incest, cannibalism and murder. There is no objective truth about human nature.[8] But philosophy points towards a particular view of human nature that, whether implicitly or explicitly, is always a prerequisite for our actions and assumptions, whether these are concerned with society, religion, justice or conflict resolution in a broad sense.

One of the leading Scandinavian legal thinkers of the twentieth century, Alf Ross, described his view of human nature clearly, in his article *Credo*, in 1974:

> 'I believe in man's limitless egoism – not exactly as something great and good, but as something important, as the reality behind the words. Love between people is just a fantastical ideal, so far removed from reality that one must be blind to believe it is more than wishful thinking.
>
> ... In the same way, I believe in people's lust for power, i.e. I believe that egoism essentially takes the form of striving for power and the possibility for the ego to express itself, to show its superiority and to rule over its own fate and that of others.'[9]

There is no doubt that Ross would be highly sceptical about mediation, and that he would be fearful of the oppression of the weak by the strong.

Goldberg's concern is, that 'if a party's frame is different enough ... something of great importance or central to another's sense of self or world can be discounted, or even invisible, to a practitioner whose frame rules it out'. The consequence is that 'remaining ignorant of these dynamics or pretending that they do not exist virtually guarantee that we will unconsciously bias our processes'.

8. See *Ken Wilber*, Up from Eden, A transpersonal View of Human Evolution, Boston 1981.
9. The article is reproduced in its entirety in Isi Foighel, Hans Gemmeltoft-Hansen & Henrik Zahle (Eds.) *Ret som teknik, kunst og videnskab*, Copenhagen 1999, pp. 383-390.

View of humanity

It is impossible to say to what extent Ross's view of humanity is shared by others, whether lawyers or non-lawyers. However, what is important is that whether or not we share Ross's view, whatever our professional background, the description applies not just to others, but also to ourselves – with the undeniable need to set boundaries in our work.

It is in this setting of boundaries that we must always be aware of our underlying values. Thus, how we give or exercise power is also an important factor in assessing the practice of mediation.

In mediation, as it is described in this book, the view of humanity is more optimistic or positive than Ross's. There is a belief that, under the right conditions, people will act appropriately both for themselves and for others. Certain assumptions lie behind mediation, including that: conflicts are a part of life and, sooner or later, we have to learn to adopt a constructive attitude towards them; the parties are ultimately those who know what is best for them in their lives, because it is they who have to live with the consequences; and that it is possible to arrive at satisfactory solutions if the parties really wish it. But mediation is not naïve. Therefore, these assumptions are explicitly and inevitably linked to the way in which the mediation process is conducted. There must be a congruence of both form and content.

Attitudes towards freedom

Attitudes towards freedom are also closely linked to the view of humanity. The concept of freedom, which is a prerequisite for mediation, can mean that each person is responsible for their own fate, and that there is a desire to give priority to freedom of contract and to reduce to the minimum the power of the state to interfere in citizens' freedom of action. It is easy to caricature this approach as saying: 'You can do what you want. You don't have to pay attention to others, unless it is to your benefit.'

The concept of freedom which is used in this model of mediation is very different. It is based on the belief that one is free to choose, but that others have the same right. One cannot believe that people have a right and a duty to choose, and at the same time try to manipulate them to choose according to one's will. As understood here, a free choice will always be one made with responsibility not only for oneself, but also with *responsibility for one's fellow human beings.*

Some critics of mediation have described it as being: either a self-obsessed, egoistical option, in which the parties can agree whatever they like in a closed room, without consideration for the outside world; or as casting a veil over inequalities of power based on social class and gender.[10]

Since mediation takes place in a closed room, and the parties often have no adviser with them, the only defence against this accusation becoming reality is for the mediator to be clear also about his/her responsibility and values, and to conduct the mediation with respect for the underlying assumptions referred to above (which implies that the role of the mediator should not be at the forefront).

If one were to ask mediators in general, I am sure that at least 9 out of 10 would agree with the basic assumptions and basic principles described here. However, principles are necessary but not sufficient. This is why there is a constantly recurring debate about how far a mediator can go in directing and steering the content of mediation – which is why it is so often necessary to compare and contrast the principles one believes in with those one practices. Is it possible to be pragmatic about one's work without being pragmatic about the basic values for one's work? And if this is so, what factors will determine what kind of mediation one practices?

Presumably mediation is applicable to many kinds of conflict, and maybe to most, *if* the parties so desire. Media-

10. See, e.g. Boaventura de Sousa Santos in Abel (Ed.), *The Politics of Informal Justice*, Vol. 2, New York, 1982; Christine Harrington & Sally Enle Merry, 'Ideolgoical Production: The Making of Community Mediation', *Law and Soc. Rev.* Vol. 22, No 4, 1988 p. 713; Ch. Harrington, *Shadow Justice, The Ideology and Institutionalization of Alternatives to Court*, London, 1985; and Øystein Gjelsvik, *Konflikt, megling og legitimitet – en sociologisk undersøgelse av rettsmegling som alternatativ domstolsbehandling i sivile tvister*, Oslo 2001.

tion presumably also has great potential, *if* it is carried out responsibly.

Evaluation the basis for mediation

It is precisely these *'if's'* that call for caution. As indicated, mediation that evaluates is contrary to the assumptions described in this book. On the other hand, what is important is to evaluate the basis for mediation, actual mediations, mediators, training and so on, which is happily something which increasingly occurs in a European context.

In the following chapter there will be a more detailed survey of the values and assumptions which lie behind the reflexive model. Thereafter, there will be a description of which elements in the existing recognised models are applicable in the reflexive model.

CHAPTER 2

Underlying values and assumptions

I. Values and assumptions

The values and assumptions that underlie the reflexive model are:

- Understanding that conflicts are a part of life. Conflicts are neither good nor bad.[1] Whether they are constructive or destructive depends on how they bare tackled;
- Trusting that the parties know best what is good for them. In other words, they are the 'experts on their own lives';
- Acceptance that there is more than one reality,[2] that dialogue is both desirable in every conflict, and the mean to the end;
- Confidence that mutually satisfactory solutions can be reached if the parties wish it;
- That individuality and relations go together; and
- That mutual interdependence leads to shared responsibility.

Conflicts are a condition of life

Conflicts are a condition of life. Most of us have had bad experiences of conflicts. They lead to power struggles, pain and misery, and if it were possible, we would profoundly wish that they did not exist. We seldom think that conflicts are often the result of poor handling of disagreements, that if conflicts did not exist there would be stagnation or bore-

1. See Chapter 4.
2. See Chapter 5.

dom, or that the result would be repression. The very essence of democracy is the existence of disagreements about different approaches to life which are resolved by a democratic process rather than by repression. It is an illusion to imagine that there could be life without disagreements and conflicts. Thus, even if it is often a post-rationalisation, we must accept that it is not conflicts in themselves that are bad, but the way we sometimes deal with them, which can either be constructive or destructive.

Experts on their own lives

The parties are the experts on their own lives. To trust that the parties are experts on their own lives is presumably one of the assumptions which it is most difficult to realise in practice. For most people who work with conflicts professionally, it does not take long from the presentation of a problem for a view to begin to be formed, either consciously or unconsciously, about what is wrong and how best to solve the problem – a solution which, in our eyes, is naturally more sensible and more responsible than the solution the parties are thinking of. However, it is easy to overlook the fact that it is the parties and not we who must live with the outcome of the conflict. Our task therefore is not to reject the irrationalities of the parties, but rather to accept and even to encourage them so they become explicit, so the parties' attention may be drawn to the irrationality of their expectations and demands, so they may arrive at solutions which are more sustainable. If mediators can restrain their views and continue the mediation with an open mind, they will often be surprised by the solutions which the parties can arrive at by themselves, and which time and again have an entirely different content and are much more creative than those which the mediator might have conceived, and are therefore much more acceptable to the parties who have full ownership of the solution.

If one is in a supervisory relationship, for example as the manager for the parties, one may naturally have one's own interest in the resolution of the conflict. In this case one is neither neutral nor independent. In Chapter 9 there is a discussion of the special conditions that apply when a manager acts as a mediator.

More than one reality

Acceptance that there is more than one reality. Generally, we all tell of our experiences as if they are objective truths. Some narratives are purely factual, while others, perhaps most, tell of events combined with an interpretation of the events. Even though we know that it is impossible to describe social relations objectively, we nevertheless argue as if it were possible. 'Either I'm right in my description, or you are.' The mediation process reveals, step by step, that the parties have each developed a different view of the course of events, and that one narrative does not exclude the other.[3]

Dialogue is desirable

That dialogue is desirable in every conflict. As their stories are told, each party gains greater insight into how the other party could have perceived the events as they did. The essence of dialogue is to express what one believes, how one sees the world, and at the same time to be ready to listen to what others believe. Dialogue thus makes it possible to expand one's view of the world.

Mutually satisfactory solutions

Mutually satisfactory solutions. At the start of a mediation both parties' claims will be sharply drawn up and their only suggestion for a solution will be that the other party should change their behaviour. In other words, the solution to the conflict is in the hands of the other party. However, it is not just the other party's behaviour or claims that are considered unreasonable; the other party is an unreasonable person who has behaved unreasonably in relation to what has happened. By means of dialogue it is possible to expand one's understanding both of one's own and the other party's view of the world. Even if one still disagrees with the other's conclusions about the basis of the conflict, one will have obtained greater understanding for how the other party could have arrived at their position. This means that, following a dialogue, the parties are no longer as firmly fixed in their views as they were before, and no longer see the other party quite so much as being the problem, but the focus is shifted towards the problem itself. In this way, not only is there often an improvement in rela-

3. See Chapter 5 on truth.

tions, but there is also a release of creativity which usually means that the parties become able to create solutions which to a certain extent address the claims of both parties.[4]

Individuality and relations

The term 'relations' is often perceived as having positive connotations. But this is not always the case. Relations can just as easily be negative as positive. We deceive ourselves if we believe that there are either positive relations or else a vacuum. Whether we choose it or not, we also have relations with people we dislike and with people with whom we have conflicts. Negative relations can be just as demanding and destructive as positive relations can be rewarding and constructive. As soon as we have any interaction with another person, a relationship will arise. It is far from certain that this will generate any clear feelings. For example, most business people would probably deny that they have any relationship with trading partners with whom they have ceased dealing because of poor cooperation etc. Nevertheless, such bad relations will cause them to refrain from involving the other party in the development of a new product for example, even though it may be acknowledged that the other party has qualifications, expertise, local contacts etc. which could be advantageous. Thus, one does not get the best out of a situation by refraining from working together, not because of the lack of qualifications of the other party, but because of bad relations. Of course, it is even more obvious when former spouses 'don't have anything to talk about' because they are divorced, even though they are parents for life. Obviously, not all bad relationships can be repaired, but it is useful to understand and to accept that bad relations can be just as important as good, which is why it may be wrong to focus exclusively on the substantive issue of a mediation, not giving the parties the chance to repair or at least understand their relationship if they want to. In order to avoid any misunderstanding, it should be emphasised here that the media-

4. See Chapter 4 on escalation, and Chapter 5 on dialogue.

tor's view of human nature neither can nor should be imposed on the parties, though they will experience the mediator's practical expression of this view in the respect shown for the individual and society through the questions asked and the empathy shown to them.

Sometimes one can have the impression that we in the West attach too much importance to being independent of others. In this book this form for individualism is considered to be a distortion of human nature and an expression of the fact that we are neither in contact with others nor with ourselves. We have established a myth in which we confuse individualism with isolationism. It is impossible, without costs, to prioritise individualism at the expense of society and relationships (as in places in the West), or (as in places in the East) to prioritise society and relationships at the expense of individualism. In both cases we are 'conflict illiterates', as the Swedish peace researcher Jan Øberg has put it.[5]

This point of view means that neither the mediation whose main priority is individualism (such as the problem-solving and agreement-focused mediation model is known for), nor the mediation whose main priority is society or the family (such as the organic mediation model is known for), live up to important elements of the new paradigm on which the reflexive model is based. There is a risk that both kinds of mediation omit important parts of human nature.

In the reflexive model, the mediator has a fundamental conviction that human life is most naturally lived in a context in which there is room for both the individual and the other party or parties.

Mutual interdependence leads to shared responsibility

More and more people express an understanding that we live in a time when the political order is in a state of change. The USA is no longer the undisputed superpower it once was, and it may no longer want to be so. The long-standing

5. See Jan Øberg & Ann-Sofi Jacobsson, *Konfliktløsning, En Litteraturguide*, Lund 1994; and Vibeke Vindeløv, *The Ecology of Mind*, Retfærd 1994.

dominance of the West as a whole is being challenged by what used to be called the 'Third World'. Climate change and the lack of resources of fossil fuel are developing faster than we can imagine, and so on. For many of us these changes give rise to feelings that human society is on the way to more a comprehensive global collapse than we have ever known. At the same time, everything indicates that we have the political, economic and technological potential to carry out the reforms that are necessary to deal with these changes. Why doesn't this happen? Or, perhaps more optimistically, where shall we find the key to resolve the paradox that consists in the fact that we know the problems, we have the possible solutions, but we don't use them?

The Danish author and historian of ideas, Jes Bertelsen writes in his book *Et essay om indre frihed* (An essay on inner freedom), that we must recognise that external and internal freedom go together. We cannot establish a better external world without changing our internal world. We cannot transform the life of a person – or a nation – just by changing the external circumstances. Nor can this be done by changing the internal circumstances alone. But since the world we live in directs its attention first and foremost to the external, physical reality, and thus away from the bodies, hearts and minds which the changes essentially concern, it is the aim of this book to draw attention to the overlooked but necessary component of an overall solution to the both threatening and promising situation which humankind faces – the development of feelings of solidarity between people.[6]

This goal cannot be achieved without a change of attitude. And we who work with conflicts have experienced that changes in attitude can overcome even the most difficult obstacles, and with common help and support it is possible to create positive and enduring changes.

Even though, for some people, this may seem unrealistic or even pretentious, this book maintains that acknowl-

6. Jes Bertelsen, *Et essay om Frihed*, Rosinante, 2010 p 9.

edgement of a change of attitude is an unavoidable necessity.

We have to find new ways not merely in relation to climate change, but also in relation to over-population, poverty, access to resources, whether in the form of water, food, land, money etc. We have to find solutions *together*, recognising that we are linked to each other, and are therefore not only highly interdependent on each other, but that also we all have a shared responsibility.[7]

And global changes are dependent on changes of each individual's attitude to the problems. At the intellectual level it appears that we have understood the mutual interdependence that characterises the world – the recognition that everything hangs together. But we fail to understand this at the level of action, and that each one of us must bear our share of the responsibility – without being sectarian about it. The resolution of conflicts from a sustainable perspective means that we too, when we are involved in personal conflicts, must think in terms of mutual interdependence, of the balance between individual wants and needs and the needs of the other party and of common needs. Global change is dependent on and begins in change at the level of the individual.

II. Paradigms[8]

The values described above can be described as a cohesive whole, which is best illustrated when it is compared with its opposite, the handling of conflicts by the courts, which often reflects the general approach to conflict resolution in western society. Litigation is characterised by authoritative norms and has a different starting point for understanding conflicts and a different sense of community.

7. Steen Hildebrandt & Michael Stubberup, *Bæredygtig Ledelse - ledelse med hjertet*, Gyldendal Business, 2010 p. 210
8. For the original explanation of these paradigms, the reader is referred to Vibeke Vindeløv, *Konflikt, Tvist og Mægling*, (Conflict, Dispute and Mediation (with English Summary)) 1997 p. 472 et seq.

It should be emphasised that this opposition of characteristics does not imply that one method for resolving conflicts is better than the other. It would be wholly unrealistic to imagine that mediation could totally displace the court system. There is no doubt that there will continue to be a need for traditional courts for many years to come, and perhaps forever. But for the first, it is argued that both mediation and litigation would be best served by them both being conducted in as 'pure' a form as possible. Clarity about the processes would benefit both parties and practitioners. Next, it is argued that it would be desirable for mediation to be given a status which is more equal with that of the courts, or some other conflict resolution system in the traditional paradigm, so they could act as true alternatives to each other.

Two paradigms

The characteristics of litigation and mediation are set out below in two paradigms, giving an overarching framework of understanding. The paradigm for the courts is called 'traditional', as it has been dominant in western culture for many years, and not just in the context of the courts themselves. The paradigm for mediation is called 'new', because the system described here is more recent in a western context, and it does not correspond to what is recognisable in mediation in earlier times or in 'original cultures'. In these contexts, the community will often be given significance at the cost of the individual, i.e., not in harmony with, but subordinating the individual.[9]

Parties' views of conflicts

The first line describes the parties' views of conflicts. In the traditional view conflicts are considered troublesome, perhaps negative, and they should be eliminated. In the new paradigm, conflicts are regarded as a condition of life, to which one should have as constructive approach as pos-

9. See, for example, Vibeke Vindeløv, 'Japan som med- og modspiller i civilretlige konflikter' (Japan as co- and counterpart in civil law conflicts), *TfR* 1990, pp. 889-906; and Vibeke Vindeløv, 'Ecology of Mind as a Decisive Basis in Conflict Resolution – A Preliminary Comparison between Japan and Denmark', Copenhagen 1994, op. cit. *TfR* 1994, pp. 66-77.

sible. Both attitudes are a basis for and a consequence of the other elements in the paradigms.

In the next line, in the traditional paradigm the parties are seen as being in opposition to each other. They are not regarded as and do not see the situation as being part of a wider context. They can be seen as having a certain animosity or even hostility towards each other. In the new paradigm the parties are aware they are part of a wider context. This does not mean that they are friends, they can be distant acquaintances or enemies, but they are aware that what one of them does has consequences for the other, and vice versa. This mutual connection is something their conflict cannot change, and something they are ready to acknowledge and to take responsibility for.

Traditional	New
Conflicts are troublesome	Conflicts are a condition of life
The parties are opponents and individuals and see no connection between the two	The parties are individuals who value relations. They see themselves as interdependent and connected in a shared conflict
Focus on result/agreement	Focus on process and possible outcome/agreement
There is an objective truth	No-one has a monopoly of truth
There are winners and losers	There should be consideration for both parties
A third party can settle the conflict	The parties must participate actively in and take full responsibility for the resolution of their conflict
There must be scope for applying sanctions	Sanctions are irrelevant

Figure 2. Paradigms

Truth

From the next entry it is clear that, in the traditional paradigm, the parties think it is reasonable to try to find the objective truth which can be the basis for the resolution of the conflict. Even though every sociologist and every sensible person knows very well that it is impossible to find scientific truth in a social context, people nevertheless argue that one party is right and the other is wrong, that one party has given a true picture of reality and the other has not. It is the strength of the argument that counts, and there is only room for one winner. The person who has not presented his evidence well and is not good at putting his argument must accept that his description of reality is wrong, and he is the loser.

The new paradigm takes account of the fact that it is not possible to describe facts objectively, other than absolutely concrete facts. It acknowledges that each party knows part of the truth, but that neither knows the whole truth.[10] Dialogue helps the parties to increase their understanding, and both parties can learn from this. Therefore, the solution will contain elements of both descriptions and will take account of both parties' view of reality.

Since no-one is willing, voluntarily, to give up his view of reality, the traditional paradigm requires a third party to decide who has presented the best case. A judge is needed. In the new paradigm no third party can make the parties' realisation for them, so no authority can decide what or who is more correct. This means that in the new paradigm there is a much greater degree of focus on the process. In the traditional paradigm the focus is almost exclusively on the product – the result.

10. Mahatma Ghandi, one of the leading sources of inspiration for new approaches to alternative dispute resolution, based his ideas on conflict resolution on the concept of *Satyagraha*, which can be understood as meaning 'the force of truth', in other words to seek and to hold on to the truth – not *my* truth, but a higher truth.. *Satyagraha*, from the Sanskrit, consists of 'sat' – natural law or being at one with the truth, and 'agraha' which means a firm hold or decisiveness. According to Ghandi, in order to resolve a conflict one must understand that there is a higher potential common truth. Each individual sees 'their' truth as a leaf on a large tree, but the higher truth corresponds to the tree. *Satyagraha*, the truth force, is a method for resolving conflicts, i.e. for recognising that our own truth is merely relative, and it is therefore an experiminetal form of conflict resolution.

As a logical consequence of the above, it must be possible, and often necessary, to exercise power in the traditional paradigm, as the loser would otherwise seldom comply freely with a decision, so sanctions may be needed. By contrast, in the new paradigm there will often be an incentive for both parties to fulfil the agreement as both parties' reality is involved in the resolution of the conflict, so sanctions are less important.

All the elements of each paradigm should be understood as part of a whole. One cannot take a bit from one and a bit from the other. Naturally, it is possible to include elements of dialogue in the traditional paradigm, but that does not alter the fact that, behind the traditional paradigm lies a fundamental view that the parties are not able, by themselves, to reach a good solution, and behind the new paradigm there lies a belief in abilities of the parties. It is impossible to believe both of these simultaneously.

Mediators must ask themselves how convinced they are of the basic values of mediation which are described here. Mediators cannot be effective and credible unless they act in accordance with the values of mediation.

III. Short descriptions of the six well-known models

a. The problem-solving, settlement-focused model

The problem-solving, settlement-focused model

This is a phased model, the primary aim of which is to get the parties to enter into an agreement based on their own interests and needs, with a 'win-win' focus extending beyond the formal rights of the parties. It is an individualistic model in which no importance is attached to relationships, or at least only as a side-effect. The feelings of the parties are regarded as disturbing to the process, so that only if it is necessary is allowance made for so-called 'venting', i.e. allowing the parties to cool off, preferably in separate meetings where much of the mediation takes place. Mediators, who consider themselves value-neutral, have a dominant role throughout the process.[11] The problem-solving mediation model grew out of negotiation theory, as formulated by *Roger Fisher & Will Ury* in *Getting to Yes* and the Harvard Negotiation Project, with special emphasis on methods for reducing the volume of litigation and achieving quicker and cheaper solutions for the parties.[12] The model is often used in a business context.

b. The cognitive model

The cognitive model

This is not a phased model in the sense described above. The mediation process is described on the basis of certain organisational principles which are regarded as being present in all kinds of mediation, regardless of the professional background of the mediator. These principles are described as hypothesising and strategising and key notions are reflective questions and neutrality understood as questions being multidimensional or bifurcated. In this model the mediator consciously works cognitively, in other words with a view to achieving increased intellectual understanding, and thus not explicitly with feelings. In the mediation, which is inspired by systemic family therapy, the questions to the parties are constructed so as to provoke the response 'think about their thinking', which is also an encouragement which applies to the mediator's own thinking. The aim of the mediation is for the parties to enter into an agreement. It appears from demonstration videos that the mediator has a very prominent role. '[The mediator] avoids unuseful parts of the story, which [we] they define as including those parts relating to the clients' legal rights or their emotions. The areas of useful conversation in mediation are about the data, the goals of the clients, and their strategies.' The mediation model is not explicit about the underlying values, but it is stated that '[clients] must own

11. See, e.g. Centre for Effective Dispute Resolution (CEDR). www.cedr.co.uk Christopher Moore, *The Mediation Process, Practical Strategies for Resolving Conflicts*, San Francisco, 1989.
12. See Fisher & Ury, *Getting to Yes, Negotiating Agreement Without Giving In*, Boston 1981

the content of the discussion and the ultimate agreement.'[13] It is emphasised that the parties demonstrate confidence in the mediators by inviting them into the conflict, and the model reflects a profound respect for the parties.[14]

c. The transformative model

The transformative model

This is an explicitly value-based and ultimately process-oriented model, which emphasises that 'purpose drives practice'. It is expected to result in a non-phased process in which the mediator follows the parties in a 'micro-flow' which is a short-running, synchronous request-response process. The main aim of the model is not for the parties to enter into an agreement, but to address their capacity to transform the quality of conflict interaction itself, so that conflicts can actually strengthen both the parties themselves and the society they are part of.[15] The mediator attaches importance to being non-directing and has a more withdrawn role, which allows room for the parties to let out their feelings, and also allows feelings to be used in the course of the mediation. According to Bush and Folger, the main focus of the transformative model is on the parties' increased feelings of self-respect, self-reliance and self-confidence, called the empowerment dimension of the mediation process, and on the ability of the process to help individuals activate their inherent capacity for understanding the problems of the others, which has been called the recognition dimension of the mediation process. According to its authors, the transformative model was developed in reaction to the limited perspective of the problem-solving model in particular.

13. Haynes, Haynes & Fong, *Mediation - Positive Conflict Management*, 2004 p. 5.
14. See note 12 the foreword.
15. Bush & Folger, *The Promise of Mediation, The Transformative Approach to Conflict*, Ed. 2, San Francisco 2005, p. 13.

d. The narrative model

The narrative model

This model rejects the idea that conflicts arise because of unsatisfied interests and unmet needs, and asserts that they arise instead from people constructing conflict from narrative descriptions of events. The narrative approach concentrates on developing a relationship that is incompatible with conflict and that is built on stories of understanding, respect and collaboration. The deconstruction of the stories of the parties takes place primarily in separate meetings. The approach is said to help mediators and their clients make sense of complex social and cultural contexts.[16] Narrative mediation arose from social-constructivist theory, a post-modern movement, as well as narrative therapy as expressed in the book Narrative Therapy in Practice: The Archaeology of Hope.[17]

e. The humanistic model

The humanistic model

The main aim of mediation which uses this model is to promote healing for the parties involved and thereby to achieve real peace. This can only be achieved by the parties engaging in a proper dialogue with each other and thereby, despite the conflict, to discover or rediscover that the other party is a human being just like themselves. The underlying assumption of the humanistic model is a belief in the connectedness of all things and the conviction that human beings essentially want to live in peace and to obtain increased self-respect and self-determination by confronting conflicts openly. Humanistic mediation is phased, beginning with comprehensive preliminary meetings with each of the parties separately, so as to motivate them for the meeting with the other party and to allow the mediator to have as withdrawn role as possible when the parties do meet. The model has distinct therapeutic elements and is primarily used by offenders and their victims of serious

16. See p. xi of the Foreword in Narrative Mediation.
17. G. Monk & J. Winslade (Eds.), San Francisco, 1996.

crimes, with a view to mediating reconciliation between them.[18]

f. The organic model

The organic model

This model has explicit values, according to which harmony and community are given higher priority than the interests of the individual. The mediation therefore aims to re-establish relations through the restoration and application of community values. The mediator has a duty to represent the values and shared interpretations of the community and therefore takes a dominant role in the mediation process and in its accepted outcome. Forgiveness is seen as being fundamental for the restoration of relationships, and the mediator is bound to seek to achieve this in the mediation process.[19]

IV. The reflexive model

A non-model

Of the models described, the transformative model is close to the non-model, because of its basis of explicit underlying values and because both the individual and the relations between the parties are considered important. However, in a Scandinavian context, it seems that the consequences for the mediation process which Bush and Folger draw from their underlying values are not all either necessary or appropriate and may sometimes even be unacceptable. The transformative model allows room for the parties to let out their feelings which, even if it is not accepted that these should develop into a physical attack, may sometimes develop into an outpouring which, at least in a Scandinavian context, can be perceived as an emotional attack, *or even an assault.* The mediator's role in this is too passive. The mediator should step in earlier, not to deprive the emotional party of their feelings, but to act as a filter and reflect the angered party's pain etc. In other words, the mediator

18. Mark Umbreit, 'Humanistic Mediation: A Transformative Journey of Peacemaking', *Mediation Quarterly* 1997.
19. See Frederic Luskin, Director of the Stanford Forgiveness Projects.

should initially undertake to acknowledge the feelings and interpretations of the injured party, after which the other party can be allowed room to step in with their reaction and possible recognition and acknowledgement.

In the course of the translation of this book it has become clear that - like so many other words, 'recognition' and 'acknowledgement' have different layers of meaning, and these depend on the context. 'I recognise your claim' might mean either recognition of the existence of your claim, or it might be capable of being understood as being admission/acceptance of the claim. In other words 'I recognise your claim' can be ambiguous. On the other hand, 'I acknowledge your claim' probably removes the ambiguity and would normally be understood as an admission/acceptance of the claim, not to be confused with agreement. For this reason 'acknowledgement' is often used in this book instead of 'recognition'.

The values and assumptions in the non-model, taken together with the elements that can be derived from the earlier models, give a basis for a process that looks as follows:

- The mediator uses phases, at least in the introduction, each of which has characteristics which can be used as a framework for the mediation itself.
- The mediation is both process- and outcome-oriented, depending on the wishes of the parties.
- The emphasis is on achieving a balance between individual needs and the needs of the other party or parties.
- The mediator's approach is that the mediation involves both the emotions and the intellects of the parties, i.e. both thoughts and feelings. Mediation should thus be allowed to work with both the substantive issue and the relations between the parties, if that is what the parties want.
- In the course of the mediation there are often changes in the views of the parties both with regard to their own and the other party's roles and the narratives which were considered to be valid at the start of the mediation. Since the parties are the experts on their own lives, this

does not refer to any deconstruction of the narratives of the parties, since each party's narrative is accepted as valid at the time and against the background of the parties at that time. Thus, the aim of the mediation process is not to *disprove* the stories of the parties, but to help them to *expand* and *supplement* their respective stories.

- The mediator plays different roles, depending on what happens during the mediation. For example, as a starting point the mediator will have a withdrawn role, but can adopt a more prominent role in order to prevent aggression, as the mediator can act as a filter by using reflection, empathy, being a role model etc. The mediator can also be active in the agreement phase, for example by helping the parties test the viability of the proposed agreement.
- The mediator uses different kinds of questions, ranging from the purely factual to hypothetical or circular questions.
- Mediators never express their own views of possible solutions or make proposals for solutions.

PART 1

Key concepts for mediation

CHAPTER 3

An overview

I. The basic principles of mediation

As a background to the treatment of the general concepts, a short introduction is given here on mediation as it is understood in this book.

Clarification of concepts

The word 'mediation' is derived from the Latin word *mediare,* meaning 'to be in the middle'.

In this book the terms 'mediation' and 'conflict mediation' are used in the knowledge that the terms are not crystal clear, and must be further defined. The term 'conflict mediation' is of more recent date, so one may hope that the term will be associated with the kind of mediation activities described in this book, and distinguished from court-based conciliation, or other forms of agency where an agent acts as an intermediary, or other intervention by third parties. Since it would be somewhat pedantic to write 'conflict mediation' or 'conflict mediator' every time, the words 'mediation' and 'mediator' will mostly be used. It is hoped that it will be clear to the reader that these words are used in connection with the basic principles laid out here, unless otherwise indicated in the text. Conflict mediation, as discussed in this book, is only one of many kinds of mediation. However, it is a kind of mediation which, in the opinion of this writer, as far as possible takes into account the basic principles and values which lie behind it, as well as regard for protection from abuse of power, not only from the parties but also from the mediator etc. which mediation should ensure. It is also a form of mediation with which this writer has long practical experience, and has obtained good results with.

This book is not intended to be a dogmatic presentation of the only correct form of mediation. As mediators grow in experience they will gradually develop their own approaches to mediation. Just as all conflicts are different, despite their similarities, mediations also have individual characteristics based on the parties, the kind of conflict, time, culture, the mediator and so on.

II. Definition of conflict mediation

Conflict mediation can be defined as:

Definition

A voluntary and confidential method of resolving conflicts where, through a structured process, one or more impartial third parties assist the parties in reaching a solution by themselves to their problem which is mutually satisfactory. The mediator provides a framework and helps conduct the mediation, but makes no substantial suggestions or decisions in the case.

The elements in this definition will be described and then discussed in greater detail in connection with the review of the individual steps of mediation.

Voluntary participation

First, the fact that participation of the parties in the mediation process is *voluntary* is important. In this context, this means that the parties themselves choose whether or not to take part, whether to make an agreement and, if there is an agreement, what the agreement shall contain.

It should be noted that voluntariness also applies to the mediator, which means that if a mediator finds that the parties breach certain ethical rules the mediator can, and possibly should, withdraw from the mediation. This is a point on which mediation is radically different from litigation before the courts, where a judge may not refuse to hear a case which satisfies the necessary legal requirements.

In some countries compulsory mediation has been introduced for some situations, for example in Norway in connection with marital conflicts. It is difficult to say to what extent compulsory participation affects the mediation process, even though there appears to be a tendency for mediators to adopt to a greater degree than normal the management of the process in the form of advising the parties etc., with the attendant risk that the process can lose the character of mediation. Compulsory mediation is not dealt with in this book.

Confidentiality

Next, mediation is *confidential,* which means that the mediator has a duty of confidentiality in respect of what takes place, and that the parties themselves must be willing to refrain from discussing the conflict with third parties, unless they agree otherwise. Confidentiality creates a space within which the parties can safely make concessions and express their wishes.[1]

Impartiality

Neutrality

The mediator must be *impartial,* meaning that they must treat both parties with equal consideration. The concept of impartiality is closely linked to *neutrality,* which means that the mediator does not take a view on how the conflict should be resolved and has no interest in any given outcome.

A resolution which is satisfactory

The definition also states that the parties should achieve a resolution which is *satisfactory,* by means of *negotiation.* Since negotiation presumes that both parties understand, they must move from their original starting point. This part of the definition means that both parties, perhaps with some help, must be able to take care of their interests satisfactorily, and that they are willing to move towards the other party, so that they too can obtain a satisfactory outcome. There can be no mediation without negotiation.

A structured process

Mediation allows the parties to express their claims, injuries, needs and expectations, and it creates a framework for closer communication than is usual with litigation. The aim of mediation is often for the parties to reach an agreement, or at least achieve clarification of their conflict. To achieve this, mediation must be a *structured* process which is not rigid, as one can move forward or backward between the different stages, though without missing out a stage, and it is the job of the mediator to maintain an overview and guide the parties safely through the process.

1. The reader is referred to Chapter 8 for a discussion of the limits to and difficulties with confidentiality.

The mediator must not take decisions in the case

Finally, the mediator sets the framework for the mediation and, however unobtrusive they may be as a mediator, they influence the process of the mediation to a greater or lesser extent. It is therefore of the greatest importance that the mediator's influence on the content of the mediation should be reduced to the minimum, so the mediator *must not take decisions* in the case, since there would then not be mediation but an authoritative form of conflict resolution, depriving the parties of their responsibility for the solution and giving rise to totally different protective measures such as openness (public access), specific requirements for the qualifications of the third party with regard to the content of the conflict etc.

Principles to mediation

On the basis of this definition it is possible to lay down the following principles which apply to mediation: a *voluntary principle,* according to which the parties can, at any time, withdraw from the mediation and seek to have the conflict resolved by some other means, for example by the courts or by arbitration; a *principle of confidentiality,* which ensures that the parties can reach the right result for them, without the intervention of external authorities; a *principle of relativity,* meaning that, within the framework of overriding ethical norms, the parties can reach any agreement which they find right for themselves. In addition to this there is the *principle of responsibility,* under which the parties may have the help of others, a lawyer for example, but may not leave the conduct of the mediation to others, since the negotiation must take place directly between the parties and an agreement can only be made by them; finally there is a *duty to contradict or respond,* and a *duty to be active and to negotiate,* which means that the parties have an obligation to express their view of the conflict and to participate actively in the process which leads to the resolution of the conflict. Thus the voluntary nature of mediation does not mean that the parties have no responsibilities.[2]

2. See Vibeke Vindeløv, *Konflikt, Tvist og Mægling,* (Conflict, Dispute and Mediation) p. 139 et seq.

Fundamental values

The definition of conflict mediation and these explanatory comments are based on fundamental values which can be expressed as respect for the individual and the individual's special characteristics, so the autonomy and dignity of the parties are important. This means that great importance is attached to the parties' own sense of *fairness and justice*.[3] In addition to this, respect and dignity are necessary for a possible *restoration* and *reconciliation* between the parties.

Assumptions behind mediation

In addition to this, as described in Chapter 2, conflict mediation includes certain assumptions which influence both its process and its content. These are:

- Understanding that conflicts are a part of life. Conflicts are neither good nor bad.
- Trusting that the parties know best what is good for them. In other words, they are experts on their own lives.
- That individuality and relations go together
- Acceptance that there is more than one reality.
- That dialogue is desirable in every conflict.
- Confidence that mutually satisfactory solutions can be reached if the parties wish it.

III. Structure and flexibility

Even though an experienced mediator must often move forwards and backwards through the different stages of the process, there is no doubt that it is reasonable to call mediation a structured process. Mediation will always have a beginning and an end with distinct characteristics and in between, sometimes with little involvement of the mediator, there will be an examination of how the parties feel about the conflict and their feelings associated with it, followed by focusing on the subject of the mediation, before the parties can work on what ways they can see out of the conflict.

For the purposes of teaching, it can help achieve clarity and it can be useful if the stages of mediation are described

3. See Chapter 10.

separately; experienced mediators can keep these steps in the back of their heads as a support for structures which later develop.

IV. The conduct of the meeting

Before the mediation meeting itself, which consists of 6 stages, the mediator must take the initiative to contact the parties in one way or another, and there must also be a period afterwards. In summary form the *structure* is as follows:

A. Before the meeting

B. The meeting itself

1. *Opening*, which consists of welcoming, presentation of the mediation process, and clarification of roles.
2. *The submissions of the parties and dialogue*, where each party gives their side of the story and learns about the other party's story. This leads to the discovery of the positions of both parties, as well as facts, feelings, interests and needs.
3. *Definition of the problem area*. The topics which require further work are identified. Perhaps priorities are set.
4. *Generation of possible solutions*. As many proposals for a solution are produced as possible – without a view being taken on them.
5. *An agreement is negotiated*. The parties negotiate on the basis of the possible solutions.
6. *The agreement is checked and approved*. The agreement is signed. Loose ends are tied up.

C. After the meeting

These various stages will be described in detail in Part 2.

CHAPTER 4

Conflicts and their escalation

Introduction

A personal challenge and a professional activity

It is not only the parties to a conflict, but also the mediator who has a set of reactions which come into play when confronting conflicts between people. Therefore, an ability to understand conflicts is not just a skill required in relation to the parties, mediators must also deal with their own reactions when they encounter a conflict. Mediation is thus an interactive process, which hopefully not only benefits the parties, but also contributes to the mediator's own development. This is why work in the area of conflict resolution can be a personal challenge and source of satisfaction, as well as a professional activity.

There are many different professions involved in dealing with conflicts, and each profession emphasises the characteristics which are special from its own perspective. For this reason, definitions of conflicts, descriptions of their developments etc., are based on studies of different disciplines, and the materials will be selected and adapted as appropriate for a book whose primary topic is conflict resolution. However, it should be emphasised from the start that some fundamental assumptions about conflicts, that are not dependent on any particular professional discipline, lie behind this book. *First,* a constructive approach to conflicts can be learnt, and it is not conflicts themselves, but the way they are dealt with which determines whether they develop constructively or destructively. *Second,* there is always some mutual dependence, or interdependence, between the parties to a conflict. If there were not some form of dependence, and one of the parties were indifferent to what the other party did, there would be no conflict,[1] which by no means implies that there is any mutual respect between the parties.

I. The concept of conflict

View of conflicts

Dealing with conflicts always involves a view of conflicts, usually implicit. It is very rare for the concept of a conflict or the characteristics of different kinds of conflicts to be described explicitly.[2] However, the different kinds of forum for dealing with conflicts should not merely be considered as 'bare forms' in which some given conflict is dealt with, but should be seen as the upholders of certain standards, for example as to whether conflicts should predominantly be considered constructively, destructively or neutrally. Similarly, each person's reaction to conflicts often reflects earlier experiences about how best to deal with conflicts. This means that, both in theory and in practice, there can be some fundamental views which affect the form of reaction and reasoning. For example, is it best to act as if the conflict does not exist, or should one retaliate? Or can one accept that a conflict is a disagreement which can be resolved by a joint effort?

Many regard conflicts as events which are almost wholly negative, so their assumptions automatically asso-

1. See, for example, H.B. Braiker & H.H. Kelley, 'Conflict in the development of close relationships', in R.L. Burgess & T.L. Huston (eds.) *Social exchange in developing relationships* (New York 1979) p. 137; W. Wilmot and J. Hocker, Interpersonal conflict, McGraw-Hill, 6. ed. 2001.
2. An important exception to this is the description of Transformative mediation where, even though the concept is not directly defined, it is nevertheless described with the emphasis on the effect which conflicts have on the parties, namely that 'it leads and forces them to behave toward themselves and others in ways that they find uncomfortable and even repellent. More specifically, it alienates them from their sense of their own strength and their sense of connection to others', Bush & Folger: *The Promise of Mediation*, 2005 p. 46.

ciate conflicts with winning or losing. Our everyday usage includes a number of expressions which reveal how explosive, exhausting and unacceptable conflicts can be: 'She'll be the death of me', 'It just blew up in my face' or the quasi-legal 'You're accusing me'.

Within the legal world it is customary for the concept of conflicts neither to be defined nor discussed, and reactions to them are basically authoritarian, i.e., conflicts are decided by the exercise of power. One can therefore assume that these reactions have an in-built view of conflicts as disruptive, overwhelmingly destructive and something to be eliminated.

Conflicts a social reality

Behind forms of conflict resolution, referred to as mediation and problem-solving negotiation, there is an assumption that conflicts will always exist, and cannot be eliminated without abandoning development, freedom or democracy. Conflicts are thus a social reality, and it is necessary to have a constructive approach to them. In this view, there is no natural law which says that conflicts must be destructive, and the ability to deal with conflicts constructively is a skill which can be acquired.

Thus, behind this book lies the normative view of conflicts that is expressed by the Chinese character on the cover of this book; conflicts contain both dangers and possibilities.

According to the ideas of Ghandi, it is necessary to reframe a conflict and neither allow it to lead to a violent outbreak nor suppress it, and according to Nils Christie conflicts must be given back to the people directly concerned, as they are best placed to resolve them themselves.[3]

3. Without doubt, the Danish/Swedish peace and future researcher Jan Øberg is right when he says that many modern problem-solvers are deeply indebted to Gandhi, many probably without knowing it; see Ann-Sofi Jakobsson & Jan Øberg, *Konfliktløsning* (Lund 1994). Refer also to Johan Galtung & Arne Næss, *Gandhis politiske etik* (Oslo 1995) as well as Arne Næss, *Gandhi and Group Conflict, An Exploration of Satyagraha, Theoretical Background* (Oslo 1974). See also Nils Christie, 'Conflict as Property', *The British Journal of Criminology*, 1977, 17, 1.

Definition[4]

As a basis for this discussion, the following definition of conflicts will be used:

Conflicts are disagreements between two or more parties which cause stress for or between the individuals concerned.

This definition requires the following further clarifications:

First, it is clear that the existence of a conflict assumes not only that there is interaction between people, but also that there is at least some view of the existence of a form of dependence between them, whether or not this view is based on practical or emotional circumstances or merely on an assumption of such dependence.

Next, it is assumed that there is a connection between the inner feeling of stress and outward conduct. This means that a conflict will exist even if only one of the parties feels the stress. Thus, it is not open to one of the parties to assert that it is only the other party who has a conflict. There *is* a conflict between them, even if the parties do not have the same feelings about it. Thus the conflict cannot be 'owned' by one party alone. The conflict must instead be seen as an individual conflict (an inner conflict) and a relational and contextual conflict.

Third, the definition describes both an issue and a relationship, since it covers both *inter*personal and *intra*personal conflicts, understood as conflicts *between* persons and conflicts *within* an individual, as well as the issue about which the parties may disagree. In the literature there is agreement about the distinction between inter- and intrapersonal conflicts, and the distinction is significant for the choice of forum for conflict resolution. Both courts and arbitration tribunals concern themselves with interpersonal disputes and only with such. Mediation is likewise concerned with interpersonal conflicts but can *also* be concerned to a limited ex-

4. There are many different definitions of conflict. For example, Folger, Scott Poole & Stutman, *Working through Conflict*, 2009, p. 4, use the following definition: 'Conflict is the interaction of interdependent people who perceive incompatibility and the possibility of interference from others as a result of this incompatibility'.

tent with intrapersonal conflicts when these spill over into the interpersonal, and clarification of the ambivalence of one of the parties in relation to means and ends can form the basis for positive mediation. However, mediation does not include therapeutic procedures, unless discussing feelings and acquiring insight into oneself are regarded as therapeutic. Maintaining the structure of the mediation process means there is no room for deeper therapeutic procedures, even though the mediator needs to recognise both kinds of conflicts and learn how to respond to what is called 'resistance', i.e. the reluctance of one of the parties to cooperate constructively in the mediation process. In the course of the mediation process, the parties will often learn something both about themselves and the other party, whereby the basis for a solution to the conflict can be created.

Fourth, the stress need not be articulated or otherwise expressed in order for a conflict to exist, though it is obvious that mediation cannot be initiated before the conflict is expressed.

Pseudo conflicts

Fifth, some writers distinguish between *genuine* conflicts and *pseudo* conflicts.[5] Genuine conflicts involve outward disagreement between the parties to the conflict. Pseudo conflicts are those where there is a misunderstanding, because a party believes the situation to be otherwise than it is in fact. These conflicts are typically based on misunderstandings caused by lack of communication between the parties, but they can be resolved if sufficient information is presented.

However, it is more convenient to define pseudo conflicts as a separate category in a positivist world view, where truth and reality are coterminous and constant, and where a fully informed observer, e.g. a judge, can consider the situation objectively. However, from a phenomenological, empirically based point of view, it is difficult for an outsider to define something as pseudo. In this case the conflict is, by definition, genuine as long as it is perceived

5. Enderud, 1987, p. 37; and Peter Berliner, *Konflitkløsning*, 1999. Others call pseudo conflicts 'mistaken' or 'false conflicts', e.g. Deutsch 1974.

as genuine by the parties.[6] New information can alter the parties' view of reality, so there will be a new situation, but this does not make the first scenario any more pseudo or false than the succeeding scenario. Pseudo for A can be genuine for B. The establishment of reality or the view of reality is lacking, since individuals' stories remain valid for themselves.

Even where there is information in such quantity for the 'objective' basis for a conflict to be eliminated, it is recognised in mediation that parties can nevertheless feel themselves injured. The information can have been provided too late, too vaguely, too casually etc. This means, in effect, that *in the context of mediation, the distinction between pseudo conflicts and genuine conflicts is irrelevant.*

***Inter*personal and *intra*personal conflicts**

Finally, the definition covers all the elements of a conflict which the parties may believe is relevant, and it is therefore broader than the concept of 'dispute' before the courts, which is characterised by the fact that all factors which are not legally relevant are excluded.

Conflict and dispute

The negative attitude to conflicts undoubtedly reflects the predominant attitude not only of the courts, but of the western world in general. Without in any way idealising conflicts, one may nevertheless ask what the world would be like if there were no conflicts. The immediate relief at the prospect of a harmonious life would quickly be replaced by the feeling of being put in a straightjacket, bound by boredom, lack of development and repression. In other words, it is more realistic to view conflicts as part of life; as soon as one conflict is resolved another springs up. Conflict is part of the human condition, but it is possible to be more skilled in relation to conflicts and to have a positive attitude towards them. This is a useful insight both for mediators and for parties to conflicts.[7]

6. See likewise Enderud, 1987, p. 37.
7. In transformative mediation conflict is regarded as an 'interactional crisis', which 'forces them to behave toward themselves and others in ways that they find uncomfortable and even repellent. More specifically, alienates the parties from their sense og their

Conflicts in context

If we adopt a contextual approach, we can use, for example, Galtung's well-known ABC triangle,

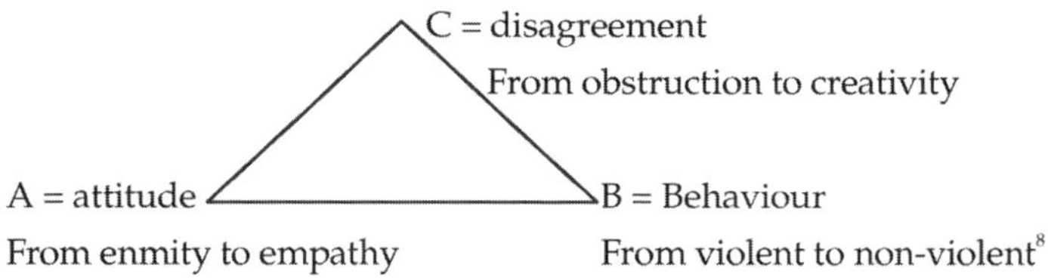

For further on these contexts, see Chapter 12. Another way in which conflicts can be seen contextually is as the connection between minor conflicts and major conflicts. For the sake of simplicity, here it can be helpful to regard conflicts as being divided into three zones: Zone 1 relates to the wider world (EU, NATO, UN, municipal authorities etc.), where we only act indirectly. Zone 2 is the area of direct relations, where we encounter everyday conflicts as actors (families, immediate superiors at work, nurses, business contacts etc.). Zone 3 is the place where one prepares and seeks to understand the big problems which affect us in our everyday lives, and where we learn and train to deal with conflicts.[9]

Reactions to conflict

Even though there is growing awareness of the potential within conflicts, there is not necessarily harmony between this intellectual awareness and our spontaneous feelings,

own strength and their sense of connections to others', R. Bush & J. Folger, *The promise of Mediation*, revised ed. 2005, p 46. In narrative mediation, which is based on post-modern philosophy, conflict is understood as a product of the differing ways in which the individual creates meaning in their life, and is thus understood 'from the outside in as the almost inevitable by-product of diversity, rather than as a result of the expression of personal needs or interests', J. Winslade & G. Monk, *Narrative Mediation*, 2000, p. 41.

8. See Johan Galtung, *Conflict Transformation by Peaceful Means*, www.transcend.org, where Galtung gives an account of conflicts which destroy as well as create.
9. Else Hammerich & Kirsten Frydensberg, *Konflikt og Kontakt*, new edition 2009, Ch. II.

just as it can be difficult to know when to answer back and when to hold one's tongue, or as Bateson has said, 'Fight and stand up for yourself, but only when it is acceptable.'[10]

Nevertheless, conflicts can have positive side effects so one should confront them more openly and constructively. If conflicts are seen as an unavoidable and natural part of life, the incentive to 'cool off' and use one's problem-solving skills is obvious. Properly dealt with, conflicts can bring people closer together, and working with people of a variety of points of view can lead to creativity and development.

Reactions to conflict

Whether conflicts are seen as predominantly good, bad or indifferent effects *how one usually reacts to them*. Broadly speaking it is possible to divide different kinds of reaction into three categories: avoidance, aggression and openness.

If one does not believe that a conflict can have a positive result, or if one can simply not be bothered, *avoidance* will be the usual reaction. One backs off, smoothes over, ignores, represses, excuses or even takes flight. This can be because one is concerned about how the other party will react to confrontation, because one does not think one has a right to object or because one does not trust one's own ability to deal with the conflict properly. On the other hand, if a person is hot-headed he may respond *angrily*, giving as good as he gets, even threatening or attacking the other party.

Both these kinds of reaction are normal and may be justified. But however much they differ from each other, they are similar in preventing dialogue and contact with the other party, and thus, at least in the short term, they hinder the parties from entering into a constructive process of conflict resolution. To shy away from and avoid conflicts can lead to escalation of a conflict just as much as aggression can, because one does not object in time.

On the other hand, if one has the confidence to *be open* to opposing views, and to investigate the basis of disagreement, one can approach the other party in a way which

10. Gregory Bateson: *Steps to an ecology of mind* (New York 1972).

does not provoke an aggressive reaction.[11] The other party has an opportunity to explain their point of view, and it can be seen how, when treated properly, conflicts can be resolved to the perhaps surprised satisfaction of both parties. It is when the parties are unable to carry through such a process for themselves that mediation can be necessary.

II. The cycle of conflict and the ripe moment

Five phases

Sometimes it seems as if conflicts have their own life cycle. The life of a conflict seems to pass through five phases, regardless of who the conflict is between or what kind of conflict it is. The phases are: 1) the hidden conflict, 2) the start of open conflict, 3) imbalance of power, 4) balance of power, and 5) the re-establishment of equilibrium.[12]

A conflict is thus presented as a continuous spiral, a helix, which is set in motion by change but which is otherwise shaped by the kind of power or context in which it is manifested. When the subject of the conflict has passed through these five phases, it has completed a circuit of the spiral and there will have been a change in the values and norms affecting the socio-cultural structures, and these changes can generate new hidden conflicts (phase 1) or move the conflict directly to phase 2. The helix starts on a new cycle, but this cycle can only exist if there are continuing relations between the actual or potential parties to the conflict.

The timing

There has been an awareness of the question of when a conflict is *ripe* for settlement, particularly with international conflicts. Such awareness can be helpful in other kinds of conflicts. The *timing* must be right if there is to be a positive outcome to an attempt to solve a conflict, otherwise there will be wasted effort.

11. See W. Wilmot & J. Hocker, *Interpersonal Conflict*, 6th ed. (McGraw-Hill 2001), Chapter 5; as well as the *Manual for Konstruktiv Konfliktløsning*, Center for Konfliktløsning, 2001.
12. R.J. Rummel, *Understanding Conflict and War*, Vols. 1 and 2, (New York 1976).

Ripe moment Especially in connection with international conflicts there has been an assumption about there being a time when a conflict is *ripe* for a solution. The ripe moment is assumed to exist when the parties reach a 'mutually hurting stalemate'. This means that the parties involved feel the conflict has stalled at an unacceptably painful level. At this point the parties are expected to be ready to resolve the conflict, and this will be the optimal stage for a mediator to enter the conflict.[13] In the life-cycle of conflicts, the conflict is ripe for resolution when passing from phase 3 to phase 4. The theory of the ripe moment has often been challenged, not least by external reality, where in continuing a conflict the extremism of the parties can appear not only destructive for the opposing party, but equally self-destructive. Since the initiative for mediation in inter-personal conflicts must necessarily be taken by the parties themselves, even if they are encouraged to take part in mediation by third parties, the theory does not always hold water. Regarding international conflicts, see Chapter 12.

III. The dimensions of a conflict

When the parties find, that there is an opportunity to try to resolve a conflict, possibly by mediation, it can be helpful to distinguish the different dimensions of conflicts. These dimensions are often mixed together, but the main emphasis will probably be in one particular place. The benefit of this is in greater understanding of what the conflict is about, and in recognising that the different dimensions of the conflict give rise to different kinds of reactions.

Apart from the dimensions already referred to, interpersonal/intrapersonal and pseudo/genuine conflicts, the following are the four main dimensions of conflicts: structural

13. See, inter alia, Saadia Touval & I.W. Zartman (eds.), *The Man in the Middle: International Mediation in Theory and Practice*, Colorado 1985; and David Druckman, 'Negotiating in International Conflict', in Zartman et al., *Peacemaking in International Conflict, Methods and Techniques*, (Washington 2001).

conflicts, instrumental conflicts, conflicts of interest and conflicts of values.

Structural conflicts

As the name suggests, *structural conflicts* concern the structure within which the conflict arises and this is often related to power. Usually these concern factors of a more overriding and enduring character, for example relations between management and workers, the grant of licences, or the allocation of resources between different groups arranged according to a hierarchy. Individual employees or members of a group will often feel powerless to affect the conflict, partly because it requires individuals to pool resources and work together to bring about change, and partly because the greater the distance and power differential between the parties to the conflict, the more there is a need for a long-term perspective. Since the structure can be said to absorb the other conflicts, they can also be seen as yet another dimension of the relationship between inter- and intrapersonal conflicts.

Instrumental conflicts

Instrumental conflicts concern disagreements about specific ends and means, for example where the family should go on holiday, how some particular task shall be tackled etc. Most people encounter numerous such situations every day, and deal with them without great difficulty. As long as the problem is kept at the instrumental level it can most often be solved, possibly through negotiation, so it is possible to proceed to the execution of the task.

Conflicts of interest

Conflicts of interest (material conflicts). The Norwegian sociologist, Vilhelm Aubert, introduced the distinction between conflicts of interest and conflicts of values. As distinct from conflicts of values, conflicts of interest are governed by lack of resources.[14] These can be lack of time, money or space, or there can be a contest for territory or other basic necessities of life. Power and influence are also resources that can be the subject of conflict.

14. V. Aubert, 1976, p. 172 and the same author, 1963, pp. 26-42. The distinction between conflicts of interest and conflicts of values is Aubert's invention, and it has remained primarily a Scandinavian phenomenon.

Conflicts of interest do not necessarily imply that the parties differ in their values, indeed, the opposite is more likely to be the case. It is precisely because the parties share the same view of the worth of the subject of the dispute that there is the basis for conflict.[15] If the conflict is to be resolved peacefully, there must be negotiations so that the good is shared according to guidelines which the parties agree are reasonable.

Conflicts of values

A *conflict of values* (*normative conflicts*) consists of 'a disagreement about the normative status of a social object (situation, position, system, person, thing etc.)'.[16] Conflicts of interests and of values can thus be said to be based on two different areas of social life, the material and the normative respectively. A conflict of values concerns the personal or cultural values one believes to be correct: moral, ethical, political and religious. These values concern one's own identity and will typically be values for which one is prepared to fight. This category includes conflicts of a more personal nature, concerning a person's image of themselves, the need for recognition and acknowledgement, the desire not to be excluded etc.[17] The more a conflict concerns personal aspects, the more difficult it can be to address it. Thus, it is often possible to be open about the values and ethical/political views one may have, but it is much more difficult to be open about, or even be conscious of conflicts one may have at a personal level.

Aubert believed that 'there must be a point of view for everyone, both with respect to normative and descriptive questions.'[18] This view is based on an idealised approach, but it has to confront the reality of lack of power and authority. But it is the use of power and authority in connection with conflicts of values which means that they are treated as if they are about conflicts of interest, even if the

15. Vibeke Vindeløv: *Konflikt, Tvist og Mægling*, Chapter 7, p. 222.
16. Aubert, 1962, pp. 89-102.
17. Some writers distinguish between conflicts of values and personal conflicts (see for example the *Manual* of the Center for Konfliktløsning) but as they are all concerned with identity they are discussed together here.
18. V. Aubert, 1976, p. 172 and the same author, 1963, pp. 26-42.

lack of resources does not relate to the points of view, but to the ability or right to implement them. A problem thus arises when one party tries to enforce their values on the other party.

Dialogue

As conflicts of value concern aspects of one's identity, they cannot successfully be subject to negotiation or the application of power. The only way forward is for both, or all, parties to acknowledge the value-based aspect of the conflict and try to understand it. Thus, the aim is to *understand* both one's own values and those of others, and the means to do this is *dialogue*.[19]

In addition to the topic which forms its basis, dialogue also includes an interaction which allows for the possibility of face-saving. This can mean that the personal relationship can be articulated directly. However, in certain circumstances this can be directly counterproductive, as it can cross certain lines or lead to loss of face. This means that the main focus should be on the respect which is an implicit part of dialogue, and the context and culture must determine whether it should include discussions of a more personal nature.

It is a common misunderstanding that recognition of another's point of view is the same as agreeing with it. There is nothing which requires a Christian to agree with a Muslim about the correct way to dress. What is important is recognising the importance of the values involved in the points of view concerned, both for oneself and for the other party, whereby recognition develops to become acknowledgment. When there is recognition, it becomes clearer what can then lead to negotiation. Recognition therefore leads away from conflict resolution based on zero-sum thinking, and towards conflict resolution based on interests and needs.[20]

There will often be several dimensions to a conflict, and the more a conflict escalates, the more the centre of gravity of the conflict will be a conflict of values. This applies re-

19. See *Manual for konstruktiv konfliktløsning,* Center for Konfliktløsning 2001.
20. For a discussion of the zero-sum perspective, see Chapter 7.

gardless of whether the conflict concerns something as direct and simple as the allocation of office space between two colleagues, or something as vital as access to water resources for two neighbouring communities in Central Africa. In both situations the conflict can have or take on the nature or feeling of survival, as in both conflicts there is a need to allocate limited resources, and only in the concrete situation will it be possible to determine which dimension will be the most appropriate starting point.

Example:[21] In the autumn of 2005 a Danish newspaper published 12 cartoons of the prophet Mohammed. Initially the publication provoked protests from Danish Muslims, partly because of the general prohibition of making images of the prophet Mohammed, and partly because of the offence caused by ridiculing the Muslims' most important prophet, not least in a cartoon which represented the prophet Mohammed with a bomb in his turban and linking him to terrorism. The protests were rejected first by the newspaper's editor-in-chief and then, as the conflict became more acute, by the Danish Prime Minister, by reference to the principle of freedom of expression and to the fact that it was not within the Government's powers to restrict a newspaper's freedom of expression. The Prime Minister also rejected an invitation to meet the ambassadors from 11 Muslim countries, as the political point was made that neither freedom of expression nor the powers of the Government were negotiable, so there was nothing to discuss with the 11 ambassadors. The Danish Government (and the newspaper's editor) must thus have had the view that the mere exchange of views in a joint meeting, let alone the possibility of recognising the injury which the other party felt would necessarily lead to concessions and thus to a 'selling out' of their own fundamental values.[22]

21. Even though the original publication of the cartoons is now some years in the past, new problems still arise in the wake of the event. The examples of this are therefore still treated as being current.
22. For the sake of completeness it should be added that, by reference to the previous legal practice, the relevant Danish Attorney-General later refused to prosecute the newspaper under Danish

The distinction between conflicts of values and conflicts of interests defines the space within which the mediator operates. The task of the mediator is to shift the perception of the parties so the subject of the conflict is a limited, fixed entity. This learning process will often swing between understanding the conflict as being about values and/or interests, and accepting that the conflict contains value-based elements which must be understood or at least accepted, and questions of allocation which must be negotiated.[23]

IV. Psychological factors in a conflict

When there is increased intensity in a conflict as a whole, it is said that the conflict escalates. Even though each party may view the escalation as the result of an aggressor/defender model, where it is only the other party who behaves aggressively while one only acts defensively oneself, this is seldom an accurate picture. It will most frequently be more accurate to describe the development as a circular movement of action and reaction, in which each side may indeed increase the intensity, but where the conflict as a whole is affected because the conduct of one of the parties provokes a reaction from the other, and vice versa in a circular process. What happens is that the conduct of one of the parties provokes a psychological reaction in the other party, whose reaction then provokes a new psychological reaction in the first party. A full description of this circular process must include both the actions and the psychological processes.

The view of opposing interests:

anti-racism laws, and that at the start of 2006 the conflict reached an unexpected and explosive level.

23. For more on the question of dialogue, the reader is referred to Chapter 5.

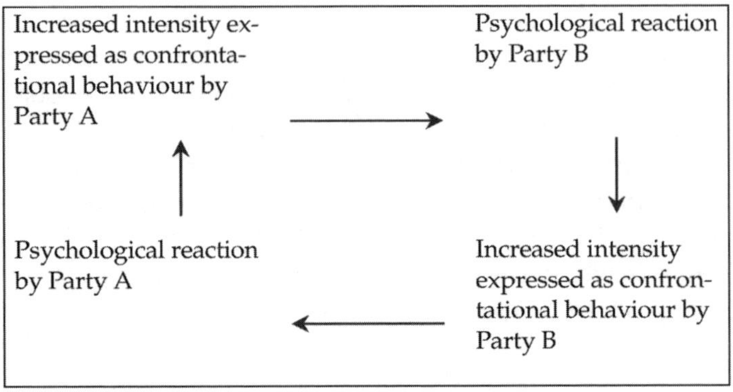

Figure 3. The circular process of escalation, with action and psychological reaction[24]

The most common psychological mechanisms which are in play in escalation is personification, leading to an escalation of a conflict, are projections and aggression often associated with anxiety and anger.

The Danish psychologist, Peter Berliner, describes part of the connection between aggression[25] and conflict as follows:

'Conflicts become destructive partly because of the nature of the problem (what is disagreed about), and partly because of the conduct of the parties involved in dealing with it. Those involved explain their conduct from a particular point of view which becomes an all-inclusive perception, a world view. This world view is often mutually confirmed by the conduct of the parties and thereby becomes established. Often, any challenge to the world view is branded as betrayal.

The world view is built up by defensive mechanisms of which the three most important are generalisation, distortion and repres-

24. This figure is taken from J. Rubin, D. Pruitt & S. Kim, *Social Conflict* (New York 1986) Chapter 5. See also R.J. Rummel, *Understanding Conflict and War*, Vols. 1 and 2, (New York 1976); and D. Sandole, who includes escalation in his definition of conflict, see *Paradigm, theories, and metaphors in conflict and conflict resolution: Coherence or confusion?* p. 6. See also Louis Kriesberg, *Constructive Conflicts, From escalation to resolution* (Boston 1998).
25. Aggression can be defined as an intention to harm the other party, see Rubin, op. cit., p. 252.

sion. Generalisation consists of seeing the other side as a homogeneous group with certain common characteristics (e.g., 'all Serbs are evil'). Distortion consists of only seeing what one wants to see (e.g., 'everything the Serbs do has an evil intention'). Repression consists of refraining from seeing or accepting anything which can rebut one's fixed point of view (e.g., 'the former neighbour, who was a Serb, was decent enough, but that's all history now').'[26]

These examples were unfortunately relevant during the wars in former Yugoslavia.

The most important feelings in conflict escalation are anxiety and anger, and these are expressed in blame.[27]

Blame

'People are good. But then, why aren't they?' Said by the Danish humorist Storm P.

Blame is the result of the desire to make the other party responsible for the conflict and to hold them liable for it. Blame is therefore both rooted in anger and in a rational desire to respond to the other party's reaction so as to prevent a repetition of the conduct. In attempting to understand the other person's behaviour and our own, we ask ourselves why the other party has acted as they have. We are often inclined to find an explanation for the behaviour of the other person in the way we interpret their *character* ('he is a rather self-important person'), and to judge our own behaviour according to the *situation* ('I had no choice; there was nothing else I could do'). This is important in the justification of our own conduct and the branding of others' behaviour as unjust or unreasonable, and it creates a basis for escalation.[28]

The more it is felt that the other party could have predicted the damaging or hurtful effect of their conduct, the greater will be the blame, as this makes it appear that the harm was intentional. When blame is felt to be sufficiently

26. Peter Berliner: *Vold og Trusler på arbejdet* (Copenhagen 2000), pp. 17-18.
27. For a more detailed discussion and further references, see Rubin, Pruitt & Kim, op. cit., p. 76 et seq.; and Deutsch (ed.): *The Handbook of Conflict Resolution* (San Francisco 2000), particularly Chapter 11 by Keith G. Allred, 'Anger and Retaliation in Conflict: The Role of Attribution'.
28. Deutsch (ed.), op. cit., Chapter 11.

justified, there will be a desire to punish the other party. The other party will often react to this with anger.[29]

Studies of aggressive behaviour show that, in order for provocation to lead to an angry response, it must be regarded as an affront to one's self-esteem and honour or as a wrong against oneself or those closely associated with one. It seems that anger stems from an unconscious reaction to an assault on one's status.[30]

Fear

It seems that *fear* follows some of the same rules as anger, even though there has been relatively little research into the topic. But fear produces a circular movement which differs from that of blame and anger. Blame and anger dominate in a *spiral of revenge*, while fear dominates in a *spiral of defence*,[31] in which each party tries to protect themselves from the threat which the conduct of the other seems to constitute, even though, from the outside, the reactions seem similar.

Threats against one's self-esteem or reputation are an especially important cause of escalation, not least when the threat concerns status, autonomy, loyalty and integrity, i.e. identity. This produces both anger and anxiety. This applies equally to nations and to persons. Therefore, when people experience threats of this kind, this ought to be taken seriously and not dismissed as unreasonable or childish – as was the case initially to the reactions to the publication of the cartoons of the prophet Mohammed.

In the conflict ladder described below the parties proceed directly to conflict, and the dominant feeling is anger resulting in outwardly directed behaviour towards those who are the cause of the anger.

Conflict avoidance

When anxiety is the dominant feeling, whether due to structural factors or to one's own personality, the conflict

29. According to Rubin, Pruitt & Kim, forgiveness is unquestionably learned behaviour which presupposes a high level of mental activity by which one party must analyse the other party's situation and motivation, and compare these with the standards of proper behaviour; see op. cit., p. 78, note 9.
30. See, e.g., L. Berkowitz: *Aggression: Its Causes, Consequences and Control*, (New York 1993).
31. See Rubin et al, op. cit., Chapter 5.

will escalate, even though attempts are made to avoid it. The escalation will be largely based on inner images and interpretations, self-reproach, coldness, rejection of contact and co-operation, as well as control and inhibition. If, in the later stages, anxiety is mixed with anger against the other party, then destructive behaviour against the other party will be expressed in the anonymous use of power, for example terrorism.

Anxiety, and anger and aggression can have, but need not necessarily have, their basis in the psychological concept of projection. According to the well-known Swiss psychiatrist Carl Jung (1875-1961), the shadow-side of the ego consists of the inputs into our personality, both great and small, throughout our life which, with the prioritising that is determined by our time and our culture, we have often unconsciously chosen to reject, refute or deny or, equally unconsciously, we have chosen to identify ourselves with and develop. Because the development of the ego is selective, it is necessary to have a suppressing mechanism The ego is a product of choice, a part of one's much more comprehensive whole, but what we choose to reject slips into our unconscious, repressed, projected state where, in order to avoid seeing or noticing the undesirable or negative in oneself, one projects it onto others. Projections can thus be called the psychological detritus of the ego.[32]

Projection thus means that one unconsciously ascribes to others some of the qualities one has oneself but which one will not acknowledge. For example, if one thinks that someone else is dominating, talks too much, is too rigid in their opinions etc., it can very well be that one does the same oneself (or does not like to admit that one would like to do so).

The theory about projection brings us to what in conflict theory, is seen as playing out in the escalation process. The description of escalation starts at the point where one no longer keeps the person and the issue separate; one becomes ever more consumed by the conflict; individual is-

32. Likewise Jes Bertelsen, *Et essay om frihed*, 2010, pp. 99-100.

sues form the basis for generalisations; and the other party begins to appear to be the Devil incarnate, without shades of meaning or mitigating circumstances; and it all ends with one creating hostile images so that it is not only justifiable, but in fact correct to cause harm to the other party.

Projection and the subsequent escalation take place equally at the individual and collective and international levels. In recent years, the tendency of the Western world, not least in Denmark, to classify whole population groups (for example Muslims) as enemies, is a clear expression of the lack of a balanced view which arises when escalation takes possession. Likewise, there is projection when, for example, one nation ascribes to another nation certain characteristics which it has itself. Thus, the introduction of the term 'rogue states' by President Bush is a classic example of collective and unilateral projection – where both sides ascribed the very worst motives to the other, and apparently did not stop for a moment to consider how these could be a mirror-image of their own.

Here it should be emphasised that consciousness of projection does not mean that disagreements or even serious conflicts cannot arise. A life and a world without projection and conflict is an illusion. On the other hand, what it could mean is that the way in which we approach conflicts will be very different when we become aware of that part of our interaction which is part of ourselves and not a part of the others.

Integrity is the connection between actions, values, methods, measures, principles expectations and results.[33] Integrity is thus the opposite of unthinking projection. Expressed simply, it can be said that projection frees us from taking responsibility for our part in the conflict – and also here there is no difference between conflicts at the individual level and the international level. If we choose to remain in the 'projection camp', it is possible to cultivate hostile images and call all Muslims 'stupid' and 'dangerous', and to refer to states as being part of an 'axis of evil', and

33. Wikipedia. 24.10.2011.

thereby feel justified in carrying out exactly the same underhand acts as those we accuse the others of. The other party 'deserves it'.

Integrity means that we apply the moral standards we think have been infringed by others equally to our own conduct, even when this is felt to be uncomfortable and restrictive for us.

If the conflict is resolved, feelings of anxiety and anger will often be overlooked or at least disappear or be toned down. However, if the conflict becomes rooted, perhaps over several generations, these feelings will develop into more general attitudes. Negative attitudes and opinions, as well as isolation and dehumanisation, seem to have an enduring character and thus influence the structures in which the parties live.[34]

Negative attitudes and negative opinions not only cover specific behaviour, but they mean that conflicts can expand to encompass the view of the other party as a person with dubious morals, personality etc. It is interesting that there is a tendency for attitudes and opinions to be the same on both sides of the question. Each side is the mirror image of the other, but this is often unacknowledged by the parties, i.e., one party distrusts the other, but does not recognise that this distrust is reciprocated, and is possibly equally unjustified.[35]

It is obvious that negative attitudes and opinions not only make it easier for one party to blame the other, but form a basis on which the actions of the other party are more readily interpreted as threatening, leaving little room for doubt and for allowing the possibility of good intentions. This also means that, if it exists at all, the motivation for considering the good intentions of the other party is weakened and this affects communication between the parties. Thus, the developments in the wake of the cartoons of the prophet Mohammed must be seen in the light of the

34. See Rubin, Pruitt & Kim, op. cit. p. 84 et seq.
35. See R.K. White: *Fearful Warriors: A Psychological profile of U.S.-Soviet relations* (New York 1984); and Rubin, Pruitt & Kim, op. cit. p. 85.

very harsh tone of the public debate in Denmark on immigrants and the role of asylum seekers in Danish society.

Negative attitudes and opinions further reduce empathy with the other side and may promote *zero sum thinking* which makes a constructive resolution of the conflict virtually impossible.[36]

Sometimes in the development of a conflict, some people have a tendency to reproach themselves for the difficulties which arise, rather than blame the other party. It seems that self-reproach is more likely at the beginning, before a conflict escalates. When conflict is intensified, blame is nearly always directed at the other side. It is much more likely for one party to see how they react to the provocation of the other party themselves than to be aware how the other party reacts to their own provocation.

V. Escalation

Circular movement of action and reaction

Conflicts go through different phases in the escalation process, and these seem to be almost universally valid.[37] There follows a short description of the escalation process, which is useful in a mediation context.[38]

Standard scenario for conflict

Even though every conflict is unique, as the parties in one conflict are never identical to the parties in another conflict and the cultural contexts of conflicts each have their own distinct characteristics, it nevertheless seems possible to write a standard scenario for conflict escalation, and to identify a pattern of increasingly destructive intensity, including the psychological mechanisms described above. Naturally, not every conflict will run through all 7

36. See Chapter 7 on the zero sum view of conflict.
37. The reader is referred to Rubin, Pruitt & Kim, op. cit., for a detailed discussion of this.
38. The model, which is based on Rubin, Pruitt & Kim has been worked out by the Northern Ireland peace workers, Diane and John Lampen, and has been tried in many different cultural contexts. The model is used in a revised version for teaching at the Center for Konfliktløsning and is printed in the Center's collected materials, see www.konfliktloesning.dk.

stages of the scenario, but the risk that it might is real and predictable, unless countermeasures are taken in due time.[39]

Step 1: Disagreement

Step 1: Disagreement

At the first step of the conflict ladder the parties acknowledge their disagreement, and attention is focused on the subject of the disagreement. The parties agree that they disagree, and both (or all) parties are sufficiently sensible to direct their efforts purely at the subject of their disagreement, and not against each other. In the literature of negotiation, this is described as *keeping the problem and the person separate*.[40]

The interface of conflict

After a period of disagreement, a certain amount of 'interference on the line' can arise and one or both of the parties can begin to feel a certain reserve towards the other.[41]

The transition to blending the person and the problem is an essential part of conflict escalation, and if it is recognised in time, it is possible to take countermeasures relatively easily.[42] It is here that escalation takes root. As shown in Figure 1, the change only seldom takes place at the same time for both parties, but has a circular motion which makes both parties responsible for the development. In order to prevent further escalation, it is therefore necessary for both parties to be aware of the change. If only one of the

39. The Austrian economist, Friedrich Glasl, has also described a conflict ladder, which is often referred to. Glasl's version of the conflict ladder has nine steps, of which the first three describe a win-win approach, the next three a win-lose approach, and the last three a lose-lose approach. See Friedrich Glasl, *Konfliktmanagement – Ein Handbuch für Führungskräfte, Beratterinnen und Berater*, Stuttgart, 1999.
40. See Fisher, Patton & Ury, *Getting to Yes* (New York 1983).
41. The emphasis of this as a separate stage of the escalation process is due to Else Hammerich & Bjarne Vestergaard, *Mindful Conflict Resolution* (Dharamsala 2001).
42. Such measures include awareness of the language used, whether one expresses oneself in the abstract, focuses on the future or the past etc. Factors which can increase or decrease stress are dealt with later in this chapter.

parties refuses to 'play along' this will often be enough to return the conflict to Step 1.

Step 2: Personification

Step 2: Personification

On the other hand, if the blending of the person and the problem is not recognised, or if countermeasures are not implemented, the conflict will escalate with the parties beginning to suspect the motives, and possibly also the character, of the other as described in IV. Each party may believe that the other is the cause of the conflict, not themselves. The parties can become doubtful and confused, and communication between them can likewise become confused and incomplete. Accusations, defences and misunderstandings become part of the transaction. The person and the problem are no longer kept separate, and there is greater distance between the parties.

Step 3: The problem grows

Step 3: The problem grows

At this stage the parties are suspicious of each other, and earlier events and unresolved differences are dragged into the picture to lend support to suspicions. New events are interpreted on the basis of mistrust, and each party focuses on the faults and inadequacies of the other. Considerations such 'he always does that' or 'they did it last time, too' increasingly shift responsibility for the conflict onto the other party and divert attention from constructive possibilities for negotiation. The stress increases and defensive ramparts are raised.

Step 4: Dialogue is abandoned

Step 4: Dialogue is abandoned

In the end communication becomes so muddled and is filtered through such negative feelings that the parties begin to avoid one another and dialogue is abandoned. 'I've said it a hundred times, and you still don't listen' is the kind of thing everyone has heard said, and it characterises this stage where each party distorts what the other says and does not listen properly. This is popularly called 'the dialogue of the deaf'. Instead of talking *to* each other, the parties now talk *about* each other to third parties, not to hear another point of view or get a better understanding of the situation, but to find an ally. Dialogue between the parties is substituted by behaviour which illustrates the distance between them, for example by failing to greet the other, avoiding eye contact, making faces to others, turning one's back, yawning when the other party says something and so on.

Step 5: Images of hostility

At this level, the view of the other party is coloured by the attitudes projected onto them, and the parties only see in each other those qualities which they do not want to recognise in themselves. The conflict is portrayed in black and white, with heroes and villains, them or us, an eye for an eye, 'you're either for me, or against me' and so on. The only thing that matters is being right, and the conflict can only be brought to an end when the other party surrenders or gives an unconditional apology.

Step 5: Images of hostility

This is no place to consider why the conflict arose in the first place. The conflict has its own gravitational pull, drawing everything towards it. The parties cannot talk about anything else. They are both repelled by and attracted by the conflict. It becomes part of who they are.

Step 6: Open hostility

Open hostility follows, which is almost autistic in nature, since the view of reality is veiled and the opponents no longer see each other as fellow human beings who suffer from conflicts and wrongdoing just like everyone else, but they are seen as monsters who must be rendered harmless. The end justifies the means and open hostility, both physical and psychological, seems justified. Actions which will damage the other party are considered justified.

Step 6: Open hostility

Friends or allies who urge moderation are seen as traitors and are dismissed by both parties. All subtlety and sympathy vanishes.

Step 7: Polarisation

Co-existence is now impossible; warfare, retiring to a ghetto, firing employees, or divorce are seen as the only way out. At best, the conflict ends when the parties no

Step 7: Polarisation

longer see each other, but at worst, they continue to assail each other from a distance, literally or metaphorically.

The scenario for escalation:

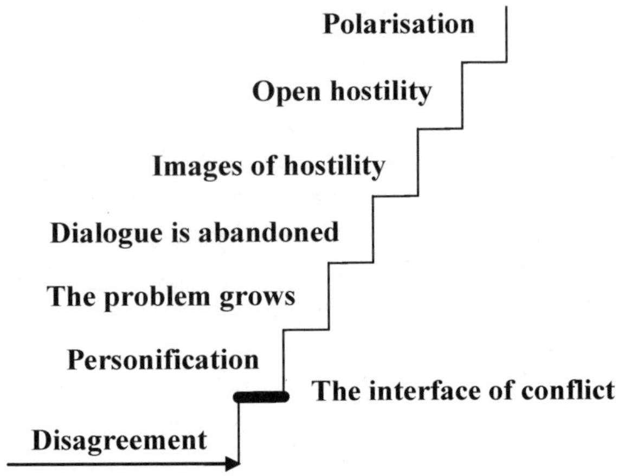

Figure 4. The conflict ladder

Scope for preventing conflict

Knowing the various steps of the scenario makes it easier to evaluate what intervention will be helpful, since it is supposed that there will be an interest in avoiding further escalation of the conflict. This supposition is important, as knowledge of the scenario increases the scope for preventing conflict, not in terms of avoiding conflicts altogether, but rather avoiding the escalation of an existing conflict to a destructive level.

The conflict ladder can also be used as an explanatory aid during mediation. The parties will usually nod in recognition of the development and it takes some of the drama out of the situation, partly because it makes it clear that escalation involves both sides of the conflict, and partly because, despite the uniqueness of their conflict, it nevertheless has things in common with other conflicts, which they may know about, and which it has been possible to solve.

'De-individualisation'

An important but little regarded characteristic of conflict escalation is the change which takes place when one no longer sees the other party as an individual but as part of a group. This 'de-individualising' has a tendency to lead to de-humanising. From here there is an almost rational acceptance of one's hostility, making it easier to behave injuriously against the other party, who is no longer worthy of being protected by the general norm that one should not harm other people.

Name-calling, for example the use of animal names (pigs, rats, snakes), is a sign that one party deprives the other of their status as a human being, that the other party is morally corrupt and different from oneself, and this makes it easier, or even justifiable, to harm them.

It is thought provoking that, in depriving another of their status as an individual, one identifies oneself with a group and gives oneself a group status (white as against black, Christian as against Jew or Muslim), laying the foundation for a corresponding de-humanisation and de-individualisation of oneself.

VI. The language of escalation and de-escalation ('Me'-oriented language and seeing things from our own standpoint)

When parties are in conflict with one another, it is usual for each to be of the view that the other side has done something wrong: 'If only you hadn't done so-and-so, or *had* done so-and-so, I wouldn't have had this conflict'.

The feeling that the other side is overwhelmingly to blame for one's misfortune is often dominant, and is seen in the expressions we use when we grumble or otherwise describe our situation. The problem with this common form of expression is that while we express our anger or pain, we ascribe motives to others which we do not know to be true. We overstep the mark, which means that the other party goes on the defensive.

It is important for a mediator to be aware of which forms of expression can have an escalating effect on a conflict, and how, by expressing oneself differently, one party can express their concerns and anger without the other party shutting out their complaints. Mediators should, if possible, use their knowledge and awareness in the mediation process to gently educate the parties in the use of non-confrontational communication.

The second person form of address

The most obvious way of expressing oneself in the language of escalation is to use the second person form of address, in other words to talk about the behaviour and thoughts of others instead of expressing one's own point of view in the first person, to interrupt rather than listen to the end, to ascribe blame rather than expressing one's wishes, to talk in the abstract rather than of the specifics, and to be personal – 'playing the man' rather than 'playing the ball'.[43]

If one starts from one's own position and stays within one's own territory, it is easier to explain one's concerns without offending the other party. If one listens, without being over-eager to put one's own point of view, new information may be obtained which may eliminate misunderstandings. If one is clear about what one wants rather than blaming the other party for something they may not have been aware of, it is easier for the other party to see if one's wishes can be met. If one is specific about what angers one, this is less overwhelming for the other party than if they are accused, for example, of 'never' being on time (which is seldom correct). If one tackles the problem, rather than telling the person that they are incompetent, it becomes possible to make the problem something which can be shared and solved in co-operation.

'Giraffe language'

The American psychologist Marshall Rosenberg, with help from Carl Rogers[44], has developed a simple method which enables people to express themselves in a way which helps them to achieve what they want without oppressing the other party. Rosenberg has named the method 'Giraffe language', because the giraffe is the animal with the largest heart and the best overview.

43. Based on *Kunsten at løse konflikter*, Center for Konfliktløsning, September 1997.
44. See chapter 5, section on 'empathy'.

Non-violent communication has four components:

1. Observation (where one states the facts, non-judgementally, without interpretation, analysis, etc.);
2. Feelings (one express what feelings these facts give rise to in oneself);
3. Needs (one identifies one's needs, without involving the other party in them);
4. Request (one asks the other party for something, but not in the nature of a demand).

An example:

'When you arrived this morning at twenty past eight' (instead of 'When you arrived late this morning'),

'I was very annoyed' (instead of 'I think you are totally irresponsible'),

'I need our agreement about when to be here to be kept to, so I can start work' (instead of 'I just don't know how I'm going to get everything done, and it's your fault')

'So I want to discuss how we can make an agreement we can stick to, about when we are to meet. Are you prepared to do this?' (instead of 'You'll just have to pull yourself together.')

The point about this method is that it makes it possible for a person to express themselves clearly and honestly, while maintaining respect and empathy for the other party. In the example given above there is scope for the other party to explain why, for various practical reasons, it is almost impossible for them to arrive at eight o'clock precisely, and that a change in the working hours would make their timekeeping more reliable, so that to meet at 8.30, for example, would be a great improvement.[45]

Giraffe language is not a tool which can be used mechanically. If one turns the four stages into a mere technique, without having a genuine intention of establishing

45. For further reading on 'Giraffe language', see Marshall B. Rosenberg, *Nonviolent Communication: A Language of Compassion*, published in Danish by Borgen, 1999. See also Bodil Weirsøe: *Girafsprog - Empatisk kommunikation i pædagogens arbejde* (Copenhagen 2002).

good communication with the other party, it is more likely that this will quickly provoke resistance and mistrust, rather than move the process forward.

In the context of mediation it will seldom be the case that all four stages will be directly applicable, unless the parties express a need to improve their communication, and the mediator is encouraged to give brief information about the method. For example, this may occur in connection with a conflict between colleagues where, as part of the solution, the parties wish to improve the communication between them for the future.

More usually a mediator will ask the parties, who by this time will probably have escalated the conflict to the point where they are full of blame for each other, to express how they perceive some specific conduct and what they want to achieve, rather than expressing blame. In this way, non-violent language can help to improve communication between the parties.

CHAPTER 5

Truth, dialogue and culture

What is characteristic of the themes of truth, contact, and empathy is that they are closely linked to each other and can all be actively engaged throughout the mediation process, between the mediator and the parties and between the parties themselves. Since understanding of these is also often affected by cultural background, this makes awareness of the nuances even more important. The mediator's understanding of this is decisive for establishing dialogue and for the success of the mediation.

Weighty tomes could be written on each of these themes, which are communicative, philosophical and value-based. Indeed, such books have been written. However, here the themes will only be dealt with in sufficient detail to enable them to be recognised and acted on during mediation. If further discussion is required, the reader is referred to the specialised literature.

Since understanding of the concept of truth is absolutely decisive for the other concepts, this will be dealt with first.

I. Truth

What is true and what is false is obviously important in mediation and conflict resolution, as in most other contexts. However, the concept of truth is much more multi-faceted than one might suspect, and since this has direct consequences for the practice of mediation, it is important to understand this.

A shared truth

It may be strange to say so directly, but what makes people seek mediation is that they cannot agree on a shared truth. Many conflicts, including wars, are concerned with claims to be in the right and attempting to convince the other party that one's own truth is the real truth. To be 'in the right' means the other party is in the wrong. This means that the concept is very black and white; it gives winners and losers. But if one accepts that truth is only objective and measurable to a limited extent, it becomes possible to develop an alternative 'truth' jointly.

The truth of each

When each side speaks on the basis of its own truth, it is the task of the mediator to listen and to believe the truth of each, and to try to see if there are any common denominators.

The following story from the Sufi tradition illustrates the concept of truth in mediation:

On the other side of Ghor there was a town. All its inhabitants were blind. A king and his followers came to a place close by this town. He had his army with him, and they made a camp in the desert. He also had a huge elephant which was used in battle, to frighten and impress people.

The people were eager to find out more about this elephant, and some of the blind people from the town were so inquisitive that they ran out to find it.

As they didn't know anything about the shape of an elephant they felt their way around and learnt about the elephant by touch.

Now, everyone thought they knew about elephants, because they had all felt some part of the creature.

When they went back to their town, the people crowded around them eagerly. All wanted to hear the truth from those who didn't know it.

They asked what shape an elephant was, and listened to what was said.

One man who had felt the elephant's ear was asked about what the elephant was like and he said: 'It is a large rough thing, flat and wide like a carpet.'

A man who had felt the trunk said: 'It's like a large hollow pipe, terrifying and destructive.'

One who had felt its feet and legs said: 'It is massive and solid, like a stone column.'

Each of them had felt only one part of the many. All had the wrong impression. None of them knew the truth. All imagined something that was wrong.[1]

And so they could argue about who was right. Each of them had created an animal which did not exist. What they had found was something which lay within the range of concepts they knew already. They had taken part of the truth to be the whole truth. From their own perspective, each of the blind people had a part of the truth, even though their information seemed contradictory. If they had listened to each other, instead of believing that only they knew the truth, they would have got a much more varied picture of the elephant which would have been closer to the truth.

The South African Truth and Reconciliation Commission worked with four notions of truth: factual or forensic; personal and narrative; social or 'dialogue'; healing and restorative.

Factual or objective truth

Personal or subjective truth

Social truth

Healing and restorative truth

Factual or forensic truth: legal or scientific information. At the individual level this means information about particular events and specific people, what exactly happened to whom, where, when and how. At the societal level it means recording the context, causes and patterns of violations; an interpretation of the facts that should at least erode any denials about the past. Disinformation once accepted as truth must lose its credibility.

Personal and narrative truth: the stories told by perpetrators and (more extensively) victims. This is an opportunity for the healing potential of testimony, for adding to the collective truth and for building reconciliation by validating the subjective experiences of people who have previously been silenced or voiceless.

Social truth: the truth generated by interaction, discussion and debate arising from experience and interaction – often culturally determined. Hearings provide transparency and encourage participation. Conflicting views about

1. This story is retold by Helen Gamborg in *Det usynlige i helbredelse* (Viborg 1991) p. 7.

the past can be considered and compared. It is the process that matters rather than the end result.

Healing and restorative truth: the narratives that face the past in order to go forward. Truth as a factual record is not enough; interpretation must be directed towards the goals of self-healing, reconciliation and reparation. This requires the acknowledgement that everyone's suffering is real and worthy of attention.[2]

In addition to these, in the context of conflict resolution, it can be useful to add another, an *existential* truth, which covers the basic conditions of existence, and is bigger than us and bigger than society, and which we can do nothing about, for example the fact that we are born, grow older and die.

For example, the factual truth may be that temperature in a room is 20 °C. The temperature can be measured by a correctly calibrated thermometer. The temperature is thus factual and objective, though one should be aware that the statement of the temperature expresses a unit of measurement which, in the mists of time, it was agreed should be expressed in this way and which may thus, to some extent, be called a social truth. If a person then says that they think the room is cold, this is an expression of a subjective truth which will not be altered by the fact that another person in the same room thinks that the temperature is just right. Finally, the existential truth in this context could be that our bodies cannot tolerate temperatures below a certain level without suffering harm.

On the face of it, one could classify both factual and existential truth as objective, but they are distinguished by the fact that, in contrast to factual truths, many existential truths are denied, despite their significance. Our culture today seems to be in denial about some of the basic truths, which we do not learn to evaluate properly.

When parties do not have the same view of the truth, what is initially relevant for mediation is not whether they are lying, but that they say what they say because they be-

2. See Albie Sachs, *The Strange Alchemy of Life and Law*, Oxford, 2009.

lieve it, or because they need to have what they say stated as the truth. All of us are blind to some extent, including mediators, so a mediator must put brackets round feelings that what has been said may not be true. What matters is that the mediator believes that the parties mean what they say, while they say it. The only thing mediator can use their 'intuition' for is as a basis for further questioning and doubt, which can either result in the party saying more, enabling the mediator to understand better, or the party or parties say something very different, so the originally expressed 'truth' is changed.

Phenomenology

This approach to truth in mediation is phenomenological. This means that it is based on subjective experience. Our view of truth is not determined merely by what we can describe, but also by our experience, who we are, what we have learnt, and our values and assets in general. Each party to a mediation will lay out their narrative on the basis of their knowledge and information, observations, interpretations, and conclusions. When one realises that so many factors have to be taken into account to reach 'the truth', it becomes easier to understand that there are so many opportunities for making mistakes, and that others can have different information, experiences and so on.

For lawyers this can be a provocative way of looking at truth. In mediation, truth is seen as a concrete concept which is defined on the basis of the individual's reality. Truth can be found in small bits, as part of the whole, and it is not found in modern legal thinking, through the application of judicial procedures, since the circumstances of witness testimony often lead to varied views of the truth. This concept of truth may also be provocative for professional groups other than lawyers.

It is precisely this view of the concept of truth which is particularly emphasised in the narrative model of mediation. The aim of this form of mediation is, as described in Chapter 2, to help the parties deconstruct their narratives in order for them to build them up again a new. Because of the decisive requirement for contact between the mediator and the parties in the non-model described here, it would be more correct to describe the mediation process as helping the parties by giving *recognition* of the narrative with the possibility of *developing and expanding* it, rather than a deconstruction, which can be understood as a rejection of it or as having the goal of changing it and thereafter reconstructing it.

Mediation and therapy

In order for there to be contact, the parties must be allowed to have their personal views of things. We must be alert to the different levels of truth which include a desire to be understood at a deeper level. In mediation, the different kinds of truth must be laid open and related to one another. Quite often, denial of the objective, subjective and existential truths are mixed together. The mediator can deal with these different areas, without being a therapist. The boundary to therapy will not be overstepped where relevant matters are dealt with, but it will be overstepped if the mediator becomes involved in something which has nothing to do with the mediation, such as the relations of a party to others outside the mediation process, drawing on previous experience in other contexts etc.[3] Briefly, therapy can be described as being concerned with a person discovering who he or she is; mediation is concerned with a person discovering what he or she should do.

If in the course of mediation the mediator succeeds in communicating this understanding of the truth, this will often give release. The debate about which of the parties is right will thus fall silent, as there will be mutual acceptance that the stories and views of both parties can both be right and have a justifiable basis. Naturally, recognition of the subjective element of truth does not mean that one can ignore the facts, whose clarification is highly important to the process. However, it is the awareness of the dividing line between what is objective and factual and what is subjective that can lead to a solution.

3. See for example, Joan Dworkin, Lynn Jacob & Elisabeth Scott, 'The Boundaries Between Mediation and Therapy: Ethical Dilemmas', *Mediation Quarterly* Vol. 9 No 2, 1991 pp. 107-119. See also Kenneth Cloke, *Mediating Dangerously – The Frontiers of Conflict Resolution*, US, 2001.

II. Contact

Definition of contact

Contact and empathy are closely connected and both are based on a view of the concept of truth described above. Contact is also a key concept in mediation because it creates confidence and promotes the ability of the parties to open themselves to the possibility of finding a solution. Contact is also important because it is only through contact that one can discover another person's view of the truth. *Contact* can be described as *a meeting between two separate people, at which there is an exchange* of feelings, words, thoughts, eye-contact, actions etc. It is an exchange which has *particular significance,* which each of the parties is able to perceive, interpret and react to. Since this exchange always takes place in a situation, in an environment and at a time, the necessary requirements for contact are; *a sender, a receiver and a situation which exists in relation to them – here and now.*[4]

Professional contact facilitators

Mediators can be considered as professional contact facilitators. This means they must have a dual awareness, directed both towards the respondents and towards themselves, because a precondition for contact is the mediator's honest presence. One cannot force oneself to have contact, or feel obliged to have contact, without absolute honesty. It may be possible in the short run, but this will be revealed and its absence will give rise to distrust between the parties and the mediator.

However, what constitutes honesty in a professional context is another matter. Honesty does not necessarily consist in saying everything, as it is possible and often necessary to select. What one should reveal to the parties is not obvious. But one should be able to stand by what is said. There is therefore a close connection between the view of the truth and an ability to make contact.

The character of the meeting is of key importance to the mediation. It is not possible simultaneously to be open to contact and devious. A hidden agenda, a particular objective in questioning, will affect the openness of the questions

4. See Hanne Hostrup: *Gestaltterapi* (Copenhagen 1999) p. 118 et seq.

asked. If one has some particular objective, one will have to put one's questions within a frame of interpretation which is shaped by one's own professional or personal background. This type of questioning can naturally also be justified in mediation.

However, if one wishes to achieve contact, one must put brackets round what one already knows, and ask questions on the basis of genuine interest, solely aimed at obtaining more information and finding out more about the worlds of the respondents. Naturally, a party or a mediator can guess or interpret, but this is not appropriate. What is interesting in mediation is what the other party and the mediator do *not* know, so the mediator must refrain from drawing conclusions too hastily on the basis of what a party says from their own frame of reference, and must continue to seek and ask questions to obtain further information. A mediator must remain on the same level as the party, and not get caught up in interpretations about what may lie in the background. The mediator must therefore be willing to say: 'Yes, that's how it is, but let's see if together we can't find out whether there is more to it.' All too often on closer investigation a conclusion drawn too rapidly is shown to be wrong. The mediator must play the detective, with genuine inquisitiveness.

This is what is meant by reacting to one's feelings with open questions. As a mediator one must be personally engaged, but this should not be confused with issues of privacy, and the limits to what should be taken account of in mediation. Thus, to be a mediator is closely linked to openness and to genuine inquisitiveness about what it means to be human.

III. Empathy

Contact is important for being able to find out how the truth appears to each individual. We exhibit empathy, or compassion, when we are *able to imagine what it is like to experience that truth.* If we are unable to imagine something, we must ask.

Definition of empathy

The psychologist Carl Rogers has defined empathy as follows: *'Being empathic, is to perceive the internal frame of reference of another with accuracy and with the emotional components and meanings which pertain thereto as if one were the person, but without ever losing the 'as if' condition.'*[5]

Empathy can arise when there is an ability to make contact and a willingness to 'imagine' oneself to be in the same position as the other person. This means that empathy is impossible without contact, for example, because one cannot believe what the other person says.

This involves understanding the sorrows and pleasures of another person as they feel them, but without ever forgetting to recognise that it is *as if* one were happy or sad oneself. If this 'as if' condition is lost, there will be a state of identification, and as a mediator one will have lost impartiality and entered into an alliance with the injured party. One must be able to discover the truth of the individual without losing one's own truth.

A *primary* precondition for empathy is willingness to be receptive to the other person's body language, facial expression, breathing, projection, etc. and to relate to the whole person with both head and heart.

A *second* element of empathy is the mediator's willingness to accept, unconditionally and positively, how the parties experience the world. If one questions the justification for a party's situation or their perception of it, then neither contact nor empathy will be possible.[6]

Ability and willingness to listen

A *third* precondition for contact and for empathy is naturally the mediator's ability and willingness to listen. This is discussed in more detail in Chapter 6.

5. Rogers in Howard Kirschenbaum & Valerie Land Henderson (eds.): *The Carl Rogers Reader* (Constable & Co, London 1989) p. 236.
6. In recent years many authors have written about empathy. See for example, Judy Gammelgaard: *Mellem mennesker – træk af indfølingens psykologi* (Copenhagen 2000); Ole Vedfelt: *Bevidsthed* (Copenhagen 1998); Ole Vedfelt: *Ubevidst Intelligens* (Copenhagen 2000); Daniel Goleman: *Emotional Intelligense*, Boston 1995; and Daniel Goleman: *Working with Emotional Intelligense*, Boston 1998.

The view of truth, contact and empathy described here is closely connected to the fundamental assumption that each party is an expert in their own lives. A truth which is revealed by a party themselves can sometimes be harsh and uncomfortable, but it will not disturb the party's view of reality, and it will therefore be less damaging than an untruth, and as a rule it will provide a better basis for the party to take decisions about how they wish to act in the future. As a mediator, one must therefore not refrain from helping the party reveal the realities out of a mistaken sense of charity, provided that the challenge is dealt with supportively.

IV. Dialogue

The understanding of truth, as described above, together with ability to make contact and to empathise, is a precondition for the creation of a true dialogue.

Definition of dialogue

Share, dare and care

Dialogue can be defined as an *investigative, unpredictable and risky discussion, in which the truth or the best solution cannot be assumed in advance.* The only thing that can be assumed in advance is that no-one can, on their own, produce a satisfactory solution.[7] Dialogue can thus be characterised by three words: share, dare and care. One must share one's experiences, competences and perspectives; one must dare to take the risk of being wrong or of being wiser by laying out one's viewpoints and fundamental assumptions to collective examination; and one must care for each other and build up proper relationships which allow room both for dialogue and for a shared future.

It is usual to consider dialogue as a form of conversation which can be used between people who are already largely in agreement. However, this is not the correct understanding of the concept of dialogue which, in its true form, can

7. See Marianne Kristiansen & Jørgen Bloch-Poulsen, 'Dialog og dialogiske kompetencer – en ny form for magt?', in Helle Alrø & Marianne Krsitensen (eds.): *Dialog og magt i organisnationer*, Ålborg Universitetsforlag, 2004, pp. 11-34.

be particularly fruitful even with those with whom one has strong disagreements, as it requires a decision to be made to listen.

Potential of dialogue

The potential of dialogue, both in mediation and elsewhere, is that it can be used to examine the rules we usually use for communication, whether we defend our views or whether we listen. With the help of dialogue we can go further and examine the deeper meaning of an opinion, statement etc., and by means of dialogue it is possible to reveal differences which then makes it possible to find common ground.[8]

Example: The Danish Government's rejection of a meeting with the ambassadors from 11 Muslim countries, after the publications of the cartoons of the prophet Mohammed in the autumn of 2005, on the clear ground that Danish freedom of expression was non-negotiable, was presumably an expression of the 'usual' rules for communication, but it showed an incorrect view of the nature of dialogue. Subsequently, this rejection of the possibility of dialogue has been one of the main criticisms of the Danish Prime Minister's handling of the issue[9].

The nature of the dialogue is not to win over the other party by argument but to make oneself available to the other party with one's knowledge and viewpoint, while being inquisitive about the other's knowledge and viewpoint. This means that dialogue provides a foundation for being better informed both about oneself and the other's view of the world.[10] With their ability to enter into dialogue, mediators must show the parties how to resolve their conflict by dialogue.

If, at its heart, the conflict concerns a violent infringement of a person's basic needs, dialogue can help at a cer-

8. See e.g. Stephen W. Littlejohn & Kathy Demenici: *Engaging Communication in Conflict*, 2000, pp 26-28.
9. See Ch. 6 on interests and needs.
10. See Vibeke Vindeløv, *Konflikt, tvist og mægling* (Copenhagen 1997), Chapter 17, 3.2. 'Kærlighedskampen', as well as Chapter **4** in this book on dialogue in conflicts of values.

tain stage – to open channels to the opponent and to find common ground for negotiation.

But if the party who is infringing the other's basic needs maintains their position and intends to carry on with their infringements, it is no longer the time for a dialogue in order to 'learn something new'. It is then time to be true to one's fundamental values, which do not allow for violence, but require respect for people's fundamental needs.[11] Anyone who takes on the work of a mediator must already have decided that they will enter into dialogue and must develop their skills for this. It is different for the parties involved. They come to mediation after communication with the other party has broken down and the conflict and the parties have taken several steps up the conflict ladder.

It is thus the first task of the mediator's to make contact with and develop empathy for each of the parties, and then to work to increase contact between the parties.

When, in the course of the mediation, the parties become more willing to look one another in the eye and to address one another in a proper manner, this is a sign that the level of the conflict has fallen, that dialogue is possible and the basis for successful mediation has been created.

V. Intercultural aspects

Members of a 'global village'

Since we all are members of a 'global village', even if we do not directly seek it, we will increasingly have parties coming to us who are from cultures that are different from our own. It can therefore be useful to look briefly at the differences in mediating between parties from different cultures and 'ordinary' mediation.

'Culture' is a difficult concept. Culture can both be inclusive and exclusive, in the sense that some people are considered as being included in a particular culture while others are outside it. The concept of culture therefore also contains some inherent tensions, as it consists of an entity

11. Hammerich & Frydensberg, p. 79.

to which we refer and have an objective relationship with, and towards which we also have a subjective relationship from the standpoint from which we speak.

Moreover, culture is often referred to both as a problem and a solution. The dispute about the cartoons of Mohammed, which is referred to several times in this book, is a good example of how the incompatibility of cultures can be an explanation for a problem and how, for example, the Prime Minister's attempt to use humour to reduce tension had more the effect of intensifying the crisis than mitigating it, when there are different cultures which do not have the same understanding of humour.

It is not an exaggeration to say that different countries have widely differing views about the place of religion in public life. Views about the secular are also vastly different, and fundamental values and specific taboos differ between countries and cultures and are often implicit.

An important element of the practice of mediation is thus the mediator's sensitivity to the cultural factors which may apply between the parties involved. Of course, the more foreign the mediator is to the culture of the parties, the more this sensitivity must be increased. Here the mediator must not only engage their genuine inquisitiveness but also their willingness to learn from the parties about their values and traditions, while the mediator must naturally be true to their own values.

For example, many cultures are far more collectivist or communitarian than mainstream western cultures, and this must have an effect on mediation. If a mediation concerns a conflict between parties from different cultures, it is important that they should 'come to understand their basic cultural differences and create commonality in their interaction which facilitates communication and problem solving' without which 'misunderstanding and breakdown in international meetings may result from the often unconscious expectations that negotiators, mediators and educators bring to these encounters from their own cultures' expectations that are not shared by their counterparts from other cultures'.[12]

Sensitivity towards the cultural factors

Even though *Kimmel's* work focuses on conflicts between parties from different cultures, his comments are just as valid in situations where the mediator is from a culture that is different to that of the parties.

A western, post-industrial, nuclear family context

Cultural differences may be seen when several parties participate in a mediation. In a collectivist-oriented culture, many more participants than the parties directly involved may have an interest in how the mediation develops. *Tony Whatling* and *Mohamed M Keshavjee* describe this vividly: 'Mediators working in a western post-industrial nuclear family context are used to recognising the importance of "significant others", e.g. parents, brothers and sisters, friends and perhaps new partners, all holding partisan views and opinions that may be important to the mediator to inquire about, if they are not to risk sabotaging any agreements created between the two parties in the mediation room. However, within the non-western cultural group, this "chorus" of opinions and concerns is likely to involve many more "stakeholders" and significant community sub-groups. Besides questions and concerns about the extent to which mediation will be fair, competent, equitable, legally binding, in the best interests of the children etc., some groups (e.g. extended family members, elders and religious leaders) will pay attention as to whether the marriage can be saved, whether the community has in some way failed this couple, whether the couple are aware of the range of support and counselling services available within the community etc. Parents and grandparents may have concerns about financial loans, investments, land rights, property given to the couple towards house purchase or business start-up funds. Employers may be concerned about the physical and psychological health of the

More 'stakeholders' and significant community sub-groups

12. Paul Kimmel, 'Culture and Conflict', in Morton Deutsch: *The Handbook of Conflict Resolution*, 2000, p. 453.

employee and the extent to which he/she will be able to concentrate on duties in the workplace etc.'[13]

A question which can fundamentally challenge the western mediator's ethic can arise when, on the basis of their cultural and historical context, the parties express a clear expectation that when all the parties to the conflict have been heard, the mediator will produce a solution to it, and if the mediator refrains from doing so, they will run the risk of being considered a fiasco as a mediator, and the mediation process will not be respected.

Mediation which involves several very different cultures unquestionably represents a challenge both for the parties and for the mediator. The American Mennonite, *John Paul Lederach*, who has given training in several South American countries, has described how 'trainer talk' can become an obstacle. 'In Panama after my first day of training someone said that mediators were like "guides" leading people through complexities. The image stuck. By the end of the week we almost never spoke of "mediators" but rather of "guides" and the process of "guiding". Language is not merely a process of communicating, but is an essential feature of the conflict experience'[14] – and, one might add, of conflict resolution.

13. Mohamed M. Keshavjee & Tony Whatling, 'Reflective learnings from the training programmes of the Ismaili Muslim conciliation and arbitration boards, globally', presented at the 5th International Conference of the World Mediation Forum, Crans-Montana, Switzerland, 2005.
14. John Paul Lederach in David Augsburger: *Mediation across cultures*, 1992.

CHAPTER 6

Active listening and movement in communication

I. Positions, interests and needs

A key element of conflict mediation is helping the parties to move the focus away from their positions and towards their interests and needs. This process can only be promoted if the mediator is able to introduce a true dialogue in which the truths, feelings etc. of the parties are acknowledged. In the following there will first be a description of the theoretical understanding of positions, interests and needs, and then of how movement from positions towards interests and needs can be initiated.

Graphically, the movement can be shown as a movement down from mountains, where the peaks represent positions and sea level represents fundamental needs.

Positions

When the parties put forward their demands and *positions*, they are each at the tops of their mountains, where it is cold, there is a steep descent and a great distance between peaks from where people can shout to each other without being heard. In the mediation process, the different interests which lie behind the claims of the parties are gradually revealed, leading to a more sophisticated understanding of one's own and the other party's reasoning. When the parties move, they move down off the mountain and the distance between them is diminished. When the underlying needs are identified, the parties reach a common ground where they can listen to each other, and where their needs are equally valued.

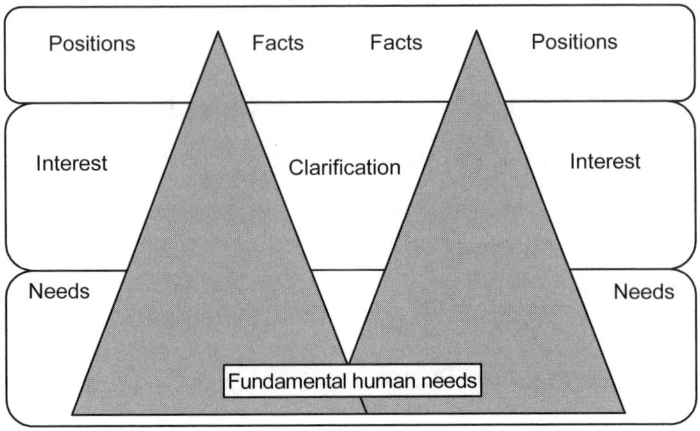

Figure 5. The 'mountains' of positions

This movement describes the psychological processes of the parties. Movement and recognising the needs of others do *not* mean that one's own needs and interests must be given up, and this must be stressed repeatedly. Even if one party still disagrees with the other party's conclusions about the unmet needs, and thus with the positions stated by the other party, the other party's motives become understandable, leading to increased flexibility and willingness and ability to find creative solutions to meet the needs and interests of both parties, so a balance can be achieved.

With positions, the parties formulate their demands and express them in a way they believe will best redress the wrong they feel they have suffered. Demands contain both an expression of the wrong suffered or feared, and a more or less well thought through assessment of a justified reaction to the wrong. Positions can vary from a demand for a neighbour to cut down a tree because it casts a shadow, to payment of money, to demanding an apology, to scrapping missiles etc.

A prerequisite for a conflict arising is that the other party perceives a demand as being unreasonable, and if not before, they would now feel wronged if the demand were met. If a conflict is decided on the basis of positions, some wrong to either or both of the parties is inevitable, as there will either be a winner and a loser, or a compromise in which both parties give way.

Interests

Interests

Positions or demands are motivated by various factors referred to as *'interests'*. These must be accommodated to some extent if there is to be an acceptable solution.[1]

Often, understanding the first level of the parties' interests is not enough to enable a conflict to be resolved. One has to look at what lies behind the surface interests, and sometimes behind these again. There will typically be a hierarchy of interests ending in basic human needs. An example of a hierarchy of positions, interests and needs is given in the figure below.[2]

Hierarchy of positions, interests and needs

Son's claims, interests and needs	**Father's claims, interests and needs**
Buy a motorbike ↓ Enjoy the sound of power ↓ Attract attention for example from neighbours ↓ Impress important people ↓ Gain self-respect	No motorbike ↓ Peace and quiet ↓ Not attracting attention ↓ Being respected by the community

Figure 6. Hierarchy of interests and needs

1. Moore, *The Mediation Process*, 2nd ed., p. 71 et seq., divides interests into 3 groups: psychological, procedural, and substantive. However, this division only indicates the *type* of motivation, and not the *importance* of that type of motivation for the individual, as this will depend on the actual conflict.
2. The example is based on Rubin, p. 180 and will be further developed.

This hierarchy shows a son's attempt to persuade his father to allow him to get a motorbike. It starts with the son's suggestion (position) and the father's rejection of it, without discussion. An analysis of the son's proposal reveals his desire for greater freedom and to have fun in the neighbourhood.

However, this is directly contrary to the father's desire for peace and quiet, and is unresolved. The next level of interest shows that the son wants to be noticed by the neighbours, but the father wants a quiet life, so here too there is no agreement with the father. The conflict is first resolved when someone (the son, mother, father or someone else) discovers a deeper motive for wanting a motorbike, which is the desire for higher status and to impress important people (the pretty girl down the way). This is important, because there are other ways for the son to make an impression on people which do not necessarily conflict with the father's interests, for example, joining the youth section of the local golf club which arranges good social events for young people. Thus, deep down in the son's hierarchy is a desire for increased self-respect. However, often it is not necessary to state this directly, which could be felt to be intrusive, and the mere recognition of this will help achieve the necessary flexibility with regard to solutions.

In this example, only the interests and needs on which the father and son disagree are described. However, there will usually be some shared interests, for example that both are concerned about the son's safety (even though disagreeing about the dangers of motorbikes), as well as a wish to solve family disagreements respectfully.

Needs

Needs

As can be seen in the above example, the son's *need* for self-respect is at the base of the hierarchy, in other words, it lies deeper than the level of interests. These underlying needs can also be ordered hierarchically or in the form of a pyramid, as first formulated by Abraham Maslow as part of his work as a psychoanalyst to understand his patients.[3]

Maslow's pyramid of needs

According to Maslow, the hierarchy is as follows: *physical* needs, such as air, water, and food are the most important, as lack of them can cause debilitation, illness and death. Next there is the need for *security*, in the form of housing, protection from danger, confidence that one's physical needs will be met etc.; lack of security leads to fear, anxiety, anger and psychosis. These two first levels are the fundamental needs. The third level of needs is the need for *belonging and affection*, to receive sympathy and to have the chance to show sympathy etc. as part of a group or family; frustration of these needs results in feelings of alienation, loneliness, and different neuroses. The next level concerns *self-respect*, which can be achieved by being affirmed, by being able to carry out tasks etc.; lack of self-respect leads to feelings of incompetence, helplessness, shame and guilt. Finally, at the top of the pyramid of needs is *self-realisation*, which includes people's need to realise their full potential in relation to others, to use their skills etc. There are also certain *meta-needs*, such as truth, inquisitiveness, justice, play etc.

Cultural factors

Even though Maslow originally described these human needs as being arranged as a pyramid, he later accepted that the hierarchy is not the same for all and that, for example, some people can put themselves at risk in order to save others whom they care for. It has also been pointed out that *cultural factors* can affect the ranking of needs.[4] For example, the action of a Palestinian suicide bomber may seem inexplicable to most westerners, but may be better understood (if not more acceptable) if one understands that the overwhelming futility of everyday life for young Palestinians is such that offering one's life for a 'good cause'

3. Abraham Maslow, *Motivation and Personality*, New York 1954. See also Johan Galtung, 'Cultural Violence' in *Journal of Peace Research*, Vol. 27, No 3, 1990, which distinguished between basic human needs and personal needs.
4. See for example, Paul R. Kimmel, 'Culture and Conflict' in Deutsch, *The handbook of Conflict Resolution*, Chapter 22.

may be the only thing that can give life some meaning. The need to find some meaning in life is universal, as is the drive to overcome its meaninglessness, whether the lack of meaning is due to the breakdown of old norms and boundaries, or whether the threat of ruin at all levels provokes a feeling of helplessness and futility. The ways in which meaning can be created can vary and can be linked to cultural and social conditions.

John Burton has taken Maslow's pyramid of needs and applied it to conflict resolution. Burton's fundamental approach is that a conflict will not be solved constructively unless the basic human needs of the parties are made visible and taken account of in a way which is satisfactory for both parties.[5] Acknowledging and making visible the needs which lie hidden in everyone's personal story often makes parts of the story familiar to the other party. This usually means that we see the other party as a person like oneself (so we descend the conflict ladder from the level of dehumanisation), and it becomes possible to create solutions which benefit both parties.

As described in the section on the dimensions of conflicts in Chapter 4, values and deeper needs cannot be negotiated, but must be revealed by dialogue and be recognised. On the other hand, it may be possible to negotiate about certain interests. In the example given above, unless some deeper need is revealed, the conflict between the son's desire for greater freedom and the father's wish for peace and quiet could be negotiated so there could be agreement about when the noise would be least disturbing to the father, but often the willingness to negotiate first arises when the needs have been mutually recognised.

Parties decide their fundamental needs

Basic needs are decisive for our lives as human beings. Some of them change over time (e.g. attitudes), while others, are more closely linked to physical survival and are constant (e.g. food and drink), but what matters is that the parties themselves should decide their most important

5. See John W. Burton, *Conflict Human Needs Theory* (New York, 1990).

needs. This avoids cultural arrogance and lack of understanding which can prevent us resolving conflicts between continents and cultures.

Again, it must be emphasised that understanding the other party is not the same as agreeing with them.

Example: In the example given in Chapter 4, of the publication of cartoons of the prophet Mohammed in a Danish newspaper, it was a serious mistake in the Danish Government's handling of the conflict that it confused dialogue with negotiation, and moreover with competitive negotiation. The Government saw it as a conflict of interests (a power struggle – in this case about values), and it therefore treated it as a traditional negotiation from a zero-sum perspective, in which one party could only gain something at the expense of the other party.

Collisions between cultures are characterised by the fact that they are not concerned with the allocation of resources. They are conflicts of values, so that dialogue is the only way. What is essential is that each party should understand the other side. In this case it would be decisive that both parties should understand that the cartoons and freedom of expression are merely symbols for much deeper and more important feelings. The focus must be shifted from the claims to something bigger.

Freedom of expression is naturally important, as it symbolises the free society we live in and value. An attack on freedom of expression is an attack on our way of life. This is what we must say to the Muslims who feel offended. In the same way, the Muslims must explain how, by printing the cartoons we are not only offending the prophet (whom faithful Muslims love with all their heart) but their whole way of life. It is there that both sides must acknowledge the depth of the conflict.

If a meeting had been held with the ambassadors for Muslim countries, it would have been possible to sit face to face and explain what was at stake for one's own side, and to give signals that one had an understanding of what was at stake for the other side.[6]

The specific reaction to the cartoons was a demand from the group of Muslims for an unconditional apology first of all from the newspaper which published them, and then from the Danish Prime Minister. Against this, the position both of the editor of the newspaper and the Danish Government was that freedom of expression in a modern democracy is unrestricted, so that there was no cause to apologise.

If we present this event in the framework of the 'mountain of positions', the interests and needs could be presented as follows: the interests of the Danish Muslims who were the first to react and who belong to a relatively radical group[7] could have been to signal to more moderate Danish Muslims that they maintained their original beliefs and had not been affected by modern norms, and to signal to Muslims in the rest of the world that their organisation characterised Muslims in Denmark. The Danish Government and the newspaper may have had an interest in showing that it would not give in to pressure from a relatively small Muslim group, and that those who have chosen to live in Denmark must respect Danish norms. If one then moves to the next level of underlying needs, it is natural to see that, on the one hand the protesting group of Muslims genuinely felt personally offended that their deeply held religious feelings had been ridiculed, and on the other hand that the representatives of the Danish newspaper and Government were deeply disturbed by the thought that recognition of the offence to the Muslims might lead to the undermining of fundamental freedoms in a modern democracy. Both parties thus felt both injury and anxiety. These are feelings which any person can feel so that once they are recognised it is possible for each party to identify with the other, even if one does not understand or agree with the *cause* of the

6. See Vibeke Vindeløv, interview in the newspaper *Mandag Morgen*, autumn 2005.
7. The Society of Islamic Belief in Denmark (Det Islamiske Trossamfund i Danmark).

other's feelings. Once such recognition has been achieved, it will usually be possible to reveal the parties' *shared* interests which, in this case, could have been both parties' desire to find a peaceful way out of the conflict, after which the parties would be able to negotiate a solution which would satisfy both of them.

Regrettably, neither side was willing to acknowledge the hurt of the other side, and the conflict developed so that more moderate Muslims also protested.

The needs described here focus only on the needs of individuals. However, there are also major social needs which are important, for example, for environmental resources, security and identity. These needs often lie at the heart of many long-term inter-community and international conflicts.

III. Facts and feelings

The mediation process is forward-looking

The movement from positions to interests and needs will usually take place in parallel with the clarification of certain facts, and feelings connected with misunderstandings or feelings of hurt will usually be expressed.

It is mistaken to believe that parties who are only operating at the level of positions are not emotional. The parties naturally bring their emotions to the whole process, but at the level of positions the emotions are usually very self-centred, whereas emotions become more open and more inclusive as one moves deeper down into needs.[8]

The whole process can be presented graphically as follows:

8. For a corresponding view, see *The promise of Mediation*, 2005 p. 53 et seq.

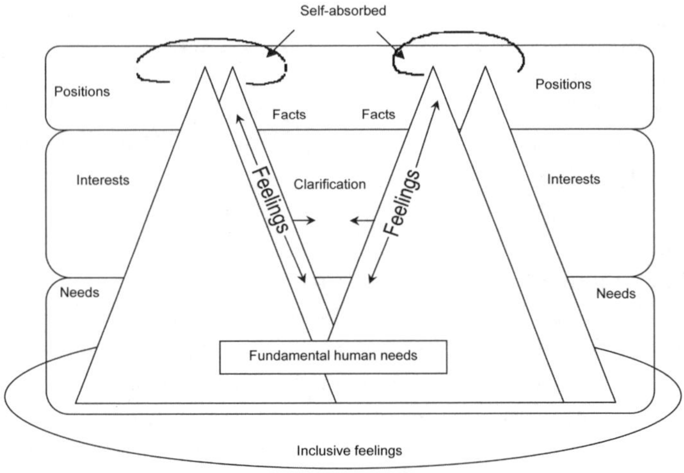

Figure 7. The connection between facts and feelings[9]

IV. Communication

Active listening

Communication involves both a sender and a receiver. In mediation the most frequently used communication tool is *active listening*. This is a strange term, as it consists equally of listening and questioning. Active listening was first described by Carl Rogers as a technique whereby a listener *decodes* an oral message, *identifies* the feelings expressed by it, and then *repeats* its emotional content in the same or similar words.[10] [11] By active listening the exchanges be-

9. Figure taken from Steen Clausen, *Kompendium i Mægling gennem dialog*, Center for Konfliktløsning, 2001 and further developed.
10. See Moore, p. 165.
11. The term 'active listening' is frequently referred to in the literature on conflict resolution and mediation, though without reference to its origin. The term presumably comes from: Carl Rogers, 'The Non-Directive Method as a Technique of Social Research', *American Journal of Sociology*, 1945, 50(4) pp. 279-283, and was subsequently developed by T. Gordon, *Leadership Effectiveness Training* (New York 1978) and J. Creighton, *Communications* (Tulsa, Oklahoma 1972), as a method for responding to people in a conflict

tween the parties are changed from discussion and argument, where they speak more than listen, to a dialogue where it is as important, if not more important, to understand than to talk.

The point about active listening is the attention which is paid both to what the parties say and to the meaning which lies behind what they say; it also concerns how questions are asked and what it is intended to achieve by them. An important pre-requisite for active listening is being attentive to the present, and not thinking about the next question to be asked. Only thus can one know what the next question or response should be.

Since Carl Rogers introduced the idea of active listening, it has been expanded to include other elements, apart from questioning. These elements include the following:

Closed questions or clarifying questions

One can ask *closed questions* or *clarifying questions* when there is a need for clear information about specific circumstances. The questioner sets the framework for which questions are asked, for example, 'When did you leave home?', 'How many times a week do you have meetings?' etc. Closed questions are suitable for obtaining factual information. Some closed questions are only answerable with a 'Yes' or a 'No'.

Open questions

Open questions can also be asked when a party needs the chance to determine the direction of their story. Open questions are good for casting light on things the mediator might not have thought of, because he or she does not have prior knowledge of the parties' stories. Open questions allow the story to unfold, sometimes in unexpected directions. Open questions are one of the best ways of getting information, and experience shows that one usually gets quickly to the heart of the matter by using open questions.[12]

situation. Danish sources include Erno Metze & Jørgen Nystrup, *Samtaletræning, Håndbog i præcis kommunikation*, 1992, Chapter 2; and Anne Suzette Humle, *En samtale - To vindere* (Albertslund 1993).

12. For the Milan Consultation Method in Mediation and types of questions derived from this model, see Larry Fong, www.fongmediate.com

Examples of open questions:

- 'Tell me something more about what happened that day.'
- 'Tell us about what you think is the most important thing.'

Open questions can be used later on in the proceedings, even though the issues have been narrowed down:

- 'What did you think, when he said that?'
- 'You said you want to be given advance notice. Can you tell us more about that?'
- Or, in the event of deadlock: 'Where do you want to go from here?'

Silence Strangely enough, *silence* belongs under the heading of active listening. There are several reasons for this: first, active listening requires a lot of concentration, and this can be a strain over a longer period. There can be a need to digest what has been said. Silence, even for as little as 20 seconds, can give a necessary break. Silence can also give those involved time to think more carefully and be sure they say what they want to say. Finally, silence can be a challenge for many people, and can create tension and expectation. Sometimes, in order to break the silence, the parties can blurt out something which is important, but which they might not have said, at least that juncture, had there not been a pause.

Summarising *Summarising* is part of active listening, and it can be useful to summarise frequently during a mediation. When, either as a party to a dialogue or as a mediator, one repeats what has been said, perhaps in one's own words, this can have several effects. First, it shows the other party that one has understood their story. Next, it show the second party that at least one person can understand what the first party is saying, namely the mediator. Finally, summarising is also an important method for slowing down the tempo of a discussion.

Summaries can be of facts as well as of interests, needs and feelings. However, it is important to ensure that summaries do not become interpretations, as in this case they can easily become a form of manipulation.

Repetition

Repetition is a variation of summarising, though it usually only refers to the last part of a statement, for example: 'You didn't telephone and say where you were, and you didn't come home until the early hours of the morning', may be followed by the repetition: '... until the early hours of the morning.' The repetition will often act as a prompt for giving further details.

Reflection of feelings

Repetition will often involve a *reflection of feelings*, so the speaker can observe their own feelings. For example, a speaker may have expressed insecurity about her job. If the listener just repeats the word 'Insecure?', this will often be seen as an encouragement to say more about why she feels insecure, why the feeling arose etc. Repetition is useful in helping more reserved people to speak. If the speaker has not been able to put her feelings in words, but the listener senses that these feelings are important and that the failure to express them is blocking the progress of the process, the listener can help by saying something like 'You're angry', in an interrogative tone. The speaker will reject the approach if she does not want to express her feelings, which may depend on the trust built up during the process, on the personality of the party, and of course on whether the listener has guessed correctly. Revealing the feelings of the parties must not develop into a therapeutic exercise.

Confrontational questions

Confrontational questions are aimed at getting the parties to get a better perspective of their situation, as they should prompt the parties to think about problems which they were not previously aware of. There is a risk that such questions could be perceived as being provocative, though it is usually more the parties' own answers to the questions that are felt as provocative rather than the questions themselves. The aim of asking provocative questions is to get the parties to see their situation in a more realistic light, and the parties themselves are responsible for the answers they choose to give.

Example from mediation: A former married couple went to mediation as the father, contrary to the mother's wish, had demanded access rights to their one year old child in accordance with the regulations. During the mediation it came out that the couple had not lived together after the child had been born, as the father had left the mother while she was pregnant. Consequently the mother had decided that the child should not know the identity of its biological father, and the mother had consistently indicated to the child that its father was her new partner. It was clear that the mother was still very angry at the father for deserting her while she was pregnant. The mother asked for a separate meeting which was then held. In the separate meeting the mediator asked the mother whether she thought it was realistic to hide from the child the identity of its biological father and, if not, when she thought it would be acceptable to let the child know the identity of its real father and how she thought the child might react if, as the mother suggested, the child was told as a 12 year old about its real father and so on. As the issue became clearer to the mother, she was faced with a dilemma between how far she would allow her feelings against the father or her love of her child to influence her decision, and regardless of the difficulty of such choice, it made the question especially meaningful for her.

It is clear that questions such as these can only be put with the greatest of care, and they require full and respectful contact and empathy, and respect by the mediator for the party's choice.

Validation

Validation is a very important part of active listening. The listener's validation of the speaker's statement does not mean that the listener agrees with the speaker, merely that the listener has heard, understood and acknowledged what has been said. Validation need not be word for word repetition of what has been said or a summary; it is a clarification of what has been heard, a kind of 'receipt' for the message. This may be by repetition, or by nodding, eye contact indicating 'I have understood', 'OK' or suchlike. Validation is not intended to get the party to expand on what they have said, at least not necessarily immediately, but to reassure the party that something important has been heard and noted.

Recognition

Several of the elements of active listening gain a special dimension from, or are perhaps dependent on, the presence of a third party such as the mediator.

As a rule, in the first instance *recognition* will be addressed by the mediator to one of the parties, for example: 'So you feel hurt by the cartoons.' In mediation it is important that the mediator should give recognition to both (or all) parties, and the recognition can eventually be repeated and expanded to cover acknowledgement of both (or all) parties at the same time, a 'double acknowledgement' for example: 'So *you* feel hurt by the cartoons and find it hard to accept the ridicule of your religion, and *you* are worried (fearful, anxious) that the values which are important to your democratic secular society will be trampled underfoot?' The aim of this is to show to the parties that they both have important interests to protect.

Any recognition should be made 'at the same level' as that at which the parties have spoken, but the linking together of two recognitions means that the problem will be raised up to a new level whereby recognition develops to become acknowledgement, and the parties will have the possibility of seeing what is important both for themselves and for the other party. This will lead to experiencing of interrelatedness, which forms the basis for establishing the themes or formulating the headings which are forward-looking and which give scope for the realities of both parties, and which thus already moves forward to the next phase of the mediation.

This level can be expressed so as to encompass both parties and for example after recognition of each of them it can be expressed as follows: 'So it's important for both of you that the way of life of each of you is respected, and that for this purpose you can agree on ways in which this can happen.'

In diagrammatic form this sequence looks like this:

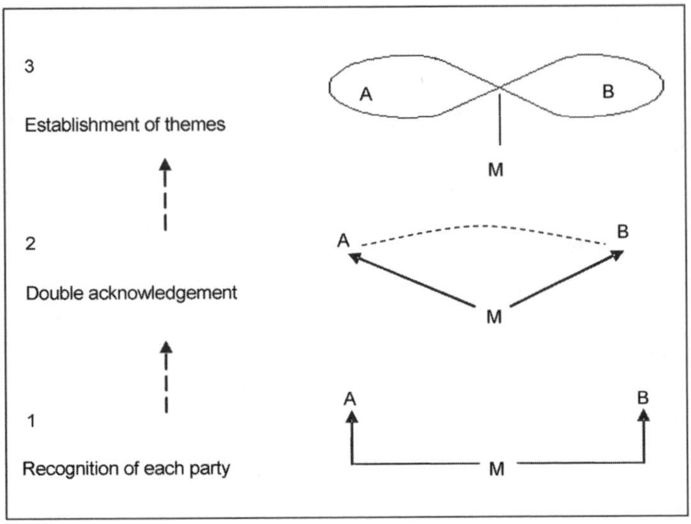

Figure 8. Double acknowledgement

A way to *build a bridge* between the parties is to get one party to express a view on what the other party has said. For example, after validating something, the mediator can ask a party about their reaction to what has been said. This can be an occasion for getting the parties to see that there are two different and equally legitimate realities. Often, in giving a reaction, a party says something in the nature of a regret or an apology which it would be hard to say directly. The mediator can – like a conductor who asks the oboe section to play a little louder – help the party express this, and ensure that the other party accepts the apology. This can lead to the parties referring directly to each other in a proper way, making eye contact etc. A mediator must be aware that the parties may have a need not just to receive an apology, but also to make one.

Reframing

Rephrasing

If a mediator believes that something which has been said includes words or phrases which do not help the mediation process, then as part of her repetition, she can *rephrase* the statement, so as to soften it. This can be done by the mediator choosing different words, to make what has been said more digestible. However, this technique can easily become manipulative or it may lack respect for the parties, so the mediator must be extremely careful in using it. A variation of rephrasing, where the mediator puts what has been said in a different frame of reference, known as *reframing*, can introduce the parties to an alternative, more positive presentation or understanding of the problem, not as a rejection of the way the parties have previously looked at the matter, but as opening up for different more inclusive interpretations.[13] Rephrasing and reframing can thus be a step in the process of enabling the parties to separate the dispute from the person. However, it is again important to avoid manipulation, and the rephrasing should be made with genuine contact with the parties so that the parties can reject the offered reframing without difficulty.

If one business partner accuses the other of being miserly, the mediator can rephrase this by saying: 'You think that X is over-concerned about finances?' Or this could be reframed by saying: 'So there are situations in which you think more money might be spent on fitting out the workplace?' Other examples of rephrasing are: 'lazy' which is translated into 'relaxed' or 'takes things calmly'; 'withdrawn' becomes 'profound' or 'thoughtful'; 'impulsive' is translated as 'assertive' or 'pro-active', etc.[14]

13. P. Watzlawick et al., *Change: Principles of Problem Formation and Problem Resolution* (New York 1974). describes reframing in as follows: 'To reframe, then, means to change the conceptual and/or emotional setting or viewpoint in relation to which a situation is experienced and to place it in another frame which fits the "facts" of the same concrete situation equally well or even better and thereby changes its entire meaning.'
14. See Anne Suzette Humle, *En samtale – To vindere*, 1993, p. 80.

CHAPTER 7

Negotiation

In some kinds of mediation, often in a business context for example, mediation proceeds directly to negotiation after each party has presented their case, often in separate meetings. As emphasised above, this form of mediation is more like a hybrid of arbitration and court proceedings than a mediation that follows the process described in this book. In the process as described, negotiation will usually first take place at a later stage in the proceedings, after the conclusion of the dialogue between the parties. Thus, when there is negotiation, which is described here in rather technical terms, it must be remembered that it should only take place after the conclusion of a fruitful dialogue, and that the negotiation should be supplemented by active listening.

Negotiation is often considered to be an activity which is concerned with one party getting the most out of a situation, at the expense of the other party. This need not be the case. Knowing about negotiation, as an independent discipline, is therefore useful for achieving as constructive a negotiation as possible.

As with conflict theory, negotiation theory is both interdisciplinary and relatively new. Some of the more important elements of the theory are described here. Those who want to know more are referred to the further literature on this.[1] Here the emphasis is on different negotiation strate-

1. E.g. Howard Raiffa, *The Art and Science of Negotiation* (Cambridge 1982); David Lax & James Sibenius, *The Manager as Negotiator* (New York 1986); Søren Viemose, *Forhandlingsteknik* (Copenhagen 1982); and Vibeke Vindeløv, *Konflikt, tvist og mægling* 1997, Chapters 5 and 6 with further references.

gies, what is meant by the effectiveness of the negotiator, and strengths and weaknesses in negotiation.

I. The negotiation 'minuet'

'It takes two to tango'

Negotiation is often described as a kind of minuet. 'It takes two to tango', and it is the same with negotiation. The role of the mediator is to keep the dance going. The techniques used by the mediator will depend on how the parties dance. In many situations the mediator's job is merely to bring the parties together and play the right music. From there the parties can carry on by themselves until the conflict is resolved. This usually presumes that the parties have a continuing relationship, for example a long-term trading relationship or regular transactions. In other situations the mediator must lead the parties through the dance, step by step; he or she must choose the music and choreograph the steps. In this situation the mediator has an active and leading role.[2]

However, a negotiation can also take on the character of a cockfight, best symbolised by spitting and scratching, with advances and retreats, and alternating victories and defeats.

Definition of negotiation

Negotiation can be defined as *a process between parties who have different aims, but have an intention of reaching an agreement, and involves changes being made to the original aims.* Negotiation thus consists both of the process and the content of communication, and the process is significant for what the content or result will be.

Movement

In a process, *movement* is a central element which influences content. A party must move from their original position towards another. However, nothing moves unless it receives some influence. Negotiation therefore consists of influencing the other party to move from their original position, so the parties can move towards each other. But in-

2. Kimberlee Kovach, *Mediation, Principles and Practice,* 3rd Ed., 2004 p. 193 et seq.

fluencing someone requires people to talk and to listen; each person must think and reflect, and it takes time to influence someone. A mediator must be aware of these aspects of movement, influence and time.[3]

In a classic negotiating situation, one wants to get something from the other party. Power, strength and cunning determine how much one can get. According to a more modern view of negotiation, introduced by Lax & Sibenius, one resorts to negotiation when it becomes clear that one cannot achieve a desired outcome on one's own. In other words, one has to try to create something, together with another party, which could not otherwise have been created. According to this conception, negotiation changes from having its primary focus on 'give and take' to becoming 'a creative process'.[4] It is a process in which it is possible to create something together with a partner: 'create and share'. With this perception, the relationship to the other party becomes very different, as they are viewed as someone who can help one to achieve one's aim. In negotiations, if they are smart, both parties focus on the potential, on what they can both achieve.

The climate in which negotiation takes place is thus decisive. Broadly speaking in negotiation, as in any form of communication, there are three possibilities: evasion/concession, meeting fire with fire/to steamroller, or to be firm on the case and open to the person.[5] Each of these possibilities is described in the literature, and their characteristics will be reviewed below.

3. See Søren Viemose, *Forhandlingsteknik – Nye muligheder gennem påvirkning og opbygning af tillid* (Copenhagen 2000), e.g. at p. 120.
4. David A. Lax & James K. Sibenius, *The Manager as Negotiator* (New York 1986).
5. Likewise, Hammerich & Frydensberg, p. 106.

II. Different negotiating strategies

The competitive negotiator

A zero sum

1. The competitive negotiator: meeting fire with fire
To assume that the parties have divergent desires and incompatible requirements affects not only the quality of the solution achieved through negotiation, but also the quality of the process by which the solution is achieved. If one prejudges that the requirements are incompatible, the scope for possible solutions will be sharply limited and will have a tendency to produce a negotiating process which puts emphasis on competition. The aim of the competitive strategy is to undermine the other party's confidence in their negotiating position. The *competitive negotiator* has a clear perception that the negotiation produces a winner and a loser, and this hangs together with the idea that the subject of the negotiation has predetermined dimensions (the cake to be divided has a certain fixed size),[6] a zero sum, and may even be indivisible. This means that a party to the negotiations focuses purely on the division of the cake, and considers the other party as an *opponent* in the negotiation.

The formulation of opposing claims and the fulfilment of the claims of one of the parties need not lead to the non-fulfilment of the claims of the other party. Negotiations which satisfy the aims of one party at the expense of the other are therefore a manifestation of power/strength and a negotiating tactic.[7]

A competitive style of negotiation is usually based on an individualist view of the world, where mutual interdependence between parties is not considered important and where it is possible that the party has subconscious assumption that their taking of power will be enduring so they will not subsequently be met with serious challenges or confrontations from the losing party.

The competitive negotiator is often characterised as being aggressive, pushy, someone who always makes high opening demands with few subsequent concessions, de-

6. See Fisher & Ury, *Getting to Yes* (New York 1981).
7. See, e.g., Gavin Kennedy, *How to Negotiate and Win* (London 1982).

manding information without giving any in return, who is not shy of practising concealment or of lying, who tries to undermine the other party's position and self-confidence by threats, arguments, breaking off negotiations, who uses deadlines and ultimatums, and who himself drafts any agreement.[8]

To be fair, it should be stated that it is of course possible to be a competitive negotiator without lying or threatening.

2. The co-operative negotiator: Who risks making concessions

The co-operative negotiator

As with the competitive negotiator, the starting point of the *co-operative negotiator* is that the subject of the negotiation has a predetermined size, so they operate with a zero-sum perspective. However, in contrast to the competitive negotiator, the co-operative negotiator attaches great importance to the relations with the other party, so they seek to move towards the other party and establish common ground for negotiation. The co-operative strategy thus generates a friendly and flexible atmosphere on the grounds that what serves the negotiator or their client best is to reach an agreement which is fair to both parties, and that this can be achieved by cultivating relations with the other party based on trust and goodwill.

Compromise

The opening offer will often be to the advantage of the party making the offer, or their client, but will not be unreasonable, and the negotiations will consists of a number of mutual concessions and the exchange of information. A typical result will be a compromise at a point midway between the two extremes of the parties' initial positions.

The competitive negotiator tends to view co-operation as a sign of weakness, while the co-operative negotiator tends to view the competitive strategy as hard and inflexible. This means that each negotiator must be aware of their own negotiating strategy or style and learn how to achieve the best results when dealing with those who adopt a different kind of strategy.

8. Williams 1983, p. 48 et seq. See also D. Gifford, 1989, Chapter 2.

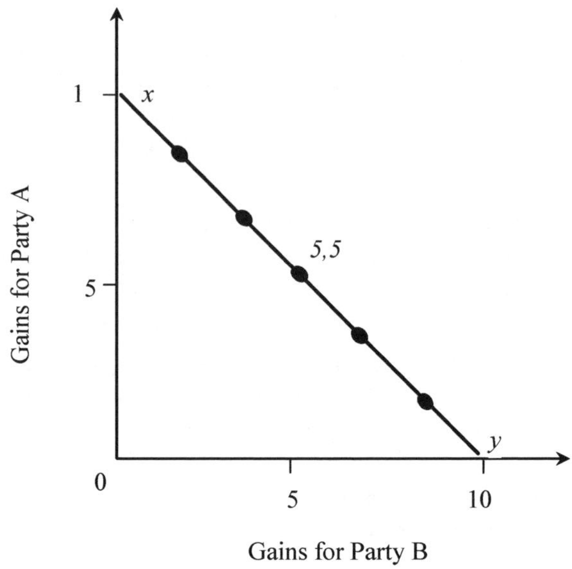

Figure 9. Zero-sum negotiation[9]

In this figure, the vertical axis represents what Party A can obtain and the horizontal axis represents what Party B can obtain. If the parties share a zero-sum resource, the division has to take place at a point along the diagonal line *xy*. Some of the possibilities for an agreement are identified as points along this line, with the point at 5.5 being an equal division of the resources.

For the cooperative negotiator, who generally has a zero-sum basis for their approach (interestingly enough, this is the most usual but least regarded aspect of this approach), there is a risk that the negotiation will be an example of the form of communication that can be characterised as evasion and concession.

9. Figure taken from Moore, *The Mediation Process* (San Francisco 1996), p. 271.

3. The problem-solving negotiator: firm on the case and open to the person.

The problem-solving negotiator

The *problem-solving strategy* operates in an integrated context which exists when the interests of the parties are not directly opposed and it is possible to make an agreement by which the satisfaction of one party is not directly linked to the dissatisfaction of the other party. It therefore seems, on the face of it, that the strategy can only be used in special circumstances. This is not the case.

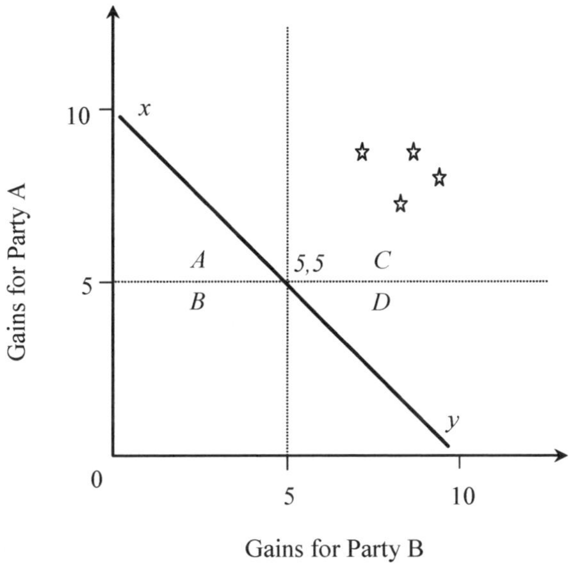

Figure 10. The problem-solving negotiation[10]

In this figure the diagonal line represents the division of assets where the parties make some compromise in a zero-sum negotiation. Point 5.5 represents an equal division of the apparent resources. The solutions which are sought by a problem-solving negotiation lie in quadrant C, which shows greater common satisfaction of the interests of the

10. See Moore, op. cit., p. 274.

parties (and therefore requires these to be taken into account) than any division along the *xy* axis.

The subject of negotiation

Instead of dividing up a cake of a predetermined size, with this strategy the parties adopt problem-solving behaviour, so they extend the subject of negotiation from a zero-sum object to one with several dimensions ('enlarging the pie')[11] with a view to finding a solution which is mutually satisfactory. This strategy consists of co-operating to identify interests and needs, and on this basis to develop creative solutions. It is the identification of interests and needs which changes the conflict from being zero-sum to being multi-dimensional, where areas can (always) be identified in which the interests of the parties are not directly opposed to each other, or where they at least evaluate the different elements differently, and there will be possibilities for discovering deeper needs and to identify with the other party, reducing resistance from the other party. This creates a basis for negotiation in which the needs of both parties can be accommodated to a certain extent.

With several dimensions

The best known guide to problem-solving negotiation is Fisher & Ury's bestseller *Getting to Yes*.[12] The book, first published in 1981, is based on experiences at the Harvard Negotiation Project, which had been founded by Roger Fisher and, among other things, its techniques were used in the 1978 Camp David negotiations between Israel and Egypt.

The essence of the theory consists of 4 elements based on very simple principles:

1. Separate the people from the problem;
2. Focus on the parties' interests, rather than their positions;
3. Generate creative options, with benefits for both parties;
4. Insist on the use of objective criteria.

11. See Fisher & Ury, op. cit.
12. First published in 1981 by Houghton Mifflin, and subsequently by Penguin Books. Fisher & Ury were the director and associate director, respectively, of the Harvard Negotiation Project.

Principle 1: Every negotiation concerns an issue and a person, so a negotiator has at least two interests, the professional and the personal. The personal and professional aspects are often mixed together; as shown in Chapter 4, this mixing together is a decisive element in the escalation of conflicts. Therefore, if one wants to create a rational basis for obtaining the best results, one must consciously work to prevent the negotiations from being influenced by personal tensions or perhaps the desire for friendship with the other party. There is a tendency, in both a positive and a negative sense, to treat the person and the problem as one. It is important, in negotiations, to be aware not only of one's own, but also the other party's reactions, and to tackle the problem and not the person.

Tackle the problem and not the person

Changing the focus from positions to interests and needs

Principle 2: Changing the focus from positions to interests and needs is important for problem-solving negotiation. If one remains at the stage of positions, then the solution which will best satisfy the wishes of each party will be a compromise between the two extremes. If, on the other hand, the interests of the parties are taken into account, there will be a much greater probability that the parties will reach a satisfactory solution, since incompatible positions contain both compatible and conflicting interests.

To illustrate the movement from positions to interests, Fisher & Ury used the well-known example of an orange. Two sisters are arguing over an orange. When their mother asks each of them why they want the orange, one says she wants it for its juice, because she is thirsty, and the other wants the peel to use in baking a cake. By identifying the interests it becomes possible to satisfy the interests of both sisters, and it can be assumed that, if she had not discovered the true interests of the sisters, the mother would have divided the orange in two.

Fisher & Ury advise us to be firm in dealing with problems but considerate when dealing with people, as referred to under Principle 1. This means that one should be just as firm when stating one's interests as one would be when stating one's position. It is seldom wise to stand firm on one's position, but it can be wise to stand firm on one's interests.

In mediation the change from positions to interests will typically take place at the second stage of mediation, with the submissions of the parties and dialogue. The distinction must also be maintained in the negotiation phase (stage 5), since a negotiation which is treated as a trial of strength between positions will create conflicts between the personal and the professional aspects.

The reader is referred to the description of positions, interests and needs in Chapter 6.

Generate several possible solutions

Principle 3: The third element of problem-solving negotiation is to generate several possible solutions, perhaps by brain-storming. The aim is to find ideas with potential and advantages for both parties. Negotiations are often one-dimensional, e.g., about the amount of salary, the price of a car, the duration of a tenancy etc. In other situations one is confronted with an either/or situation, which gives a particular advantage to one or the other of the parties. Fisher & Ury point out that when we work with solutions we are often inhibited by taking a view too early, and focusing too much on the only 'right' solution, in the belief that the cake has a predetermined size, or the belief that is for the other party to solve his own problems. One must be aware of these inhibitions and make room for what, in Step 4 of the mediation process, is called *vertical thinking*. The reader is referred to Chapter 18 for further discussion of this.

Use of objective criteria

Principle 4: The fourth criterion for problem-solving negotiations is the use of objective criteria. In this context, objectivity is not meant in a scientific sense; it means that the parties agree to negotiate on a basis which is independent of their strengths. This means, for example, that when the parties agree to call on the opinion of an expert, neither of them knows which of them will be more favoured by the expert's opinion. The criteria must be both justified and practical. For example, it can be agreed that the opinion of an expert (for example a technical institute) shall be used, or that a divorce shall affect the children as little as possible.

Fisher & Ury emphasise that the use of objective criteria is a method for achieving a solution. This is on the basis that a fair solution is better than no solution, and that an objective aim can be used to bring the parties to a solution without them negotiating on the basis of their positions. Where the parties use objective criteria, they will reach a solution similar to a compromise, even if it does not meet their needs.

A series of steps for negotiation

Fisher & Ury can perhaps be understood as proposing a series of steps for negotiation: first, the parties try to accommodate each other's interests. If this is not successful, perhaps because there really is a clear conflict of interests, then objective criteria can be introduced, rather than the parties negotiating on the basis of their positions or taking the case to litigation.[13]

4. The Tit-for-Tat Strategy

The Tit-for-Tat Strategy relies on the tendency to reciprocate in conflict interaction. In this strategy each party tries to match the moves of the other party. The theory and research on Tit-for-Tat demonstrates that simple matching can generate cooperative behaviour in a wide range of circumstances. Most strikingly, studies show that matching can induce even extremely competitive parties to cooperate.

Tit-for-Tat can apparently foster cooperation in large groups, even entire societies, provided that small clusters or individuals base their cooperation on matching and interact regularly.[14]

This strategy, and its theoretical basis, is not discussed further here.

13. See Carrie Menkel-Meadow, *Towards another view on negotiation* (1984) p. 816 note 243.
14. See R. Axelrod, *The evolution of Cooperation*, New York, 1984; and E. Apfelbaum, 'On conflicts and Bargaining', in L.Berkowitz (ed.), *Advances in experimental social psychology* (New York 1974), Vol. 7, pp. 103-156.

III. Effective negotiation requires preparation

Preparation is an essential part of any negotiation. A negotiator who knows what he or she wants from a negotiation, and is ready for what he or she may encounter will be more composed and have a better overview than a negotiator who has to improvise in an unknown situation.[15] The less prepared one is, the greater the risk that one will act inflexibly and hard, even if one knows inside that this is often not the approach which gives the best results.

The preparation should include both the *facts* about the subject of negotiation, and *feelings* in relation to the prospective negotiation and the other party, what is at stake, what interests and needs are involved, and what outcome one believes would be good or acceptable.

It is also important that the preparation should not only involve considering what one wants from the negotiation oneself, but also what one imagines the other party wants from the negotiation.

The aim of the negotiation

Part of the preparation is to get an idea of the aim of the negotiation. The aim of negotiation is what a party wants to achieve in the course of negotiation. It *can* mean 'to maximise gains', but in many negotiations a party will not have a goal which involves maximum gains.

Assumptions that the parties have divergent wishes and incompatible requirements not only affect the quality of the solution achieved by negotiation, but also the process by which the result is reached. If one prejudges that the requirements are incompatible, the scope for possible solutions will be limited and this will lead to a negotiation procedure with an emphasis on competition. The effectiveness of a negotiation can only be judged, if at all, by comparison with the ideal aims which the negotiator may have set themselves.

This question can be illustrated by the following research, undertaken by Gerald Williams, into the behaviour of 40 attorneys in practice in the state of Iowa. The attor-

15. Likewise Hammerich & Frydensberg, p. 106.

neys were split into 20 pairs who all undertook to carry out negotiations in a case of a non-contractual claim for damages, for example for personal injury. The parties they represented were the injured person and the insurance company of the person causing the injury, respectively. The attorneys representing the injured party received identical information and materials, as did the attorneys representing the insurance company. It was stated that the circumstances of the case took place in Iowa, that Iowa law was applicable, and that any litigation would go before the court in Des Moines, Iowa. In order to ensure that the attorneys put their professional reputations at stake, the participating attorneys were told that the results of the negotiations would be made public. After 2 weeks preparation, the attorneys met, and were given time to negotiate. Afterwards they were asked to fill in a form, giving each party's opening offer and the result of the negotiation.

14 out of the 20 pairs were willing to fill in the form; 3 of these had not reached agreement. As for the rest, the opening offers of the injured parties had varied between $32,000 and $675,000. The opening offers of the insurers varied between $3,000 and $50,000. The resulting settlements varied between $15,000 and $95,000. The highest figure resulted from a negotiating zone starting between $675,000 and $32,150. The average settlement was $47,318.[16]

The attorneys differed, not only in their apparently differing views of the value of the claim, but also with regard to their persuasive powers or the skills with which they sought to achieve their aims. On the face of it, those attorneys who gained the highest payment were the most effective. But is this right?

The basis for effectiveness

This example has the weakness that it only measures effectiveness in terms of money. Other factors can be just as important. For example:

16. Gerald Williams, *Legal negotiation* (1983), p. 5 et seq.

a. What were the costs (in time, money and psychological costs), and what was the relationship between the costs and other possible ways of solving the problem?
b. Were all matters in dispute cleared up, or was something left for later?
c. How did the agreements affect the relations between the parties?
d. Did the agreement minimise the damage and maximise the return for both parties? In other words, was the agreement economically effective and socially productive?
e. Would litigation, arbitration or mediation have been better?[17]

We know nothing about these issues, even though the answers to these questions can often have a decisive influence on the assessment of effectiveness. If these questions were included in preparing for negotiations, they would help to justify the negotiator's ends and means, regardless of whether they are negotiating on their own behalf or, like the attorneys and trade union representatives, acting on behalf of a client.

IV. Negotiating strength

Strength is always relational and measured against someone or something

An essential part of a party's preparations for traditional negotiation is assessing their own strengths and those of the other party. Negotiating strength is often defined as *the ability to influence the decision of the other party in a direction which is positive for oneself.*[18] This means *first* that negotiating strength is *relative,* and *second,* that negotiating strength is only effective if the other side perceives or believes that one

17. Gerald Williams (1983), p. 9.
18. See R. Fisher, 'Negotiating Power, Getting and Using Influence', *American Behavioral Scientist,* Vol. 22, No 2, Nov/Dec. 1983, p. 150. For comparison see D. Gifford: *Legal Negotiation, Theory and Application* (St. Paul, Minnesota 1989), p. 3.

has strength.[19] The strength of one party is therefore directly related to the strength of the other party, whether that party is a person, an organisation or a nation state. Strength is not a statistical variable, but it can vary over time.

Power or strength can take different forms, including the relationship between the parties, their hierarchical structure, their patterns of behaviour, their relative financial positions, status and authority, the relative probability of success if the matter were to be brought before the courts, greater access to relevant information, greater ability to damage the other party or the interests of the other party.

Strength can also be more or less evident, for example, having a position which is morally strong even though doubtful in law, the ability to withhold co-operation, the possibility of damaging the other party by damaging oneself (e.g., the ability of debtors to damage a creditor at risk by declaring themselves insolvent, or a spouse's threat to commit suicide), or the power of the irrational – a party may react unpredictably and irrationally, with uncertain consequences, unless a given outcome is reached.[20]

Even though strength can be real, it can be veiled by the opinion of the parties of their own and the other side's strengths. According to the definition, negotiating strength is only effective if the other party perceives or believes that one has strength. Power is not a detachable characteristic of an organisation or person, but it is an important quality in a relationship. In negotiations, parties can use their power directly in the form of an actual or implied threat, or indirectly by allowing the other party to understand that one has power. However, there is seldom power on one side only. When one analyses power relations more closely, there is usually more of a balance, even if it appears super-

19. See Morton Deutsch: *The Resolution of Conflict: Constructive and Destructive Processes* (New York 1973). See also Søren Viemose, 1992, p. 78.
20. See H. Brown & A. Marriott: *ADR Principles and Practice* (London 1993), p. 98.

ficially that there is power only on one side, so it is necessary to approach the question with caution.

Imbalance of power

For example, if there is a conflict between a multinational company and one of its franchisees, there appears to be a clear imbalance of power. The multinational company probably has greater financial resources, can employ a top lawyer, and can be economically unaffected by the result of the conflict, whereas the small franchisee can be financially ruined. However, other factors can be significant and can alter the balance of power. The legal position may be to the advantage of the franchisee, giving it good prospects of winning despite its weak resources, or other franchisees can be interested in how the multinational company treats its franchisees, so the handling of the conflict becomes a politically delicate matter. The multinational company can also be sensitive to public reactions to images of David and Goliath, and the struggle of the small man against the multinational giant. A dispute in Denmark between 'big' McDonalds, and its desire to enforce its trade marks against 'little' McAllan, the name given to a hot-dog stall, is an example of this.[21] There are many factors which can be relevant, and which can make it more attractive for the multinational company to negotiate an agreement allowing the franchisee to carry on his business, rather than imposing a decision through the exercise of power.

Correspondingly, a conflict between a superior and a subordinate can involve complex power relations which are not easy to interpret. Here, the subordinate's fear of losing their job may be balanced against the superior's need to be recognised as a popular manager, and fear of grumbling and general insecurity in the workplace. The reader is also

21. The conflict arose between a man called Allan, who had a small hot-dog stall under the name of 'McAllan' in a town square in a provincial town in Denmark and the multinational giant McDonalds, which brought a case against the hot-dog seller in order to stop him calling himself (or his business) 'McAllan'. McAllan received solid support in the Danish media, and McDonalds was ridiculed. The case ended legally by McDonald winning the case in 1995.

referred to the discussion of power in mediation in Chapter 10.

V. BATNA

Best Alternative to a Negotiated Agreement

A separate stage of preparation and in assessing one's own strength and the strength of the other party in a negotiation is to consider what the alternative would be if one did not achieve one's initial aim in the negotiations. In the literature of negotiation this is referred to as BATNA (Best Alternative to a Negotiated Agreement),[22] and has since been supplemented by WATNA (Worst Alternative to a Negotiated Agreement).[23]

Experience shows that in developing one's BATNA (or WATNA), one often sees other possibilities, which one has previously been unaware of and it thereby becomes possible to develop a stronger and more persuasive basis for achieving a good negotiated result. In this way one can protect oneself from entering into agreements which ought to be avoided, and in fact strengthen one's negotiating position, as the relative negotiating strength of the parties primarily depends on how attractive it is for each of them to reach or not to reach an agreement. It is just as important to try to guess the other party's alternatives as to consider one's own.

Whether or not it is a good idea to let the other party know about one's BATNA naturally depends on how good it is, and on the negotiating environment. If a negotiation is focused on competition between the parties, the parties will usually only reveal an alternative if it is good.

As referred to in several places in this book, a change in power relations takes place in negotiations - as well as in

22. The concept of BATNA was introduced by Fisher & Ury to describe what they called principled negotiation, but it appears equally applicable to other negotiating strategies. See Fisher & Ury, *Getting to Yes*.
23. WATNA is described by John & Gretchen L. Haynes in *Mediating Divorce* (San Francisco 1989), p. 11.

mediations - when the focus is changed from positions to interests and needs. If it is possible to identify the basic needs of the parties, the reasonableness of their needs will often be understood by both sides, and the negotiations will not result in the suppression of one party's needs by those of the other. This explains why differences in mediation strengths are often referred to at length in theory and why there is a deal of scepticism about this among those who have never attempted conflict resolution, but why it is not seen as a major problem by experienced mediators. In essence, the task of the mediator can often be simply to dissolve the effect of any differences in strength by helping the parties reveal their needs and the different dimensions of the conflict, and thereafter to negotiate about matters where there is a lack of resources, see Chapter 4 for a further discussion of this.

VI. Causes of failed negotiations

Failed negotiations

When negotiations fail every negotiator will try to find the reasons for the failure. In Chapter 4 several causes are given for understanding conflicts, their escalation and lack of solution, including the 'ripe moment', and these are discussed here.

The 'ripe moment'

Despite deploying all their negotiating skills, a negotiator can meet insurmountable resistance from the other party, so that every proposal for a solution seems impossible. In this situation, the negotiator must question whether the time is ripe for negotiation. The negotiator must analyse the situation in the hope of finding out whether the 'ripe moment' has arrived. If not, one might just as well refrain from trying to negotiate. The topic of the 'ripe moment' is dealt with relatively briefly in the general literature on negotiating,[24] while it is a recognised topic in the

24. See, e.g., David A. Lax & James K. Sibenius, *The Manager as Negotiator* (New York 1986), pp. 59-60.

literature on international conflicts.[25] On the one hand, the term indicates that one may just as well refrain from seeking a negotiated settlement unless the time is ripe, and on the other hand, it indicates that it can be expected that sooner or later the point will be reached where the opposing parties recognise that the conflict must be resolved. If the situation is tolerable, it will not yet be ripe for resolution or negotiation.[26] Whether the concept of 'ripeness' is fruitful is questioned by some authors. On the one hand the 'ripeness' idea has the attraction of simplicity, on the other hand it is argued that it gives too much weight to the power relationship between the parties and fails sufficiently to take account e.g. of changes within the parties or changes in the context which may also foster a propensity to negotiate.[27]

Differing assessments of risks and losses

Another aspect of understanding why negotiations are sometimes unsuccessful can be found in the *differing assessments of risks and losses* which probably exist in most of us. In negotiation theory an attempt has been made to explain the parties' lack of ability to reach optimal solutions on the grounds of their behaviour in relation to winning or losing. The theory is based on research with students who were subject to two experiments. In the first experiment, students were promised a choice between the *certainty* of earning a given lesser sum of money and the *possibility* of earning a given greater sum. In the second experiment the students could choose between the threat of losing a given smaller amount and the risk of losing a given greater amount.

It was shown that the students reacted differently in the two situations, giving rise to a theory of 'risk aversion' and

25. See, e.g., Zartmann, *Ripe for Resolution, Conflict and Intervention in Africa* (Oxford 1989); and Peter Wallensteen, *Från krig till fred, Om konfliktlösning i det globala systemet* (Eskilstuna 1994), Chapter 8. The reader is also referred to Chapter 12 below.
26. See the section on the cycle of conflict and the 'ripe moment' in Chapter 4.
27. See Ramsbotham et al., (eds.) *Contemporary Conflict Resolution*, 2005, p. 165.

'loss aversion'.[28] Unsurprisingly, according to this theory, most people prefer the certainty of a smaller gain to an uncertain larger gain (the bird in the hand is worth two in the bush). However, what was interesting was that when it came to the risk of loss, most of the students reacted differently. To the extent that this lesson is applicable outside the classroom, it means that we tend to do what we can to avoid a certain but relatively small loss, but that we are prepared to accept the risk of a much greater loss. What this means is that we will not gamble to make gains, but we are willing to gamble to avoid losses.

Cognitive barrier

This 'cognitive barrier', as it is called, is regarded as a partial explanation for why some people are willing to spend so much on litigation in the hope of winning a case, (even though the result of litigation can be so uncertain as to amount, virtually, to gambling, and even if the return on a successful outcome can be less than the costs incurred). It should be noted that what is decisive for whether something is regarded as a gain or a loss depends on the point of reference, and that the point of reference can be flexible. For example, the pleasure of buying a desirable piece of furniture can change to disappointment and regret about having paid too much for it if, a week after buying it, the same item is available in a sale at half price. It is this 'manipulability' that can sometimes make it possible for a party to make a breach in stalled negotiations, by expanding the frame of reference of the problem.

If one experiences that the other party sabotages the negotiation, the best thing to do is to do nothing. One should neither strike back not give in. If possible one should take a break which can be used to get an overview of the situation and analyse what the cause can be. Is the time not ripe? Has one failed to discover the needs of the party – or possibly one's own needs? Has one failed to recognise the importance of these needs? Has one wandered too far from the solid facts, etc.?

28. See Robert Monookin, 'When Negotiations Fail: An Exploration of Barriers to the Resolution of Conflict', *The Ohio State Journal of Dispute Resolution*, Vol. 8, No 2, 1993, pp. 235–249.

Thereafter the new assessment of the situation will make it possible to return to the negotiation and more openly address the situation that one believes has been the cause of the failure to progress.

CHAPTER 8

Voluntariness and confidentiality

I. Voluntariness

First, the fact that the participation of the parties in the mediation process is *voluntary* is important. In this context, this means that the parties themselves choose whether or not to take part, whether to make an agreement and, if there is an agreement, what the agreement shall contain. Voluntary participation means the parties can leave the mediation whenever they choose, and they are not bound by anything (except the expenses incurred in the first part of the mediation) until the final agreement is signed. It should be noted that voluntariness also applies to the mediator, which means that if a mediator finds that the parties breach certain ethical rules the mediator can, and possibly should, withdraw from the mediation. This is a point on which mediation is radically different from litigation before the courts, where a judge may not refuse to hear a case which satisfies the necessary legal requirements.

However, one can reasonably ask what voluntariness amounts to and when something is voluntary. There is no doubt that a party can feel pressured to participate in mediation. One can feel pressured by an employer, a spouse, financial pressures and so on. But is the fact that one feels pressured the same as saying that one doesn't have free will? What is the alternative?

In philosophy, free will is defined as *the possibility that the actor could have acted differently.* The essence of this is that one has a choice. The choice may not be very attractive, for example one could lose one's job by not agreeing to participate in mediation, or there could be fear of a divorce.

However, the point is not that free will and choice should be seen as presenting a choice between heaven and hell; it can just as well be the choice between the lesser of two evils. There is nevertheless a choice. The difficulty of accepting that this is a choice is presumably more the difficulty of accepting that one finds oneself in such a difficult situation and that one must take the responsibility for choosing. Whether or not it is what one desires, one has a problem that will not go away by refusing to take responsibility for making a choice.

Finally, it should be borne in mind that participation in mediation does not necessarily mean that an agreement will be reached, as the voluntariness applies both to participation and to the outcome of mediation. With regard to the conclusion of mediation and any agreement made, it is also necessary to consider the full range of choices available.

II. Confidentiality

The extent of confidentiality

Confidentiality is another of the essential requirements for mediation. This does not mean that the concept is clear-cut. The extent of confidentiality can vary. It is important to consider the purpose of confidentiality. The aim is to secure a safe space around the parties' treatment of their conflict. In principle the confidentiality covers both the identities of the parties and the content of the mediation.

The parties will often accept it, without question, if the mediator suggests a rule that everything that takes place in the mediation shall be confidential. However, equally often, the parties will question the extent of confidentiality. The mediator must be ready to explain the extent of confidentiality, and treat it as part of the mediation to obtain agreement on the issue before moving on to dealing with the substantive conflict which is the cause of the parties coming to mediation.[1] A thorough discussion of the need for confidentiality, and its extent etc., can even be a good opportunity, at an early stage, for mediators to demonstrate their listening skills and ability to promote dialogue and get the parties to reach an agreement.

Confidentiality can be synonymous for 'secret' so that nothing of what takes place or is said at the mediation is communicated to others. However, such an interpretation of confidentiality is probably not realistic; it is as well to acknowledge that most people will need to share their mediation experiences with a confidant.

Controlled variation from absolute secrecy

When discussing confidentiality, it is more realistic to agree that it is natural and permissible for a party to discuss things with someone close to them, a friend or a spouse. The mediator may also need to confer with another about the proceedings, and should make it clear at the start that they may need to discuss the proceedings with a colleague, though naturally without revealing the identities of the parties. All those present should accept this form of *controlled variation from absolute secrecy.*

Confidentiality towards the wider world is different. The assumption must be that the parties must be able to behave and speak in mediation proceedings without fear of later being confronted with what they say or do, for example at their place of work, or in the media. Thus, confidentiality in a mediation between two work colleagues must clearly cover colleagues at their work-place. Confidentiality will also prevent either party approaching or answering questions from the media, even though the conflict might be considered 'good copy'. Obviously it would not be considered a breach of confidentiality to refer to a trade union representative or a lawyer for advice. The trade union representative and lawyer will be subject to their professional rules on confidentiality.

In conflicts that are of wider importance, whether between trade union leaders on employment agreements or

1. On the special circumstances applying to confidentiality and the holding of separate meetings, see Chapter 15.

between political groups, the media are often used as a channel of communication and pressure, or even manipulation. In this situation negotiations will often take place on several parallel levels, so communications are intended to inform both the outside world, the other party and those involved in parallel negotiations on one's own side. The problems arising in such a situation will not be discussed further here.

It is usually not difficult for the parties to agree on a rule of confidentiality while the proceedings are in progress. But when the mediation is over there may be a need to notify the outside world. This can include the parties' employer who may have facilitated the mediation, or it can be work colleagues, who may be aware of a conflict between the two parties and aware that there has been mediation. In these cases it can be a good idea for the parties to agree what the outside world should be told at the end of the mediation, or even at the end of each mediation meeting. Information should only be given about what the parties agree on, and the rest should be kept confidential.

The mediator may have agreed with the employer, prior to the mediation, to give information on whether an agreement is reached or not. The parties will already have been told about this agreement with their employer at the start, so this should not create problems during or after the mediation. It is, of course, unthinkable to minute any details from the mediation itself, including any assessment by the mediator about which of the parties must have been most 'reasonable'; such would express the mediator's departure from neutrality and impartiality.

If the mediation is unsuccessful and there is no agreement, there is a risk that the conflict will end up before the courts. The obligation to give evidence is a key question for the mediator.

Confidentiality is an essential pre-condition for creating not only a secure space within which the parties can work on resolving their dispute, but also for obtaining as good a solution as possible. If there is a risk that the mediator may be called as a witness, this can diminish the scope of the parties to put forward creative suggestions and the mediator's scope for confronting the parties in reality testing, and even the desire of the mediator to assist in mediation.

Not all conflicts are legally defined at the start of mediation. For example, there may be mediation between two work colleagues who have problems working together, without the parties yet being dismissed or giving notice; or two companies may disagree about the quality of products supplied. If the mediator feels that the conflict could develop into litigation, then before the process starts, the mediator ought to obtain the agreement of the parties that he or she will not be called as a witness in the event of litigation.

Obligation to give evidence

In countries where it has not been confirmed by a decision of the court that a mediator can be exempted from the obligation to give evidence, there is no doubt that it would strengthen the position of the mediator if the parties agreed this.

The EU directive on certain aspects on mediation in civil and commercial matters

At the present time it must be noted that the questions of confidentiality for the parties and the mediator, as well as the obligation of the mediator to act as a witness, both remain largely unclarified in the individual EU Member States. In 2007 political agreement was reached on an EU Directive on international commercial disputes, which had to be implemented by the Member States by 2011 (Directive 2008/52/EC on certain aspects of mediation in civil and commercial matters). The Directive applies to all Member States except Denmark; see Article 1(3). The purpose of the Directive is to make mediation a more accessible and attractive form of alternative dispute resolution. Article 7(1) provides that: 'Given that mediation is intended to take place in a manner which respects confidentiality, Member States shall ensure that, unless the parties agree otherwise, neither mediators nor those involved in the administration of the mediation process shall be compelled to give evidence in civil and commercial judicial proceedings or arbitration regarding information arising out of or in connection with a mediation process'. This is followed by some very broad exceptions from this main rule, and it is stated that the provision does not prevent Member States from adopting stricter rules.

Section 4 of the European Code of Conduct for Mediators, states that: 'The mediator must keep confidential all information arising out of or in connection with the mediation, including the fact that the mediation is to take place or has taken place, unless compelled by law or grounds of public policy to disclose it. Any information disclosed in confidence to mediators by one of the parties must not be disclosed to the other parties without permission, unless compelled by law'.

The apparent lack of congruence between the Directive and the Code of Conduct, together with the open question of what exceptions to confidentiality may have been adopted by legislation in the individual Member States, means that the question of confidentiality has still not been entirely clarified.

This lack of clarity should not alter the fact that confidentiality in connection with mediation is vitally important, and in response to this lack of clarity, when being called as a witness in litigation, many mediators have found that they have suffered from acute amnesia.

CHAPTER 9

Neutrality and impartiality

I. Understanding the concepts

Nearly all definitions of mediation, including that used in this book, include the concepts of neutrality or impartiality. These concepts are also usually referred to in the ethical rules that accompany mediation. Both concepts are problematic. As pointed out by Kowach, there is no consensus in the literature on mediation about the precise content of these concepts, and they are seldom the subject of comprehensive treatment. It seems that they are concepts that are at one and the same time both assumed to be well known and ambiguous, so there is a need for clarification.[1]

Definition of neutrality and impartiality

'Neutrality' can be defined as neither taking a position on how the conflict should be resolved, nor *having an interest in achieving a specific result*; and 'impartiality' can be defined as not favouring one party above the other, but treating both parties with respect. Thus a mediator must not favour either one particular party or one particular result. Undoubtedly, while both are admirable goals, fortunately it is becoming more widely acknowledged that, realistically, they are impossible to achieve in practice.[2] In the absence of specific rules or norms which a mediation agreement must contain, mediators have no specific indicators for identifying what agreement will be the right one. But if

1. K. Kovach, 2004, 211 ff
2. See, for example, Bush & Folger: *The Promise of Mediation*, p. 105; as well as Larry Fong, *Cognitive Mediation*, as mentioned in Chapter 2. See also S. Cobb, 'Einsteinian Practice and Newtonian Discourse: Ethical Crisis in Mediation', in Kressel & Pruitt (eds.) *Mediation Research: The Process and Effectiveness of Third-Party Intervention*, San Francisco 1989.

neither neutrality nor impartiality are possible, how is it possible to protect the parties from manipulation and the exercise of power by the mediator?

Instead of rejecting the whole concept and the qualities which mediation undoubtedly has, one should instead redefine the concept of neutrality so as to take account of the inevitable influence of the mediator on the process and its content.

It is inevitable that, by their mere presence and by leading the process, a mediator will affect the mediation in certain directions and thereby will indirectly come to influence the solution. For example, this can occur if a mediator asks more about one thing than about another, so that some elements of the conflict are uncovered while others are not. Ultimately this can affect how the parties choose to resolve their conflict. However, there is a difference between whether this is an unavoidable side-effect of leading the process, or whether the mediator intentionally steers the parties in a particular direction.[3]

On the face of it, neutrality and impartiality can be seen as attitudes which a mediator can freely choose whether or not to adopt. However, a mediator cannot divest him or herself of their values, experience and attitudes and put on a cloak of incorruptible neutrality and impartiality. It is quite usual that in the course of the mediation the mediator will have a view on the conflict and believe that it would be obvious to resolve the conflict in a particular way. This can be based on experience, knowledge of the law, knowledge of the parties or something else. It will also be normal, in the course of a mediation, for a mediator to come to regard one of the parties more favourably than the other, and this can switch back and forth in the course of the mediation.

For these reasons, what matters is that the mediator should acknowledge these natural reactions, and as far as possible avoid carrying these attitudes into the mediation. The precondition for this is first, that mediators should try to be aware of their own values and attitudes, and second,

3. See Lin Adrian, unpublished Ph.D. thesis 2011.

that they should work actively to keep them to themselves during the mediation. Thus, both neutrality and impartiality have both internal and external dimensions, where the internal dimension concerns what goes on inside the mediator's head, and the external dimension concerns how the mediator acts.[4]

Different concept of neutrality

Bush & Folger propose a different concept of neutrality, according to which mediators undertake to use their influence exclusively to ensure the parties' ultimate control over any agreement they make. Neutrality thus means that a mediator's only interest is in using their influence to ensure the control of the parties over the result of the mediation. This interest is not neutral in the sense of being without influence, and it is only influential in the sense of not affecting the result of the mediation, whether by defining the problem or by showing how different aspects of the problem should be solved.[5]

Whether we like it or not, as mediators we cannot help influencing the parties by our mere presence – an influence which must be limited as far as possible with regard to the content of the mediation, but which cannot realistically be avoided entirely.

In Bush & Folger's *Transformative Mediation*, the emphasis is overwhelmingly on the insight and growth which the parties can obtain from the mediation process. Another possibility, which is used in cognitive mediation, is to ask so-called 'bifocal' questions, meaning that the same questions are asked of both parties who are then not only required to answer for themselves, but also to consider the answer of the other party.

A realistic and non-dogmatic way to deal with the fact that impartiality and neutrality are impossible has been developed by the Centre for Conflict Resolution (CCR) in Cape Town, which in the post-apartheid period, when seeking 'justice for all', became increasingly aware of the difficulty, if not the impossibility, of remaining impartial,

4. See Lin Adrian.
5. Bush & Folger, p. 105.

yet despite this has had great success in mediating in all kinds of conflicts, including major and violent conflicts.

Process advocate

One of the ways in which the CCR has tackled the dilemma of impartiality and neutrality has been to emphasise the moral justifiability of the position of a 'process advocate'. The process advocate's task is to focus on the fairness and effectiveness of the process of mediation in the belief that, through the dynamics of an appropriate process, the parties will reach an understanding that meets their needs and interests (and thus serves the demands of justice and fairness). This enables mediators to suspend their own views and feelings for the duration of the process. 'Good process' becomes almost a value in itself. Commitment to 'good process' transcends the more immediate feelings and values because of the inherent faith in its ability to achieve a fair outcome.

Moral impartiality and technical impartiality

According to the experience of the CCR, a distinction can be made between *moral* impartiality (which is impossible and unacceptable) and *technical* impartiality. Technical impartiality refers to the mediator's ability to treat all people with respect, to manage the mediation process fairly and even-handedly, to listen carefully to what each party says, to identify their deeper emotions and needs, and, by skilled validation etc., to ensure that each party has been adequately understood by the other party.[6] It is thus not a precondition for living up to these requirements that the mediator should have a wholly unobtrusive role.

However, as emphasised by the CCR, it is not enough to emphasise that a mediator should be a process advocate. The extent to which a mediator's perception of a 'good process' is influenced by their own deeper values and experiences is often unacknowledged. Mediators need to be in touch with their own feelings and recognise their own prejudices. If one accepts that impartiality is impossible, the negative effects of this can be countered most effectively when mediators are aware of it in their own hearts

6. Andries Odendaal, *Modelling mediation. Evolving approaches to mediation in South Africa*, Track Two 7:1 (April 1998), pp. 11-14.

and minds and are therefore able to control it. The technical ability to be impartial thus requires a level of psychological maturity in the mediator. According to CCR, this means that training to be a mediator can never be only about acquiring technical skills, it must also be about personal growth and maturity.[7]

II. Neutrakty in international conflicts

The concept of neutrality has naturally also been debated in connection with mediation in international conflicts. In particular, there has been reflection on the comments of Dag Hammarskjöld, the second Secretary-General of the UN, who died in an aircraft accident while on UN service in 1961. In a speech given at Oxford University he said as follows:

'There can be no such thing as an impartial civil servant in this deeply divided world; the kind of political celibacy which the British theory of the civil servant calls for, is, in international affairs, a fiction.

The international civil servant is not requested to be neutral in the sense that he has to have no sympathies or antipathies, that there are no interests which are close to him in his personal capacity or that he has no ideas or ideals that matter to him. However, he is requested to be fully aware of those human reactions and meticulously check himself so that they are not permitted to influence his actions.' [8]

On his method for dealing with his own values, Dag Hammarskjöld expressed as follows:

'Far from demanding that we abandon or desert ideals and interests basic to our personality, international service thus puts us under the obligation to let those ideals and in-

7. Andries Odendaal, op. cit., p.13.
8. From the speech 'The International Civil Servant in Law and in Fact', at Oxford University, 30 May 1961, in W. Foote (ed.), *The Servant of Peace, A selection of the Speeches and Statements of Dag Hammarskjöld*, The Bodley Head, London, 1962 p. 329.

terests reach maturity and fruition in a universal climate ... To represent frankly and consistently what survives or emerges as one's own after such a test is the greatest contribution to international life that anyone can render'.[9]

However, this has two consequences. First, that 'international service requires intellectual and moral courage to admit that you and those you represent are wrong when you find them to be wrong, even in the face of a weaker adversary, and courage to defend your conviction even when you are facing threats from powerful opponents'. And second, 'if we stand firm in spite of criticism, we achieve inner security in the form of self-respect.'[10]

The observations of Dag Hammarskjöld and the CCR are fully in accordance with the view of the connection between values and professionalism which is described in several places in this book. Even though social divisions and injustice are not as obvious in our social context as in South Africa, and the conflicts are not as extensive as international conflicts, as human beings we nevertheless form opinions and have attitudes which may be less apparent because of their more subtle nature. A mediator must therefore constantly be sensitive to their own sympathies and antipathies, and reflect on how these may affect the actions of the mediator in the mediation situation and thereby increase the chance of this not happening. The mediator will thereby act as a reflective practitioner which is the requirement for true professionalism.

The ultimate test of whether the mediator has lived up to the requirement for impartiality and neutrality is therefore the attitudes of the parties, who are free to break off the mediation at any time if they lose confidence in the mediator's ability to conduct the mediation satisfactorily

It must be emphasised that the understanding of neutrality appears to be very different in a more agreement-oriented model of mediation, as represented for example by Brown & Marriott. Here it is believed that neutrality can

9. Dag Hammarskjöld, International Service.
10. Dag Hammarskjöld op cit.

be compatible with the mediator actively taking a view as to whether the conflict should be resolved in one or another way, for example by predicting judicial outcomes.[11] The understanding of what is meant by impartiality does not vary to the same extent as it is generally agreed that a mediator may not favour one party more than the other.

III. The manager as mediator

When discussing the qualifications of mediators, one should consider whether to include the possibility of managers conducting mediation for their subordinates. Since this is naturally the kind of question which can reasonably give rise to an extended discussion, here it is merely briefly noted that, because of their powers to appoint and dismiss, managers cannot be regarded as fulfilling the requirements for neutrality and impartiality which are necessary for a mediator.

However, the situation appears to be different for middle managers. Thus, it has been seen that it can be appropriate for middle managers to act as mediators in departments other than their own. This means that it is possible to exchange mediators between different departments at a workplace, so that middle managers can exercise their mediation skills where they do not have the power of appointment or dismissal. Naturally, in these cases there will still be a requirement for confidentiality about the mediation proceedings.

However, managers can benefit greatly from learning about conflicts so their approach to conflicts and their ability to deal with them can be improved. Usually the question of mediation in the workplace is raised very late in the course of a conflict, as generally there have not been the mechanisms or the culture for dealing with conflicts constructively earlier. This is why it is often apparent that there is a need to develop a conflict culture at work, making it

11. See Brown & Marriott, pp. 349-350.

permissible to have conflicts. In the same way as many workplaces develop a policy on older workers, a smoking policy, and a policy for dealing with stress, the time seems to have come to develop a conflicts policy, and the manager's role will be key in supporting such an initiative.

CHAPTER 10

Power and justice

I. Introduction

Concepts such as power and justice are central to mediation, and since these concepts have a certain internal coherence, it is necessary to try to define what they mean. This chapter attempts to do this briefly; those with a particular interest in this topic are referred to the specialist literature.

II. Power

The question of power and the balance of power in mediation is naturally an area of great concern and one which sceptics use as a reason for dismissing mediation as an acceptable procedure and for preferring the resolution of conflicts in some other forum such as the courts.

The classic questions are: Can mediation be undertaken if the parties have unequal power? Is there such a thing as symmetrical power relations? Can the mediator balance the powers of the parties and remain neutral etc.?

Illusions about power

These problems concerning power are often more theoretical than practical (see below), and some of the assumptions behind these questions are illusory. The *first illusion* is that power-free relations can exist at all. There is always power in relations, or as expressed by the Danish theologian and historian of ideas K E Løgstrup, 'One person always has more or less of the other person's life in his power, and to imagine that it is possible for there not to be power is just wishful thinking and has nothing to do with reality.'[1] The *second illusion* is the assumption that people are equal or can be made equal. Whether we like it or not, it is a fact of life that we are not born equal and can never become so. But we can have equal worth, i.e., we can respect and accept each other's personal integrity and personal opinions and values. *Finally*, the debate is based on an illusion that power differences can be evened out in other forms of conflict resolution. Not even the judicial system, with its inequality of access to the skills of advocates, unequal ability to conduct a case etc., can smooth out inequalities of power, as has been shown time and again and has always been a matter of debate.

However, these objections do not remove the need to consider how power is exercised in mediation, and how the abuse of power can be avoided. Before looking at this in more detail, it must be made clear that, as stated in the introduction, the parties to mediation must be able and willing to express their views on their dispute and to participate actively and personally in the process which leads to the resolution of their conflict. If a party cannot satisfy these conditions, for whatever reason, mediation cannot be undertaken, at least for the time being.

1. Distinations in power

The concept of power is both abstract and ambivalent, even if its consequences are real. Subjects such as philosophy, history, sociology, politics and psychology are all concerned with the concept of power, so there are as many different definitions of power as there are authors who have written about it.[2]

Structural power

A distinction can be made between structural power and individual power. *Structural power* refers to differences in power attributable to the structure and institutions of a society. These can have historical origins and relate to social class, gender, religion, politics and so on; they mean

1. K E Løgstrup: *Den etiske Fordring*, Copenhagen 1966, p. 65 et seq.
2. See Peter T. Coleman, 'Power and Conflict' in M. Deutsch: *The Handbook of Conflict Resolution*, San Francisco 2000, Chapter 5, p. 109.

that a person's membership of one or other of these groups pre-determines the power which that person starts out with. The structural basis and understanding of any society is related to its hierarchical structure. The higher up the hierarchy, the greater the privileges, so there will often be competition for the relatively limited resource of higher status.[3]

However, this does not mean that just because a person or a group has access to resources, they can use these to influence others. A resource is only effective as a means of power if others endorse the resource. A resource is only a source of power because importance is attached to it in the context in which it is used. According to Coleman, another way of looking at power is to follow four perspectives on power, in which power is seen from the perspective of the individual, independently of the structural perspective:[4]

Power over

1. *Power over*, meaning that a person has the ability to make another person do something which that person would not otherwise do. This implies that the power involves some coercion, competition or manipulation. This form of power can also consist of a strong leader exercising authority to give orders, in which case the strong leader also makes use of structural power.

Power with

2. *Power with*; rather than competition or coercion, this refers to the possibility of combining powers for mutual benefit. This power is also referred to as co-active.[5] For example, if one is subject to some form of structural power, it is necessary to work together with others in the same situation in order, jointly, to have enough power to alter the balance of power.

3. See, for example, C.I. Barnard, 'Functions and Pathology of Status Systems in Formal Organizations', in Whyte (ed.), *Industry and Society*, New York 1946. See also Coleman op. cit., p. 119 et seq.
4. Coleman, op. cit., p. 110 et seq., with references.
5. This interpretation was developed by Mary Parker Follett, who was in many ways the mother of alternative dispute resolution. See, for example, M.P. Follett, 'Power', in Fox & Urwick (eds.), *Dynamic Administration: The Collected Papers of Mary Parker Follett*, London 1973 (first published in 1924).

Powerlessness and dependence

3. *Powerlessness and dependence.* Even though powerlessness and dependence are different concepts, they are often closely connected. Dependence can be both positive and negative; it can help meet some of the needs of the weak, but it can also be repressive and abusive.

Power to

4. *Power to* can be seen as the opposite of powerlessness and dependence, meaning that one has enough strength or power to achieve what one will without being unduly hindered by others. This position, which can also be called *empowerment and independence,* strengthens feelings of self-worth and confidence and leads to increased ability to act.

A closer look at these four perspectives will reveal and confirm that power is always seen in relation to a person and his or her circumstances. Thus, power is not determined just by the characteristics of the person or persons involved in a given situation, or by the situation as such, but is determined by the interaction between them. Power is thus relational and relative, and is only effective if others recognise that a person has power or strength.[6] Specifically, this means that the study of power is the study of relations.[7]

A third, and sometimes more operational way of looking at power, is to distinguish between direct power, indirect power, power over thought, and institutional power. [8]

Direct power is power that is exercised directly in a decision-making process, where A can ensure that B does what A wants. This corresponds to *power over*, referred to above.

Indirect power means that A can determine what cases or what information B can decide on or have knowledge of. The American researchers Bachrach & Baratz describe indirect power as non-decision-making – power to avoid decisions or to avoid the consequences of decisions. [9] This form of power can presumably be listed as a subset of *power over*.

Power over thought exists where A can influences B's preferences, so that B thinks they are pursuing their own

6. See Chapter 5 for a discussion of negotiating strength.
7. Likewise M. Foucault, Le Pouvoir, comment s'xerce-t-il? Chicago, 1982.

interests when in reality they are pursuing A's interests. This form of power, which is often very subtle, is seen as being an element of structural power, if not exclusively so. Thus, for example, to change the words 'experiments on embryos' to 'experiments on fertilised eggs' will presumably persuade many to change their attitudes to the acceptability of such experiments. Similarly, in the Law on social services the term 'compulsory measures' has been changed to 'assistance measures without consent', etc.

Institutional power is described as the power that is a consequence of unreflecting following of routines, customs, norms etc., and acceptance of the framework created by society. This means that there is unquestioning acceptance of the view of reality created by the institutions of society. This power is presumably not exercised, as it is incorporated in the actor, in the same way as norms, so this form of power must be regarded as a variant of structural power.[8]

Effective power

Coleman describes the conditions for effective power as requiring *control* over the resources that give power, *motivation* to exercise influence over others, the *ability* to convert the resources into power, and the *judgement* to use the power to fit the situation. The distinction between the availability of power on the one hand, and its effective use on the other hand, is very important in connection with conflict resolution.[9] The mental images which we associate with the concept of power have considerable influence on how we react to each other and how we view conflicts. What is important, in this connection, is not which perception is right, but avoiding too close an identification with any one of them, and instead considering what may be possible and effective in the given situation.

Another way to describe different concepts of power is to emphasise how power is acquired: by threats, by exchange or through love. On the basis of this distinction one

8. Se Peter Bachrach og Morton Baratz, Decisions and Nondecisions. An Analytical Framework, 1963 p. 265.
9. Coleman, op. cit., p. 112.

could classify the different forms of power as destructive, productive and integrative.[10]

III. Power in mediation

Whether they like it or not, mediators usually constitute a power in themselves, purely by virtue of their authority, knowledge, familiarity with the mediation process, experience, linguistic skill etc. A mediator does not have the power to produce a solution, such as the parties might hope for at the start of the mediation, as that is a power which only the parties themselves can exercise. Instead, the mediator has responsibility for using both their own powers and the powers of the parties in the service of the objectives of the parties, and when possible to foster the empowerment of the parties.[1]

Influencing the process inevitably means influencing its content. The mediator's activity should therefore be considered in the context of the duty to remain impartial and neutral. Even though mediators are in principle neutral in relation to the parties, and impartial with respect to the outcome of the mediation, in trying to establish a balance of power between the parties they become directly involved in pushing the parties towards making an agreement. As a mediator is prohibited from directly arguing on behalf of a party, this can cause a dilemma for the mediator.

Different styles of mediation will deal with this dilemma in different ways. One school of thought argues that the mediator has a duty to help find solutions which are reasonable and fair, and so should help empower the weaker party so they can obtain a fair and reasonable agreement.[1] Another school of thought argues that mediators may do very little, if anything, to influence the power relations be-

10. See Kenneth Boulding, Three Faces of Power, CA, 1989; as well as R. J. Rummel, The conflict Helix: Principles & Practices of Interpersonal, Social and International Conflict and Cooperation, New Brunswick 1991.

tween the parties, partly because this would put their impartiality at risk, and partly because mediators, as in transformative mediation, find that it is only the parties themselves who can obtain empowerment through the mediation process.

It is up to the individual mediator to determine which approach to adopt, subject to the fundamental principles and values of mediation being maintained. However, it seems critically important to distinguish between a situation in which a mediator helps a party identify and organise their existing resources, and a situation in which the mediator becomes an advocate for a party and helps them generate new power and influence.

The reader is referred to Chapters 6 and 15 for a description of how mediators can (empower) bring the parties together and take possession of resources during the course of mediation.

IV. Justice

Justice is multi-faceted

To a lay person it might appear, on the surface, that the purpose of mediation is not so much to do with justice as with finding a compromise or surrendering certain rights with a view to creating peace and harmony, or saving time and money. Thus, critics of mediation often argue that mediation sacrifices a just outcome, meaning an outcome which is in accordance with adopted and accepted legal and social norms. Nothing could be more wrong, among other things because such critics ignore the multi-faceted nature of justice.

Rather than sacrifice justice, a mediator has a unique opportunity to help those who have the most intimate understanding of the complexity of their own situation to find a solution which they themselves find fair and just. Both for parties and for mediators the practice of mediation is deeply concerned with questions of justice or fairness: whether an injustice has been committed, what would be a fair response to some harm that has been caused, how there can be a fair allocation of available resources, how stable relations can be re-established between the parties after what has happened, and what the mediator must do in order to ensure that the process itself is fair.

A mediator must consider these and other questions of justice or fairness before, during and after the mediation. There are several reasons for this. *First*, a sense of injustice is a frequent source of conflict. *Second*, if the process or the outcome is felt to be unfair, its solution will probably not last and will sow the seeds of new conflicts. *Third*, the conflict may be about whether something is just or not.

An individual's basic view of what is right and wrong is formed early in life, and it acts as a thread running through life and informing their sense of justice. However difficult it may be to define what is just, it is much easier to describe when we experience something as being unjust. We react in this situation, and the need for restoration and balance arises.

1. The concept of justice

There is a difference between how the question of justice is seen in law and in the work of conflict resolution.

In law, justice means that the result is in accordance with the applicable law, and not necessarily what an individual might feel is just or unjust. In the work of conflict resolution, there is much more focus on how one deals fairly and reasonably with each other, and the goal of mediation is to clarify this.

Social science theorists distinguish between four different kinds of justice:[1]

- *Distributive justice*, which uses the criterion of whether one has received a *fair share*, for example whether employees have received a fair share of the profits.
- *Procedural justice*, which is concerned with whether a person feels that they have been *treated fairly*, with dignity and respect.
- *The sense of justice*, which focuses on which factors determine whether an injustice is experienced as such (for example, if a woman does more than an equal share of

the housework, what determines whether she feels that this is unfair or not?)
- *Retributive and reparative/restorative justice*, which concerns how one reacts to the infringement of moral norms and how one makes good any harm done.

Distributive justice

Distributive justice permeates a major portion of social life. However, it is not so easy to decide what criterion should be used to make a share fair. Should it be based on the *principle of equality*, so that all get the same, or on the *principle of reasonableness*, so that all receive in proportion to their contributions, or even on the *principle of need*, so that those who need more get more, and those who need less get less?

In virtually every situation where allocation is to be made, these three principles will conflict.

Apart from these principles, deciding whether someone has had a fair share will often have a comparative dimension (adapted reasonableness), assessing whether a person's share is comparable with that of others who are in the same situation.

The criteria that are used as the basis for any distribution will often differ from case to case, without it being clear what underlies the subjective assessment of fairness.

Procedural justice

Procedural justice seems to be just as important as the content of the solution, as the psychological perception of the fairness of the process gives confidence that the outcome of the process will also be fair. Even where people may be disappointed with the content of a solution, they show greater willingness to accept it if they have been treated with respect in the course of the proceedings.

The sense of justice

The sense of justice, is closely linked to a party's desire to retain a positive self-image, and can be linked to specific ideals, such as what a mother feels she ought to do for her family, a manager for their employees, etc.

Retributive justice

Retributive justice of special relevance in criminal cases can serve several different purposes:

- The infringement of a moral code can weaken that moral code. Retribution therefore aims to re-establish the strength and value of the moral code.

- Retribution can also be cathartic.
- It can have a deterrent effect both on the actual offender and on potential future offenders (special and general prevention).
- It can act as a 'forced' rehabilitation and reform of the offender.

Restorative justice

Restorative justice focuses on three elements: the needs of the victim, the responsibility of the offender, and the needs of society for both parties. Thus, in this version of justice the focus is less on the question of guilt and more on who has suffered. In other words in the first instance the focus is on the harm done to the victim, but thereafter also on the harm experienced by offenders and communities. The goal of restorative justice is to provide an experience of healing for all concerned. Therefore, restorative justice also emphasises the accountability and responsibility of offenders.

As emphasised by Howard Zehr, retributive and restorative justice are not necessarily opposites as both acknowledge that a balance has been upset by some wrongdoing. Consequently, the victim deserves something and the offender owes something. Both approaches argue that there must be a proportional relationship between the act and the response. They differ however with regard to what will fulfil the obligations and right the balance. Retributive theory believes that pain will vindicate, restorative justice argues that what truly vindicates is acknowledgement of the victim's needs combined with an active effort to encourage offenders to take responsibility.[11]

What is decisive for both forms of justice is that some injury has been caused and what is done cannot be undone. It is impossible to return to the balanced situation that existed before, so a new balance must be established.

Retributive and restorative justice can consist of requiring one or more of the following actions from the offender: a full confession, a sincere apology, compensation (contri-

11. Howard Zehr, The little book of Restorative Justice, Good Books, 2002 ch. 1.

tion or restitution), or if possible some re-education of the offender (self-reform). With restorative justice, a victim and offender can put together an acceptable plan to repair the damage done. In addition to repairing the damage done, an agreement can also help the offender back into society as an equally respected member.

b. Justice in the courts and in mediation

Concept of justice within and without the court system

The concept of justice is not generally a major part of the literature on mediation. However, whether or not one is a lawyer, it cannot be denied that the forum with which mediation is mostly compared is the court system. It can therefore be useful to consider and compare how the concept of justice is viewed both within and without the court system. This will here be done with reference to the Danish context.

For some years 'justice' has led a rather shadowy existence in Danish legal science, primarily due to the fact that the Danish legal philosopher, Alf Ross, considered justice to be an irrational concept which has very little to do with law. He was a leading proponent of the view that law, in accordance with positivism, ought only to be based on rational considerations.[12] Despite the efforts of Ross, it remains the case that justice plays a vital role for lawyers, who primarily see justice as the application of legal rules within a legal process. Legal rules, knowledge of legal method, and procedures for the application of laws are all aimed at achieving the ideals of law and justice, regardless of how the concept is regarded in the world of legal philosophy. How far this is successful is a matter of constant debate, giving rise to new laws and legal reforms.

However, justice in mediation is different from justice in a court case. In contrast to the role of a judge, a mediator does not decide on the dispute, and a mediator does not have some pre-determined norms as the basis on which to decide the case. The task of the mediator is to create a process in which the parties are helped to see the reasonable-

12. Alf Ross, Om Ret og Retfærdighed (About Law and Justice), Copenhagen 1953.

ness of differing views of justice and to work towards a solution which corresponds with the parties' perceptions of what is a fair and acceptable resolution of the conflict.

Legal justice and personal justice

A Danish poet, Christian Richardt (1831-92), has fittingly described the difference between legal justice and personal justice in his *Ode to Justitia*, the goddess of justice:

'She keeps watch over obedience to the word of the law;
But once in a while she lays aside her judge's gown,
Puts down the book of rules, takes up the torch of justice,
And points silently to the law written in her heart.'

Justice from above

Justice in the courts comes from *above*, by the application of accepted norms to facts selected by the judge using the accepted procedure. Mediation does have certain parallels with this, but it also has many very different aspects. The rules, standards, principles and opinions which lie behind a mediated solution are the parties' own. The parties can choose what norms they will apply; these can be legal, moral, social, religious, etc.

Justice from below

Thus, in mediation, justice comes from below, from the parties themselves, even if, for example, they use integrated religious norms. Likewise, mediation has different procedural rules than those of the courts. The parties can talk about what they find important; they can introduce any information into the discussion at any time, if they think it is important. The parties are not restricted by rules of procedure. On the other hand, the norms of procedural justice are vital both for a mediator and a judge, as both should be seen as impartial and neutral, and they must give each party equal opportunities to present their cases and viewpoints and pay equal attention to both.[13]

For a judge, both the formal procedure and the legal norms are important sources of justice in the courts. For a mediator it is similarly important to acknowledge the mediation process as a source of justice, so the mediation becomes a true forum of justice. This comes from respecting

13. See Jonathan M. Hyman and Lela P., Love If Portia Were a Mediator, Clinical low Review, Vol. 9, no. 1, 2002, s. 160.

and honouring the priorities of the parties with regard to values and decision-making.

The view of justice 'from above' is not irrelevant to the view of justice in mediation. Sometimes parties can reach an agreement which they compare with the result they could expect if the matter were put before the courts. Some practitioners of mediation even take the view that mediation would be unjust if its results differed too much from what the parties could have obtained through the courts. Were the parties ignorant of their rights? Was one of the parties overpowered by the other? Did the mediator lack impartiality or skill? These questions raise the issue of whether the parties ought to be informed about the possible outcome of the conflict, if it were to be dealt with in the court system.

In reflexive mediation the view is that, even if they are a lawyer, the mediator may not combine their role as a mediator with their knowledge of the law. It is the parties who determine whether they want to know what a legal outcome of the conflict might be, and if this is what they want they must get this information and assessment from a legal expert, not from the mediator. Only in this way the mediator can keep her neutrality.

As for the involvement of justice in mediation, the reader is referred to Chapter 16.

CHAPTER 11

Reconciliation

I. Trust and reconciliation

In recent years it has become ever more common to use the term 'reconciliation' in everyday speech, in a political context for example. Reconciliation has also frequently been the subject of national and international seminars and conferences.[1] Apart from bringing a more scientific approach to the subject, these have also helped disperse the aura of sentimentality which had previously surrounded the concept, even if the seriousness of the concept continues to exist.

In any case, reconciliation must be seen as something special, more than and different to mere everyday forgiveness or tolerance, and much more than the mere practice of conflict resolution. Reconciliation is only relevant when something important is as stake. It is a process that is linked to painful feelings and serious injustices.

The concept of reconciliation

The concept of reconciliation is often thought of as being linked to religion, particularly Christianity, as personified by Archbishop Desmond Tutu who was the chairman of South Africa's Truth and Reconciliation Commission. It is therefore important to realise that reconciliation is not an exclusively Christian concept, but can be found, if not in all religions, then at least in all the major religions such as Christianity, Buddhism, Islam and Judaism.

1. See, for example, Paul Leer Salvesen, *Menneske og Straff*, Oslo 1991; and by the same author, *Tilgivelse*, Oslo 1999; as well as Vibeke Vindeløv, 'Forsoning – som alternativ til judiciel konfliktbehandling', *Retfærd* 93, 2/2001, pp. 113-129.

Furthermore, not only philosophers and psychologists, but ordinary people in the western world are increasingly persuaded that a person's identity is formed by their relations with others. A man without relations is nothing.[2] It seems that the motivation for reconciliation emanates from a deep commitment to some higher values and principles about human conduct and relationships or from unbearable pain. Belief in some profound commonality among human beings, including those who are perceived to be enemies, and a sense of accountability for one's behaviour to a larger entity or community greater than oneself, seem important motivators which generate a desire for reconciliation. Implicit in the notion of reconciliation is an acknowledgement that a person's conflictual behaviour could be unacceptable by the standards of those higher principles, even if such behaviour might be justifiable on utilitarian grounds or on the grounds of protecting one's own narrow self-interest.[3]

Thus there seems to be a basis for enabling the parties to a conflict to repair their relations with each other, without necessarily entering the realms of religious belief or being unduly sentimental. The quality of reconciliation is a human universal and is not linked to any specific religion.

For the purposes of the following, 'reconciliation' is defined as: the re-establishment of personal relations on the basis of acknowledging the pain caused, forgiveness and acceptance of forgiveness. It may seem strange that the definition includes 'acceptance of forgiveness', but this requires acknowledgment that there is a need for such for-

2. See, for example, Martin Buber, *I and Thou*, (written 1923), Touchstone, 1996 as well as the German/American Jewish philosopher, Hannah Arendt, who wrote in *The Human Condition*, New York, 1958, p. 145: 'If I am not for myself, who will be for me? And if I am not for others, what am I?'. Hannah Arendt's saying is adapted from the original saying of Rabbi Hillel. Hillel's saying exists in two different translations. In the first it appears as: 'If I am not for others, what am I?' In the second it appears as 'But if I am only for myself, what am I?'
3. Professor Hizkias Aseffa, Nairobi Peace Initiative, Reconciliation and Healing, November 1995.

giveness, which in turn means that one accepts one's responsibility.[4]

II. When is reconciliation relevant? – an individual perspective

The aim of mediation is to help the parties resolve their conflict. A conflict can be resolved at different levels; it can be resolved at a practical level or at an emotional level. While most mediation processes allow for solutions at a practical level, only some of them, as previously described, allow the parties to work on the emotional aspects of their conflict.

In the latter case, the mediation process makes it possible to re-establish relations between the parties, and to release them from the thraldom of anger etc. However, this is only possible if the parties are able and willing to do so, and it is naturally necessary to respect the limits set by the parties.

Facilitated discussion

In some kinds of conflicts, especially those relating to criminal law, even the use of the words 'conflict' and 'mediation' can be considered offensive. For example, parties who have been subjected to rape or sexual assault can find it difficult to understand that they have a 'conflict' with their attacker, as they find the term 'outrage' more appropriate. Regardless of the term used, they can be interested in a meeting with the offender, but without intending to work towards forgiveness. In these cases the use of the term 'facilitated discussion' may make it easier for the parties to be brought together, rather than 'mediation' which may imply expectations of forgiveness.

Damaged relations not only occur when there is a serious offence. Even in apparently minor conflicts the parties can often feel they have been wronged. They may deny

4. At the Centre for the Study of Violence and Reconciliation in South Africa (www.csvr.org.za/papers/paphd12.htm) forgiveness is defined as 'the key processes of contrition, remorse, apology and forgiveness.'

that they feel wronged and may be more inclined to say that they have lost their trust in the other party. However it is expressed, the fact is that the relations that previously existed between the parties have broken down. This not only refers to relations between people who are close to each other, such as family members, neighbours and work colleagues, but also to relations between people who do not have an enduring relationship, but who may have entered into a contract for example, or have agreed the payment of compensation for some injury. Here too, the initial trust which the parties may have had in each other can be breached, so the parties feel wronged.[5]

Some injury will have been caused

If there is a need for reconciliation, some injury will have been caused. The injury may be physical or psychological, real or imaginary, but such that the two parties in the mediation have the roles of injured party and offender, or they both feel they are the injured party and neither are offenders.

Even with minor offences there can be a need for rebuilding trust and reconciliation, but out of respect for those who have been involved in serious assaults we must also be sensitive to the fact that this is a process of a totally different character. Regardless of the form of assault committed, it must be acknowledged that reconciliation can never be required of anyone, that it is sometimes possible that others may be able to make some forum available to the parties, and that the reconciliation process is a matter for the parties alone. Reconciliation takes place within the individual, it comes from within, goes beyond the normal ego, and is not a collective event. For this reason, reconciliation cannot be anticipated, cannot be directed and cannot be reduced to a formula.[6]

Last, but not least, we must respect the fact that reconciliation is a process that takes time, and no-one can force its pace.

5. See K.E. Løgstrup, *Om spontane livsytringer i System og Symbol*, Copenhagen 1997, Ed. 2, p. 113 et seq.
6. Hammerich & Frydenberg, p. 146.

III. The basis for reconciliation

The offence may involve pain or suffering, whether physical or psychological. The common reaction of the injured party is anger, hate and a desire for revenge. Usually the offender wants to forget or even deny having done anything wrong. However, it is a pre-condition for reconciliation that the pain caused should be acknowledged. Thus, there will be no reconciliation if the attitude of the offender is that 'It doesn't matter' or 'Let's forget about it and get on with life,' whether or not the offence was deliberate.

If the offence is real, there will be a need for forgiveness before there can be reconciliation, so one can say: the fact I have been wronged cannot be changed, the clock cannot be turned back. I cannot remove your guilt, but in spite of this I am ready to start on a process which can restore our relations.

In the context of mediation, reconciliation means the restoration of relations on the basis of acknowledgement of pain, forgiveness and acceptance of forgiveness. Thus the injury caused must be articulated, recognised and acknowledged. In the case of serious offences, the victim can have a need to hear from the offender an explanation of why he or she in particular was the victim, or the victim's family can have a need to know exactly what happened. Knowing what happened is therefore essential for reconciliation.

Often, in the context of mediation, one party has a need to receive an apology, or at least an expression of regret, and sometimes a party can feel a need to make an apology. Many mediators have witnessed how a sincere apology can totally turn round a situation. But even though the most sincere apology cannot change what has happened, it can immediately open up contact between parties who have previously seemed to lack sympathy for each other. This is also the case with serious offences. An apology can give the victim trust that the offender will not repeat the offence and has shown willingness to learn from what happened, so there can be the beginnings of laying the foundations for new confidence. However, this is subject to the clear condition that the apology should be seen as being genuine.

An apology is not necessarily a precondition for forgiveness, but nor can an apology compel forgiveness. Forgiveness and power are linked in another way. The power to forgive or not to forgive belongs solely to the injured party; forgiving means that the injured party will no longer be able to exploit the forgiven wrong as a lever of power. A decision to forgive often involves a decision to include the other party in the relationship of trust which one normally assumes applies to one's fellow human beings.[7]

As an overwhelming rule, reconciliation and forgiveness are linked to a need for a certain kind of justice. In this case, the injured party will often expect the offending party to accept some form of penance, if for no other reason than to show the sincerity of an apology or expression of regret. The penance may only be small, but it will relate sufficiently to the offending party's capacity so as it to be noticeable for them, but without doing them real harm. These are the ideas which lie behind the concept of *restorative justice*, since the penance has the effect of re-introducing the offender to society as someone who takes responsibility for their actions, and makes recompense, but without subjecting them to burdens which would make their future life difficult. For both victims and offenders this is a step in the re-establishment of human dignity.

Where there is forgiveness and reconciliation, without the demand for any form of compensation, this will amount to an act of 'true mercy', and the basis for this lies outside the scope of this book.

An unwillingness to see oneself as human, with human faults and defects for which there can be a need for forgiveness, is a hindrance to reconciliation. This offends against both one's own self-image and widely accepted views of justice, according to which one expects the other party first to admit their fault and then to do some pen-

7. See K.E. Løgstrup, *Om spontane livsytringer in System og Symbol*, Copenhagen 1997, Ed. 2, p 113 et seq.

ance. Only when the other party has performed some penance, so one's own sense of justice is satisfied, can one accept the desire for forgiveness.

Reconciliation and empathy

It has been observed that victims can find it so difficult to forgive that they nurse their pain within them, so there is a risk that they make themselves victims twice over. For offenders it can be difficult for them to see their offences for what they are, because this undermines the image they have of themselves, so that it is literally or figuratively impossible for them to change their picture of themselves as being 'a hero in a holy war' to seeing themselves as a 'common murderer'. However, such attitudes do not lead to reconciliation. It is key to the reconciliation process that each party should both acknowledge their own sufferings and be receptive to the other party's experience of their actions, as well as having respect for the suffering which the other party has also experienced, rather than regarding it as well merited punishment. Reconciliation is impossible unless there is empathy – both for the other person and for oneself.[8]

But empathy, in turn, depends on contact. If one takes cover behind well defended ramparts, then images of hostility will spring up like weeds. Reconciliation can only arise from a willingness to forgive and from empathy, even love. Empathy and love cannot be imposed by force, but must be freely given.[9] This means that voluntariness in mediation is vital if the parties are going to be able to repair their relations, and there can only be reconciliation if the parties meet and the mediator is able to facilitate contact between them. Preparatory work can be done in separate meetings, but the reconciliation itself requires the parties to meet.

8. Paul Leer-Salvesen, who has worked with murderers in Norwegian prisons, has experienced that those who have generally had the most difficulty forgiving have been the murderers themselves, because it is an almost impossible thing to accept that they were a person who could commit murder. See also Vibeke Vindeløv, 'Forsoning – som alternativ til judiciel konfliktbehandling', *Retfærd* 93, 2/2001, pp. 113-129.
9. See Karsten Fledelius, *På vej til Grazz*, 1997.

In his book, *God has a Dream*, Tutu says that human beings can cope with suffering, but they are unable to cope with a life without meaning.[10] A fulfilled reconciliation process has been shown to give energy to victims as well as offenders to work to remove the conditions in society that gave rise to the injuries caused.

The following summary of the criteria for reconciliation is based on experiences of the South African Truth and Reconciliation Commission (TRC) as well as a study of the literature:[11]

Criteria for reconciliation

1. A statement of or knowledge of what has happened or has been experienced.
2. Recognition of the harm done to the injured party.
3. Acknowledgement of the offence by the offending party.
4. Acceptance by the offending party of some kind of penance, for example making an apology, as a symbol of his acceptance of responsibility.
5. Acceptance by the victim of the offender's sincere apology
6. A meeting between the parties.
7. Time.

IV Reconciliation in a societal context

From the point of view of *society*, there seem to be sufficiently pragmatic reasons for seeking to establish a framework for enabling reconciliation to take place, among other things because reconciliation is a personal process which can never be demanded from others or given on behalf of others. In these cases, attempts to induce reconciliation risk being seen as a further infringement of rights, so they will not merely demonstrate a lack of respect but will be directly counter-productive.

However, there are some pragmatic factors which should be referred to and which, from the point of view of society, can help establish the framework for reconciliation.

10. Desmond Tutu, *God has a Dream*, 2004.
11. See Vibeke Vindeløv, op. cit., with references.

First, it can be inappropriate for perpetrators to serve their sentences in prison and be prevented from using their skills and other resources for the benefit of society. Similarly, victims who are consumed by their sufferings often need a lot of help from others to move on with their lives. From a utilitarian point of view, it can be a benefit to society to make use of the perpetrators' and victims' resources for restructuring and restoration.

For victims and perpetrators, the social and personal aspects complement each other. Through a process of reconciliation, the victims can obtain release from their pains and anxieties and can function better in their daily lives; perpetrators will also get relief by accepting their responsibilities and obtaining forgiveness for their acts. In this way, both victim and perpetrator are freer to move on with their lives.

In South Africa, considerations of this kind were natural as most of the perpetrators were well educated and white, occupying positions which it would be difficult to fill at short notice if their places were to be taken by educated black people. This argued in favour of an arrangement with individual amnesties, which became one of the TRC's innovations.[12] It required a high degree of acceptance of reconciliation, especially from black South Africans, to accept that people who have committed wrongs should continue in their original posts.

A second reason for establishing a framework for reconciliation can be that violations have a tendency to give rise to new violations. In war or civil war, the wronged group will try to gain the upper hand, often by means of violent acts at least equivalent to those to which they have been subjected. When a legal system intervenes and deals with a conflict, the special preventive effect relating to the perpetrator is slight. If it is possible for the parties to be reconciled, the motive to repeat or continue the previous conduct will be reduced.

12. In his book, *No Future Without Forgiveness*, London 1999, Desmond Tutu calls the general amnesty 'national amnesia'.

Reconciliation usually requires knowledge of what has happened. This means that reconciliation also includes some documentation of the violations and makes them visible. This, in itself, helps to prevent history repeating itself.

Finally, the risk of overloading the judicial system can also be a reason for establishing a separate forum for reconciliation. However, the South African Truth and Reconciliation Commission was a very expensive process, which would not have been possible without international financial support. There is not necessarily a financial saving in establishing a reconciliation forum, but the judicial system will be kept free to deal with more traditional cases so the customary functions of the judicial order can be maintained.

However, reconciliation and justice should not be seen as being contradictory but as preconditions for each other. It is within the framework of truth, mercy and justice that the bridge to peace is found, and a balance between the three is a process as well as a goal.[13]

Against this background it is important that the lessons learnt from the South African TRC should not glorify the process. One of the greatest deficiencies of the arrangement was the absence of a requirement that the perpetrators should accept personal responsibility for what had happened. The amnesty obtained was a bare amnesty, without any obligation to contribute to compensation for the victims. Among other things this has meant that the victims have not received reasonable compensation and this has

13. Examples of other books which describe the new paradigm, and thus the new approach to violent conflicts, include: William Zartman & J. Lewis Rasmussen, *Peacemaking in Interntional Conflict, Methods and Techniques*, Washington, 2001; John Paul Lederach, *Building Peace, Sustainable Reconciliation in Divided Societies*, Washington 2000; Adam Curle, *Another Way, Positive Response to contemporary violence*, Oxford 1995; Johan Galtung & Carl G. Jacobsen, *Searching for Peace, The road to transcend*, Virginia 2000; Louise Diamond & John McDonald, *Multi-Track Diplomacy*, Connecticut, 1996; and Simon Fisher et al., *Working with Conflict*, Birmingham 2000.

led to a high degree of bitterness and continued imbalance. It is presumably not contested that the arrangement of the TRC contributed to the peaceful transition from apartheid to democracy. However, it is a big question how far the reconciliation process has come today.

CHAPTER 12

Mediation in international conflicts and the link between major and minor conflicts

I. Introduction

International conflicts are a clearly separate area for research and practice, and this book does not attempt to cover them. However, it is the argument of this book that there are similarities and connections between conflicts between individuals, conflicts between groups, wider social conflicts and international conflicts. This author is not alone in believing this. Previously it was possible to make clear distinctions between: the literature on mediation and conflict resolution dealing with personal conflicts and, perhaps, conflicts between organisations; the literature on international mediation and conflict resolution; and the literature on international politics. Recently, these topics have grown more alike and sometimes they draw on each other for insight and inspiration. In parallel with this, more and more people consider themselves to be 'citizens of the world', suggesting that one is a citizen of two different societies: the national, into which one is born or brought up; and the universal, to which one belongs by virtue of being a member of humankind.[1] Thus the world becomes ever smaller and there is ever a need to understand both the local and the global, both minor and major conflicts. It has

1. See Peter Kemp, *Den nye Verdensorden*, 2007, p. 21.

also become more common to explain foreign political events in socio-psychological terms, for example. This prompts the question of whether experience gained at the micro level can be applicable at the macro level, and whether it can be necessary to involve non-state actors (such as transnational companies, banks, NGOs and so-called 'illegal combatants') in both political and strategic discussions about political measures.[2]

The aim of this chapter is to refer, briefly, to some of the similarities, differences and connections between what may be called minor and major conflicts.

II. The link between international conflicts and individual conflicts

Formal structures

The *formal* handling of conflicts *between private citizens* takes place within a national court system in which the laws of the land are enforced. Depending on how well the judicial system of a country functions, the courts are guarantors of the equal treatment of its citizens on the basis of objective norms. Thus, the courts both give citizens rights and impose a duty to comply with the country's laws. What is decisive for the effectiveness of a court's judgments is that they should be enforced and sanctioned in accordance with the appropriate laws. Each country has authorities which undertake this executive function.[3]

2. The Swedish Folke Bernadotte Academy, which is under the Swedish Foreign Ministry, is an excellent example of an initiative which is aimed at mediating dialogue in violent international conflicts. For examples of generative dialogue see, www.generative.dialogue.org. For examples of the contributions of NGOs and other private initiatives to the resolution of violent conflicts, see Paul von Tongeren et al. (eds.), *People Building Peace II, Successful Stories of Civil Society*, 2005; and IDEA (UNDP), *Democratic Dialogue – a Handbook for Practitioners*, 2006.
3. In some cases there are quasi-supranational legal systems, such as the EU legal system and the Federal system in the USA, in which legislation adopted at a supranational level can have direct effect on citizens in the countries or states which are subject to the su-

International conflicts

International conflicts are by their nature different, by virtue of the fact that there is no plausible guarantor for enforcement and sanctioning. As a general rule, a state is neither subject to laws adopted by others, nor is its security guaranteed against other states. In relation to potential conflicts, states therefore act at least in part with an expectation that they will have to look after their own interests, that they are responsible for their own security and have to find allies, since appeals to international organisations do not provide a sufficient basis for security.

III. Explanation of concepts

It may be helpful to define 'conflicts' and 'conflict resolution' in relation to international conflicts. International conflicts range over issues such as rights over territory and, as with conflicts between individuals, conflicts about ethnic and religious identity, human rights, and basic human needs. At the heart of these conflicts is a concern about limited resources, so conflicts concern control over resources, confirmation of identity and security. There are also conflicts about fundamental changes to the existing world order.[4]

Definition

We will start with Peter Wallensteen's definition of a conflict which is *a social situation in which at least two parties strive simultaneously to acquire the same limited resources.*[5]

Compared with the description of conflicts given in Chapter 4, it is clear that, also in an international context, concerns about scarce resources and a conviction that a

pranational association. Those countries or states which are part of the supranational system have agreed to enforce judgments handed down by the supranational court.

4. See J. Lewis Rasmussen, 'Peacemaking in the Twenty-First Century', in *Peacemaking in International Conflict*, Washington 1991, p. 26. See also O. Ramsbotham et al. (ed.), *Contemporary Conflict Resolution*, 2005.
5. Peter Wallensteen, *Understanding Conflict Resolution*, 2nd Ed. 2007, p. 15.

conflict can only be resolved if one party's needs are satisfied at the cost of another, are the basis for conflict.

However, an international conflict can also be seen as a process which is driven by collective needs and concerns, or fears that these needs will not be satisfied. These needs can be material, physical and psychological, and are articulated in group and international contexts through *identity groups*, reflecting their *collective* nature.[6] If conflicts are long drawn-out these concerns will become existential, as in the struggle for survival of an identity group.[7]

As stated in Chapter 4, conflicts can also been in their context, as described by Johan Galtung in the late 1960s. According to this, conflicts are to be seen as a combination of attitude (A), behaviour (B) and contradiction (C), which interact in a dynamic process.

Figure 11. ABC triangle

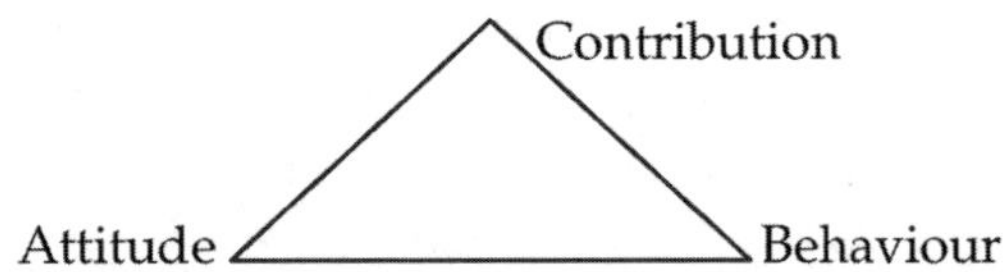

Galtung supplemented his description of the ABC triangle in 1990 by distinguishing between direct violence (e.g. the murder of a child), structural violence (a child dies from poverty), and cultural violence (which makes us blind to violence or seek to justify it).

Figure 12. Expanded ABC triangle

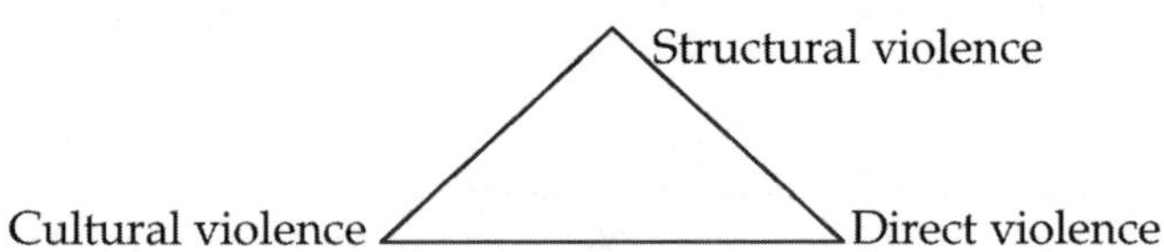

6. Herbert Kelman, 'Social-Psychological Dimensions in International Conflict', in Zartman & Rasmussen (eds.), *Peacemaking in International Conflict*, 1997, p. 194.
7. See also E. Azar, 'Protracted International Conflicts: Ten propositions', in Azar & Burton, International Conflict Resolution: Theory and Practice, 1986.

Direct violence ends when we change our behaviour; structural violence ends when we remove structural contradictions; and cultural violence ends when we change our attitudes.

IV. Differencer between the micro and macro level

a. Escalation

Escalation

Theories about escalation are also fully comparable between micro and macro levels. However, the fullest extent of escalation is displayed in international conflicts so that the first three steps in the conflict ladder described in Chapter 4 are often described merely as pre-conflicts when they relate to international conflicts. The step concerned with *images of hostility* is referred to as *confrontation,* the step concerned with *open hostility* is referred to as *crisis,* and *polarisation* is referred to as the *outcome,* since a crisis can either result in a ceasefire, in surrender or in negotiation.[8]

Dilemma of security

The dilemma of security seems unavoidable, because conflicts have a tendency to escalate to a level that threatens survival. Since war is a clear possibility in international politics, speculations about worst-case scenarios are much more systematic in international politics than at the micro level. It is precisely because it is not possible to ensure obtaining the protection or legal enforcement of others that it is regarded as 'necessary' to a certain degree to exercise extra caution, but this in itself can lead to conflict. This results in the security dilemma, where one party takes precautions in its security policy (for example, increasing armaments and forming alliances), and these are precautions which increase the feeling of insecurity of the potential opponent, and this causes the potential opponent to take its own precautions, which further increases the fears of the first party etc. In these cases an escalation takes place which neither reflects a specific conflict, but nor can it be said to be a sim-

8. See e.g. Simon Fisher et al., *Working with Conflict,* London, 2000 p. 19.

ple misunderstanding – it is more the case that there is a fundamental lack of transparency and unpredictability in international politics which follows a tragic pattern where unnecessary conflicts become almost inevitable.[9]

Escalation as a rational development

Escalation can still be described and explained in socio-psychological terms, but there is an additional element of rationality which is clearly based on zero-sum thinking and which was classically described by the great theoretician on war, Carl von Clausewitz. According to Clausewitz, in war the complex questions of aims are pushed aside by the question of winning or losing, which makes it necessary to choose the most advantageous route, regardless of whether this involves unreasonable risks, since the only choice lies between victory and defeat. Even the most seemingly irrational escalation is therefore not necessarily irrational, but may be dictated by a strategic analysis.[10] Escalation is thus not perceived as a mistake, but as a rational development whose purpose is to render one's enemy defenceless.

There are several problems with this rationale: *first*, the decision-makers can easily deceive themselves over their trust in their own well-balanced calculations, so that the rationality may not be quite as obvious as they assumed initially; theories rooted in psychology have a growing number of suggestions to explain this process. The reader is referred to the discussion of projection in Chapter 4 also at the collective level, as expressed in the term 'rogue states' for example. *Second*, as pointed out in Chapter 4, an important and often underappreciated characteristic of the escalation of conflicts is that a change takes place when one no longer sees the other party as being an individual, but as part of a group. This 'de-personalising' also has a tendency to lead to a de-humanising. In this way there arises an al-

9. John H. Herz, 'Idealist Internationalism and the Security Dilemma', World Politics, Vol. 2 (1950), pp. 157-180; and Herbert Butterfield, The Tragic Element in Modern International Conflict, first published in 1950 and reprinted in Butterfield, History and Human Relations, London 1951, pp. 9-36.
10. Carl von Clausewitz, *On War*. See e.g. Daniel Druckman, 'Negotiating in the International Context', in Zartmann & Rasmussen (eds.), 1997 op. cit., Chapter. 3.

most rational acceptance of one's hostility, and this makes it easier to take measures which are harmful to the other party, who is not regarded as being covered by the more universal norm that one should not cause harm to one's fellow human beings; and at the same time one depersonalises oneself, and by this means evades one's responsibility.

b. Neutrality

Neutrality is not absolute in international conflicts

There appears to be a difference between mediation at the micro level and mediation at the macro level with regard to the requirement for neutrality. As described in Chapter 9 on neutrality, the concept is far from unproblematic at the micro level as it is probably unrealistic to have a requirement for dealing with the difficulties of the concept, so that the mediator should concentrate on the conduct of the proceedings while leaving responsibility for the solution of the conflict to the parties, and at the same time require the mediator to ensure that the parties have an opportunity for discussion and reflection. According to Berkovitch,[11] in international conflicts the requirement for impartiality and neutrality is now questioned, and appears to go further than is yet the case at the micro level. Thus the requirement for neutrality is not absolute in international conflicts, and perhaps not even desirable. In any case, it will vary from conflict to conflict, and perhaps even change in the course of the mediation, so that a mediator may be tempted to use manipulation such as increasing or filtering information, threatening or persuading etc., which are regarded as legitimate in this context to some extent. It is important to emphasise *that* neutrality is not rejected because it is regarded as impossible to achieve, as is the case at the micro level, but because it is considered inappropriate in certain

11. Jacob Bercovitch, 'Mediation in International Conflict An overview of Theory, A review of Practice', in Zartman & Rasmussen (eds.), Peacemaking in International Conflict, 1997, p. 125 et seq. See also Bercovitch (ed.), *Studies in International Mediation*, Harvard, 2002.

circumstances,[12] *that* it may be possible to replace neutrality with a requirement for independence from the parties, and finally *that* there is far from general agreement that manipulation by mediators is acceptable, and it might be more appropriate to demand that there should be transparency with regard to the process and confidentiality with regard to the content.

Berkowitch's assessment of the need for neutrality and impartiality corresponds at the individual level to that of problem-solving mediators, and it expresses a conservative view both of the desirability and the possibility of acting neutrally which is not in harmony with, for example, Dag Hammarskjöld's demand for more universal values as the driving force and yardstick for his work.

The explanation for Berkowitch's approach is probably that it can be more difficult, if not impossible, to ignore the power dimension in international politics. Instead of positing high ideals, in the manner of Dag Hammarskjöld, he finds it more appropriate (and pragmatic) to keep an open mind on whether in the given situation it is preferable for the mediator to be neutral, or whether it can be appropriate, as for example in the case of the USA with regard to the Israel-Palestine conflict, that the USA can exert pressure on the parties to participate in mediation by virtue of the dependence of the parties on the USA. Perhaps the difference in perspective is also due to the fact that national mediation is primarily comparable with judicial decisions, whereas international mediation is seen as one of a broad repertoire of means for dealing with conflicts, ranging from negotiation, to international law and to war.

However the author of this book finds that it is essential to accept responsibility to the greatest possible extent and to demand that the universal values championed by Dag Hammarskjöld should be lived up to; see the Foreword. Only in this way is it possible to establish a more long-term

12. On the difficulties of international mediation, see 'The failure of international mediation in African civil wars', occasional paper in Track Two, Vol. 8 No 2, Cape Town, 1999.

perspective and to contribute to sustainable development, also in the context of international conflicts.

c. Difficult negotiations

The ripe conflict

A question to which more attention has been paid in international conflicts than in conflicts at the micro level is: when is the time ripe for settlement or mediation of a conflict? The subject has been discussed relatively briefly in the literature on negotiation,[13] and it is a recognised theme in the literature on international conflicts.[14] The idea is that, sooner or later, conflicts reach the point where the disputing parties recognise that the conflict must be resolved. There are many different descriptions of this: war weariness, loss of the will to fight, and concerns about steadily mounting losses,[15] and both parties have a feeling that the conflict could soon develop catastrophically for all parties. It has been argued that this was why the people of South Africa supported peaceful settlement in the form of the Truth and Reconciliation Commission. In other words, to reach this stage a situation must be intolerable. If, on the other hand, the situation is tolerable, the time is not ripe for settlement or negotiation.

According to Wallensteen the ripe moment is characterised by the fact that the parties argue in the same way both inwardly and outwardly. If the parties can do this, this it means that contact with the counterparty is firmly based, and the parties have the appearance of being both honourable and trustworthy.[16]

When the parties to a conflict have incompatible or over-optimistic views of their alternatives to a joint solution, the conflict is not ripe for negotiation. In such cases

13. See e.g. David A. Lax & James K. Sibenius, *The Manager as Negotiator*, New York 1986, pp. 59-60.
14. See e.g. W. Zartman, *Ripe for Resolution, Conflict and Intervention in Africa*, Oxford, 1989; and Peter Wallensteen, *Från krig till fred, Om konfliktlösning i det globala systemet*, Eskilstuna 1994, (2008) Chapter 8.
15. Wallensteen, op. cit., p. 274.
16. Wallensteen, op. cit., p. 280.

there is not much purpose in bringing the parties together, because potential proposals or themes for negotiation will seem inferior for at least one of the parties. An example of this was the conflicts in the Western Balkans in the early 1990s where a significant part of the problem was that the parties involved – Croats, Serbs and Bosnians – had shifting hopes of victory due to their expectations of their international supporters (whether Germans, Russians or Americans), so that war-weariness did not occur at the same time for all the parties.

Instead, efforts should be invested in activities away from the negotiating table which can pave the way for a change of attitude to the conflict, and thereby generate potential solutions. In such situations informal diplomatic measures are necessary.

The conflict between Israel and Palestine casts doubt on the tenability of the theory that there will always come a time when a conflict is ripe for settlement; it raises doubts about whether, in some situations, the time will ever arrive, or whether the parties will destroy each other. Often, it can be difficult to believe that any of the parties to this conflict believes their behaviour increases the likelihood of obtaining a good solution. At least there seems to be very little understanding on both sides that their own security is depending on the others side also feeling secure.

V. The solution of international conflicts

So-called 'realists'

Until now, so-called 'realists' have played the dominant role in international conflict resolution, where power and aspects of dominance have been decisive, and the arena of conflict resolution has accepted the existing international order as given. The 'realists' are still those who set the tone; see American foreign policy, for example. However, other ideas for conflict resolution at international level are gaining ground. According to these, knowledge about conflicts in general as well as socio-psychological factors play a much greater role than traditional power politics, and the links between major conflicts and minor conflicts become clearer.

As for international conflicts, it is also possible to have a neutral or positive view of conflicts, and this is decisive for the method chosen for resolving a conflict. According to Herbert Kelman, even at the macro level, the aim of conflict resolution is not to eliminate conflicts entirely, which is neither possible nor desirable as conflicts are 'potentially constructive forces within a society or region and serve as the basis for essential social change'.[17]

The 'Copenhagen school'

The 'Copenhagen school' of security studies has contributed to a view of international conflicts that makes it immediately possible to understand the connection between conflicts at the micro level and conflicts at the macro level. What is new about the ideas of the Copenhagen school is that they point out that much of international conflict behaviour is negatively driven; in other words, it is driven by fear rather than by motivations of a more imperialist nature, such as a desire to obtain something, primarily power.[18]

According to the Copenhagen school, the fact that existential elements are often identified as being a critical point in an international context is fully in accordance with what is revealed by insight into the needs of individuals and by understanding the dimensions of a conflict. This means that a solution requires the existential elements to be addressed, so that anxiety is removed as a cause of conflict.

As described above, many theories of conflicts and negotiation in international politics are based on a view of differing parties who want to achieve something, and where these aspirations are regrettably in collision and are

17. Herbert Kelman, 'Social-Psychological Dimensions in International Conflict', in Zartman & Rasmussen (eds.), *Peacemaking in International Conflict*, Washington, 1997, p. 197.
18. Ole Wæver, 'Securitization and Desecuritization', in Ronnie D. Lipschutz (ed.), *On Security*, New York: Columbia University Press 1995, pp. 46-86; Barry Buzan, Ole Wæver & Jaap de Wilde, *Security: A New Framework for Analysis*, Boulder CO, Lynne Rienner 1997.

mutually exclusive. The task is therefore to find the areas that overlap and outcomes that both can accept, or at a deeper level, to solve problems in a way which gives the parties the feeling of having satisfied their goals. However, the parties to a conflict are seldom strategic thinkers whose starting point is to think how to optimise their situation; the reality is usually quite the reverse, and the conflict is usually driven forward by images of threats. Therefore, understanding of conflicts can draw on the central idea of the Copenhagen School that security problems arise when an actor (*the securitising actor*) convinces a given audience (for example, the population of a country) that someone or something (*the referent object*, for example a nation, a state, nature, our values) is threatened existentially, and it is therefore necessary and legitimate to resort to extraordinary means – otherwise it will be too late.

Often, conflict resolution will be hindered by the fact that more extremist groups on each side will paint pictures of worst-case scenarios of what the other side wants, so they imply that any concessions will surely lead to defeat.

The traditional trap naturally lies in acknowledging the idea of 'a nation' experiencing anxiety, and not acknowledging any holder of authority similarly. Regardless of whether a majority of the population in a given society experiences anxiety in a particular situation, it is not the nation in the abstract that experiences anxiety, but the sum of its individuals, and not least the holders of authority and decision-makers.

The dynamic in such identity-driven conflicts is often that on the one hand political leaders present a vision in which 'the nation' is threatened, and on the other hand they promote broader cultural nationalism in which the personal identity of the individual depends on the collective survival of the society: 'I can only truly be myself in a free X-land.' The experiences of the Mohammed Crisis described above, where the Danish Prime Minister described the threat to freedom of expression as an attack on the nation, and the offended Muslims described the cartoons as an attack on their religious way of life, are clear examples of this.

It is therefore that one of the key measures for breaking this negative spiral of conflict can often be to remove the basis for these representations, even if for outsiders they can sometimes seem to be ridiculous. An example of this is part of the proposal for the solution to the conflict in Northern Ireland, which includes the removal of some paragraphs from the Constitution of the Republic of Ireland which refer to the inclusion of Northern Ireland in the Republic of Ireland. In much the same way, in mediation between individuals we seek to create new representations, new narratives which each can identify with and which bring each party's experiences within a more constructive framework.

Another aspect is the necessity of identifying the different stakeholders, as society as a whole must be involved in the process of resolving the conflict. This is often forgotten. Thus, sufficient care is seldom taken to ensure that the justifications, which the people in power (the main negotiators) find sufficient for entering into a peace agreement, filter down to the general population so that they can understand the change in attitude. An example of this is the peace agreement entered into between Egypt and Israel at Camp David in 1978, when many of the Israeli soldiers who had to evacuate the occupied areas in the Sinai desert did not understand, and thus had not really accepted, the basis on which the agreement was entered into, even though they followed their orders.[19]

Conflict resolution at international level

Peter Wallensteen believes there will be conflict resolution at international level when *the parties to a conflict enter into an agreement which resolves the central issue of the dispute, accept each other's continued existence and cease all belligerent actions against each other. The agreement can be expressed or implied.*[20]

The definition of conflict resolution seems to contain a number of elements which are recognisable from the micro level:

19. This information was given to the author at a conference by Israeli soldiers who had participated in the evacuation.
20. Peter Wallensteen, op. cit., p. 9.

Each party accepts the existence of the other

First, it is a pre-condition for the resolution of a conflict that each party accepts the existence of the other. If the parties jointly find ways to deal with important questions through measures which build mutual confidence, this will give them a sense of fairness.

Second, the criteria for a mutually satisfactory solution are that the fundamental needs of both parties should be addressed, so neither of them has to give up what they consider essential, and they are reassured on matters about which they feel insecure.[21] With a positive or neutral view of conflicts, and a focus on the needs of the parties, it becomes possible to see one party's security as a pre-condition for the other party's security, rather than one party's security being at the expense of the other's. The idea of 'enlarging the pie' also applies in an international context.

However, international conflicts are not just conflicts between governments or states. They are also conflicts between societies, and they affect the daily life of each individual in the societies in conflict. Attention must be paid not only to the military and diplomatic dimensions, but also to the economic, psychological, cultural and social dimensions. The needs and concerns which drive a conflict are a collective expression which must be satisfied at a collective level, but they are experienced at the individual level. Therefore, conflict resolution must also take place at the individual level.

Fundamental needs of both parties should be addressed

Improving relations between the parties

Third, at the micro level we are concerned with the desirability, not merely of resolving the conflict, but of improving relations between the parties. It is argued that this is equally important at the macro level. Thus, with reference to many well-known international conflicts, in her book *Multiple Realities of International Mediation* Marieke Kleiboer says that effective conflict resolution (and mediation) must involve freeing oneself from ideas of fixed definitions of immutable structures and institutions, and focus-

21. See also Kelman, op cit., Chapter 6; and Azar, op. cit.

ing on 'restructuring relationships'.[22] The aim is thus to seek 'consensual change' and this must be brought about by facilitating a 'Dialogue for Change'.[23] [24]

Substantive fairness
Procedural fairness

By observing these three elements, emphasis is put on what has been found to be decisively important in mediation at the micro level, and this is that one should not focus only on substantive fairness, in other words on the conflict and its solution. It is just as important for the parties to experience procedural fairness, in other words that they have been involved in the process which has led to the resolution of the conflict. It is only in this way that the parties can obtain ownership of the solution and become engaged in putting it into practice.

In addition to this, it is decisive for successful mediation that actors at several levels should be involved, whether diplomats, businessmen, academics, the media, the military or civil society. Regrettably there is often a great distance between the state apparatus, let alone supranational organisations like the UN, and the civil population, sometimes to such a degree that it appears that they have opposing interests. The Swedish Folke Bernadotte Academy (under the Swedish Foreign Ministry) has taken the initiative to bring together representatives from diplomacy, business and, not least, civil peace movements in courses on conflict resolution. This has helped to remove many of the hostile

22. Marieke Kleiboer, *Multiple Realities of International Mediation*, London 1998, p. 67 et seq.
23. Examples of successful mediation include Biafra, see Adam Curle, *Tools for Transformation*, Worcester, 1990; and Mozambique see Cameron R. Hume, 'A Diplomat's View', in Zartman, op. cit., pp. 319-336.
24. Op. cit., p. 73. An example of unsuccessful international mediation is the attempted mediation between Rwanda's armed forces (*Forces Armées Rwandais* – FAR) and the guerrilla forces (RPF – *Rwandan Patriotic Front*), where the Tanzanian government acted as mediator. Arguably, the main reason why the mediation failed was that the parties did not accept ownership of the final agreement entered into in 1993; see Gregory Mthembu-Salter, *Mediation and Genocide: the case of Rwanda*, Centre for Conflict Resolution, Cape Town 1999.

images and thus created a basis for constructive cooperation rather than destructive opposition.

VI. Dilemmas over the choice of form of conflict resolution

Hopefully the foregoing will have made it clear that, whether we talk about conflicts at the micro or the macro level, it is possible to view conflicts in different ways which have decisive consequences for how conflicts are decided or resolved.

A conscious choice

It is often possible to make a conscious choice between two approaches to conflicts, probably more often than would appear. But such choices constitute difficult dilemmas, both for states and for individuals.

To go to war and to work for peace require equal measures of courage

The difficult choice, for belligerents and for politicians, is to put peace on the agenda, to substitute the hope and desire for victory with the desire for peace. Victories and heroes go together in the paradigm of war, where suppression of the enemy is naturally accepted as a necessity. To negotiate with the enemy is seen as a sign of weakness, so the only thing that can be negotiated about is unconditional surrender. The paradigm of peace considers dialogue, negotiation and agreement with the enemy as being a victory of all parties, while a return to hostilities is seen as a defeat. In the paradigm of war, the way is war and the end is peace. In the paradigm of peace, the way is peace and the end is a more peaceable world.[25] To go to war and to work for peace require equal measures of courage.

States and nations can act as independent legal persons and are thus bound by treaties they have ratified, declarations etc. There will be an undermining of responsibility if one fails to note the connection between the micro and the macro levels. By noting this connection and combining it

25. For a discussion of the paradigms of war and of peace, see Steen Clausen, 'Dialog og Dilemma', a paper published on the occasion of the 10th anniversary of the founding of the Center for Kon@iktløsning, October 2004.

with political science, international law and socio-psychology, it is possible to avoid nations denying responsibility for the actions (whether good or bad) which their leaders should be held to account for. Neither a dictator nor a president can remain in power without some support from among those citizens who are just as interested in power and position or just as fearful as the dictator or president. It is important to hold on to this focus, otherwise in the worst case the responsibility of the voters will simply evaporate, or in the best case will only be ascribed symbolic value with the eventual condemnation of the dictator or president.

Thus, the dilemma unfolds as a quite ordinary human dilemma, about whether we have the courage to hold on to our belief in peace, which to a large extent concerns how we relate to the evil in ourselves, and to the hate which sometimes wells up in us when we feel injured. In the paradigm of war we believe that evil only exists in others and that it can be eliminated, and we allow ourselves to be possessed by fear. In the paradigm of peace we acknowledge the existence of evil and our own limitations, and thereby also our own responsibility to contribute to a peaceful solution.

Finally, it must be emphasised that a constructive approach to conflicts and conflict resolution should not be thought of as being some kind of mystic affair, where the actors are guided only by their intuition or by higher powers. Constructive conflict resolution is both a science and an art. This means that, on the one hand, there are a number of techniques and tools which can be taught and developed under supervision and by experience in the field. And on the other hand, conflict resolution cannot be carried out mechanically or formalistically in accordance with a preordained script. Instead, whether they work nationally or internationally, individually or in groups, the actors must act flexibly and on the basis of their general knowledge of conflicts and their development, and as far as possible they must act in accordance with that constructive approach to conflict resolution which most claim to have.

VII. The traditional and the new paradigms in international conflicts

At the international level, in connection with the settlement of wars or civil wars, there can be reactions, even with regard to gross violations of human rights, which can differ so as to produce parallels with the two paradigms described in Chapter 2. Some examples are given below which illustrate this in simplified form.[26]

The Nürnberg War Crimes Trials

Example 1: The Nürnberg War Crimes Trials that followed the Second World War were decided on by the allies, and were imposed by the victors on the vanquished. This meant that actions of the victors, such as the bombing of Dresden, were not dealt with by the tribunal. Apart from punishing the guilty, the proceedings were also an expression of both justice and revenge, and it is likely that the motivation for the trial included a desire for deterrence.

United Nations tribunals

Example 2: After the genocide committed in Rwanda and in the former Yugoslavia, the United Nations decided to set up tribunals to punish the guilty by means of a legal process. Thus the initiative for the tribunals was taken by the international community which wanted the tribunals to signal to the world that the events which had taken place were unacceptable and should be punished. As distinct from the Nuremberg Trials, the accused were all those who violated human rights, regardless of which side they were on. Tutsis and Hutus, Serbs, Croats and Bosnians, were all to be treated on the same terms.

The Nuremberg War Crimes Trials and the tribunals in The Hague and in Rwanda were or are set up as traditional courts, with prosecutors, defenders and judges. The aim of the proceedings can be summarised as being to find the guilty parties and to punish them. The overriding desire was for justice (however that may be defined).

26. The reader is referred to Vibeke Vindeløv, 'Konfliktråd, tribunaler og sandhedskommissioner', in Flemming Balvig & Jørn Vestergaard (eds.), *'Med lov....', Retsvidenskabelige betragtninger*, Copenhagen 1998.

Another way to approach gross violations of human rights is to set up a truth commission. Several different models of this have been used with varying degrees of success in different places around the world, for example in Argentina, El Salvador and in South Africa. The following looks at the Truth Commission in El Salvador.

El Salvador

Example 3: After the end of the civil war in El Salvador it was decided to embark on the democratisation of the country with the help of the UN, and to guarantee full respect for human rights and reunite Salvadorean society. An important part of the ensuing peace process was the setting up of a Truth Commission to carry out systematic investigations and give accounts of the worst human rights abuses since 1980. The *aim* of the Truth Commission's work was to produce an authorised account of the abuses which had taken place. In addition to this, there was a desire to create a basis for justice, i.e., to find and punish the guilty. However, the abuses against the majority of the population had been countless; official figures showed there had been 75,000 civilian deaths, 8,000 people had 'vanished', and over 1 million had been driven from their homes. It was thought unrealistic to investigate and punish everyone in the police and the military who were the major offenders, so the parliament agreed to grant a general amnesty, i.e. a collective remission of punishment for the crimes committed. This parliamentary decision was taken without consulting the people, who did not support the decision. 'Official' society thereby complied with the interests of the powerful in society.

It is typically the case, in connection with wars, civil wars and crimes, that the victims want justice or revenge and the perpetrators want to forget and move on. Both reactions are understandable and human. Bearing this in mind, it is now possible to consider the similarities and differences between the three examples given above.

The *differences* are that one model, tribunals, appears to be concerned primarily with the interests of victims and of the international community, as their aim is to punish and exact revenge. The second model, truth commissions, is seemingly set up in the interests of the victims, to document the acts committed, but under proceedings which are adapted primarily to serve the wishes of the perpetrators to have the events forgotten. The two models differ with regard to the consequences of the proceedings, involving either punishment or amnesty. When an amnesty is made general, there is a conflict between the establishment of guilt and the encouragement of forgetting.

The *similarities* are the desire for justice and recognition of the need to hold past actions to account. Also, there is the important but often overlooked similarity that both approaches neglect consideration for the other party and thereby deprive the relationship of meaning. Regardless of which of the two approaches is used, they overlook the fact that both the victim and the perpetrator have not only been through a war together, but they must also, sooner or later, live side by side in a shared future.

A new and just society can neither be built on a desire for revenge nor freedom from punishment. The quality of the accounting for the crimes of a previous regime is vital for the future sense of justice and the establishment of judicial practice. Should the past be revenged or repressed, or should it be remembered and acknowledged? The answers to these questions are decisive for the structure of the institutions of society and thus for the scope for the parties' shared future in the reconstructed society.

Truth and Reconciliation Commission (TRC) in South Africa

Example 4: On this basis, the Truth and Reconciliation Commission (TRC) in South Africa is unique, because it was an attempt to consider the interests both of the perpetrators and of the victims. The composition of the TRC followed an open democratic debate, and was based on a conviction that the parties had a shared history and must now construct a shared future, and that they would try to eliminate each other unless this conviction was widely recognised. Using previously used terminology, the time was ripe for a settlement of the conflict, and the connectedness of the parties was acknowledged.

The aims of the Truth and Reconciliation Commission's (TRC) work were expressed in four points:[27]

- To establish as complete a picture as possible of violations of human rights in South Africa between 1960 and 1993, by means of investigations and hearings;
- To grant individual amnesties to persons who made full disclosure of their politically motivated participation in such violations;
- To give victims an opportunity to make public the violations they had suffered, and to recommend measures for the reparation, rehabilitation and restoration of the human and civil dignity of victims or their relations; and
- To make a report on the violations which had taken place in the period in question and which had been laid before the Commission, and to make recommendations aimed at preventing the commission of gross violations of human rights.

It is outside the scope of this book to undertake a more detailed description of the work of the TRC. However, it should be noted that, despite the TRC's undeniable defects (for example, the absence of proper compensation for victims, lack of compliance with the principle of legal certainty etc.), South Africa today stands as a shining example, partly because the extensive and public proceedings made it impossible to deny that many violations did take place, and partly because its structure gave insight and inspiration for any future settlement of such conflicts and attempts at reconciliation.

27. Act No 34 of 26 July 1995, Promotion of National Unity and Reconciliation Act.

Form of settlement	Who decides	Aims	Outcome	Consideration taken for
Nürnberg War Crimes Trials	The victors	Justice (Prevention?)	Punishment	Victims of the losers (victims on the losers' side were not considered)
Rwanda and Former Yugoslavia Tribunals	The international community	Justice (Prevention?)	Punishment	All victims
El Salvador Truth Commission	UN + national government (without democratic involvement)	Authoritative description of events	General amnesty	Perpetrators
South African Truth and Reconciliation Commission	National government with democratic involvement	Comprehensive account + reconstruction + prevention	Individual amnesty + victims give their account + restoration	Victims and perpetrators from both sides

Figure 13. Different settlements following wars and civil wars

CHAPTER 13

Ethics and liability

As described in the first two chapters of this book, there are several different kinds of mediation, just as there are several different opinions about what is meant by 'correct' mediation. Differences can concern questions such as whether it is right for a mediator to evaluate the strengths and weaknesses of proposals made; whether separate meetings should be allowed in mediation and, if so, to what extent; whether lawyers can represent the parties in the mediation process; and whether the mediator should have special knowledge of the subject of the dispute etc.

One might have thought that the debate about what conditions should be fulfilled in order for an activity to be defined as 'mediation' would be passé. However, this is still not the case. The title of 'mediator' is still not a protected designation in most if not all countries. This means that, regardless of their professional background, anyone who wishes can call themselves a mediator. And it also means that mediation is a multi-disciplinary business, where it is difficult to reach agreement about criteria and requirements.

The following discussion of what is necessary in order for some activity to be called a 'mediation' takes its point of departure from two remarkably clear articles in the *Harvard Negotiation Law Review*. These are Leonard Riskin, 'Understanding Mediators' Orientations, Strategies and Techniques: A Grid for the Perplexed', 1996, Vol. 1, pp. 9-52; and Kimberlee Kovach & Lela P. Love, 'Mapping Mediation: The Risk of Riskin's Grid', 1998, Vol. 3, pp. 71-110. Even though these articles are not the most recent, they nevertheless remain highly topical and have since been followed by similar discussions by other authors.[1]

This is the origin of the two key questions which will be discussed later:

1. To what extent does the form of mediation used comply with the values and assumptions which are the basis for the mediation activity in question?
2. Can the concept of mediation reasonably include activities which are essentially different, both in their form and their basic values?

I. The expert and the reflective practitioner[2]

To illustrate the different versions of mediation, Riskin constructs a matrix by reference to two related characteristics which each span a continuum: one concerns the themes which are included in mediation and can range from the relatively narrow to the broad; the other concerns the actions of the mediator and can range from evaluative to facilitative.

Narrow mediation

In a very narrow mediation, which Riskin calls the first level, the primary goal is to settle the conflict by agreement. This largely corresponds to a court process, but is quicker and cheaper. The subject matter of the conflict will often relate to money and the process will mostly be concerned with the strengths and weaknesses of each side, seen from a legal point of view.

1. See, e.g., Dorothy J. Della Noce, 'Seeing Theory in Practice: An Analysis of Empathy in Mediation', *Negotiaton Journal*, 15:3, 1999, pp. 271-301, in which there is a discussion of whether, and if so how, ideology plays a role in mediation practice.
2. A Google search shows that both the terms 'reflexive mediation' and 'reflective mediation' are in use. In this chapter the term 'reflective practitioner' is used – a usage endorsed by the title of Donald Schön's book. There seems to be no linguistic grounds for preferring one to the other, but this author has preferred generally to use the term 'reflexive mediation'.

The second level of the same continuum includes other commercial considerations which would probably not be considered in a normal court case. This will include considerations such as whether a fee or the quality of a product is reasonable. At this level, it may be recognised that the parties have an interest in maintaining their business relations, perhaps because of mutual dependence, and questions about their cooperation etc. may be addressed. Matters may also be included which will make it possible for the parties to consider how to improve their future cooperation in ways they would not previously have thought about.

Broad mediation

The third level focuses on questions of a more personal kind. For example, the heads of two companies may have developed such personal antagonism towards each other that it damages business relations between their companies. Bad relations between the two managers may lead to anxiety and even loss of self-esteem. At a purely instrumental level, such personal relations can act as a barrier to making an agreement between the parties. In addressing the issue of personal relations in mediation there can also be a desire to enable the parties to learn and to change themselves, for other than purely instrumental reasons.

The fourth level widens the sphere of interests even further, taking into account the interests of the local community or other related elements together with those more directly associated with the mediation. For example, society can have an interest in two violent gangs resolving their differences. Or there may be some conflict within the computer industry which may have more general relevance, so that in resolving their conflict the parties can take account of how the solution may affect other similar undertakings.

It is the nature of the interest which is the primary focus of the mediation which determines its level. It is possible that the relationship between the parties will be re-established even if the mediation is at the first level, but repairing the relationship is only of secondary importance, and neither the mediator nor the parties will have focused on this possibility.

Evaluative mediation

The second continuum concerns the strategies and techniques used by mediators to achieve the goals of the mediation. At one end there is evaluative mediation and at the other end there is facilitative mediation. The evaluative mediator assumes that the parties want advice about what would be a suitable solution, based on the law, the custom of the trade etc. Evaluative mediators consider themselves qualified to give such advice as they have the necessary training, experience and objectivity.

Facilitative mediation

The facilitative mediator assumes that the parties are able to look after their own interests in the mediation and they understand their situation and the conflict better than the mediator. The parties are regarded as the experts in their own lives, and the aim of mediation is to improve communication between them so they can find a solution themselves. In the extreme view, the goal of facilitative mediation is merely to enable the parties to communicate with each other in order to achieve better understanding.

On the basis of these classifications, it is now possible to give a more precise description of the different kinds of mediation. With the mediator's different techniques, and with the different interests taken into account, the mediation can move in different directions up or down the continuums described:

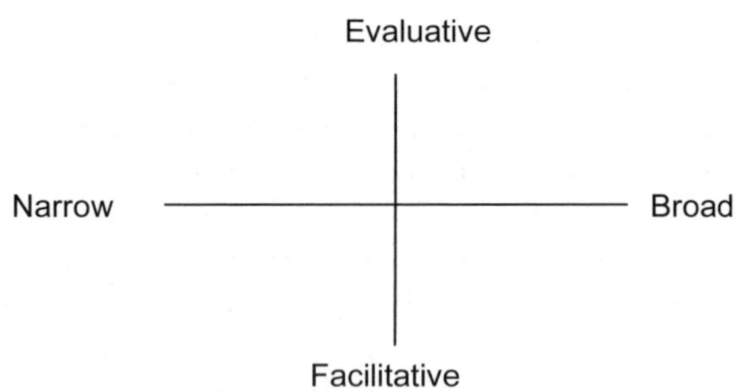

Figure 14. Riskin's Grid

Narrow-evaluative

If the mediation is *narrow-evaluative*, then in order to advise the parties on their strengths and weaknesses, the mediator will study the relevant documents thoroughly, will typically ask the parties (or their lawyers) to present their cases, will primarily use separate meetings, will propose or work towards compromises based on the positions of the parties, and typically put pressure on the parties to get acceptance of some specific proposal or room for manoeuvre.

Facilitative-narrow

If the mediation is *facilitative-narrow*, the mediator will use the same strategy as above for getting the parties to understand the strengths and weaknesses of their cases and the costs of not reaching an agreement. However, the mediator will not put pressure on the parties in the form of his or her own evaluations, proposals etc. This means the mediator will study the documentation less closely than in the previous scenario, and instead ask questions about the strengths and weaknesses of the cases and of proposals for a solution etc. Such a mediator will maintain that the parties are responsible for solving the problem, so the parties must be responsible for proposing solutions. The process can include elements of an educational nature, empowering the parties and helping them develop a sense of their own abilities to deal with conflicts, and perhaps some acknowledgement of the position of the other party.

Evaluative-broad

According to Riskin it is more difficult to describe *evaluative-broad* mediators, as they can vary both in what they include in the mediation and how evaluative they are. The main focus for this kind of mediator is probably to learn as much as possible about the parties, their interests and the circumstances surrounding the conflict, so the mediator can give the parties qualified advice about how best to resolve the conflict, having regard for the relevant interests.

Facilitative-broad

The *facilitative-broad* mediator will help the parties define the basis of their conflict in terms of needs and interests, and help them develop their own solutions to satisfy these needs and interests. Many mediators of this type will take the opportunity to help the parties to educate or adapt themselves or their frame of reference, local community etc. in a positive direction. Bush and Folger's transformative mediation is an example of this kind of mediation, where the focus is explicitly put on the parties' increased ability to understand each other's position, and to recognise it. Here the focus is on a kind of moral growth or transformation, and includes empowerment (a sense of their own capacity to handle life's problems) and acknowledgement (accepting or empathising with the situation of the other party). In addition, the parties may re-establish their relations with each other, for example by forgiving each other and recognising their mutual dependence, and each may obtain better insight both into their own position and that of the other party, and stop being angry or seeking revenge etc. As stated above, Bush & Folger believe that making an agreement is less important than the personal growth enabled by the mediation.[3]

Riskin argues that, whether they are aware of it or not, most mediators conduct their mediations on the basis of assumptions which are often grounded in their own personalities, education, training and experience. As a result, there is a tendency for mediations to take on the characteristics of the process to which they should be an alternative.[4] This means there is a certain assumption that, for example, court-based mediation will be narrow and evaluative.

A mediator who practices a narrow approach to mediation may perhaps offer the parties the opportunity to widen their focus to take account of other interests if the process becomes becalmed. In this way the mediation can become interest-based. Correspondingly, a mediator with a broad approach can, if necessary, encourage the parties to narrow their focus if it seems unlikely they will be able to reach agreement on the many interests involved.

In their article 'Mapping Mediation: The Risk of Riskin's Grid', Kimberlee Kovach and Lela Love criticise Riskin's Grid. The criticism is not so much directed against the de-

3. See Robert Bush & Joseph Folger, *The Promise of Mediation, Responding to Conflict Through Empowerment and Recognition*, San Francisco, 1994 and 2005.
4. Deborah Kolb, 'How Existing Procedures Shape Alternatives: The Case of Grievance Mediation', *Journal of Dispute Resolution*, 1989 p. 59.

scription itself, which they find to be a model of clarity, but against the fact that Riskin is apparently ready to accept, uncritically, that both *narrow-evaluative* and *facilitative-broad* can be categorised as mediation. Kovach and Love *question not only whether this is appropriate, but whether it is justifiable* for mediation to be considered to include such incompatible variants, and they argue that processes which belong in the evaluative part of the spectrum, whether narrow or broad, should use other designations such as 'arbitration' or 'Early Neutral Evaluation'. Broadly, Kovach and Love's argument reflects the fact that the history of modern Alternative Dispute Resolution (ADR) should discourage mediators from using evaluation, and that evaluation is contrary both to the ethics and the standard training for mediation.

ADR arbitration

On the development of ADR, Kovach and Love refer to the experience of arbitration. Arbitration started as a clear alternative to litigation, but it gradually took on more and more of the form of litigation. Arbitration started as an informal, quick, confidential, commercially-oriented way of resolving conflicts in specific areas by involving experts in those areas. For many years arbitration was a process one could opt for if one wanted a cheap, quick and fair solution. However, in time, lawyers became more and more involved in the arbitration process and transactions became more complex, so arbitration became more and more legally oriented, more drawn out and more expensive. Eventually, the original advantages of arbitration seemed to have become so restricted that even lawyers began to consider either going back to court litigation or looking for an entirely new approach.[5]

Quasi-litigation

Kovach and Love, who, like Riskin, are law professors, describe the development of mediation in the USA in two different directions: the first is 'non-legal', where the mediator is facilitative and works to enable the parties to find their own way to solutions which are mutually satisfactory,

5. Refer to the Postscript for a description of the historical development of mediation from 1795 onwards, with corresponding characteristics.

and the second, which is linked to the court system and is 'legal' (in the sense that the mediators are all trained lawyers and largely use their traditional negotiating style) is confrontational and usually evaluative. Both forms appear to be used for conflicts of all kinds, and not only for commercial cases.

Kovach and Love suggest that one of the reasons why lawyers fall back on the evaluative form is that they believe that the parties expect, or justice demands, an outcome which is very close to the result which would have been arrived at by a court. As has been argued before, one of the ways of overcoming this difficulty is for the parties and the lawyers to be sufficiently well informed about the essence of the mediation process, so they do not have any illusion that it is a kind of quasi-litigation.

While the use of mediation has increased, understanding of what mediation consists of has correspondingly decreased, and this is a risk to its future development.[6]

As for the ethics of mediation, Kovach and Love point out that many mediators do not have the legal training or knowledge which would allow them responsibly to give an opinion, that, regardless of their professional background, no mediators have the safety net of an appeal tribunal, and that mediation's requirement for confidentiality can protect bad mediators. Also, as noted in connection with court-based mediation, judgments given after a full review of the evidence will often be very different from proposals made at some earlier stage in the process, as in mediation, where giving evidence has not been carried through.

This description of the problem is all too recognisable from the Danish or even Nordic experience. When one takes into account the developments in Denmark and Norway (described in the Postscript) with reconciliation commissions dating back to 1795 which were gradually absorbed by the court system and then disappeared, there are grounds for fearing that the current discussions are only

6. Joseph Stulberg, 'The Theory and Practice of Mediation: A Reply to Professor Susskind', *Vermont Law Review*, Vol. 6, p. 85 (1983).

too relevant, and that mediation will be exposed to distorting pressures, unless it is made very clear what mediation is and how it should be practised.

Discussion

Compliance between values and assumptions and form of mediation

The question has been asked above, to what extent the form of mediation used complies with the values and assumptions that are the basis for the mediation activity in question, and whether the concept of mediation reasonably include activities which, both in their form and in their basic values, are essentially different. In this context it is remarkable that the settlement-driven mediation model, which generally accepts that mediators exercise more control over the process and often offer evaluations, is distinguished by its complete lack of explicit values and assumptions about conflicts, human nature etc., and only emphasises the advantage of agreements being entered into as quickly and as cheaply for the parties as possible. However, the settlement-driven mediation model usually emphasises the potential of the mediation process for allowing the parties to have a direct influence on the process, even if the influence is only slight, which must reflect some confidence in the parties' abilities and willingness to make qualified decisions on the matters which are the subject of their conflict.

As for whether the concept of mediation ought to include such widely differing activities as described by Riskin, some guidance can be obtained from a report made of a two-year study of court-based mediation in New York.[7] The report found that mediation was used in an extraordinary variety of forms. Next, the report stated that 'blurring the lines among mediation, neutral evaluation and even arbitration, can have deleterious consequences.' The consequences prevent the parties from clearly under-

7. Judith S. Kaye, New York State Court Alternative Dispute Resolution Project, State of New York Unified Court System, Court Referred ADR in NY State, Final Report of the Chief Judge's New York State Court Alternative Dispute Resolution Project 51-53 (1 May 1996).

standing what they can expect from mediation, and prevent mediation practitioners from clearly understanding what constitutes 'good practice'. The report also recommended that 'mediators (should) not advise litigants on the law or likely court outcomes'.

Mediation and mutation

It is important that the flexibility which is characteristic of mediation should not be confused with an attitude of 'anything goes'. Obviously, the more that mediation activities are linked to a demand for effectiveness, the greater will be the risk that the process will become evaluative, because there will be more focus on the parties making an agreement, even if it is brought about by applying pressure. It is impossible to imagine that a conflict which comes before the courts or is referred to arbitration should end without a decision. However, if one allows oneself to indulge in a flight of fancy in which an arbitrator could take part in a process in which the parties were not assured of a decision, there is no doubt that this process would not be called arbitration. One cannot mutate arbitration into mediation and still call it arbitration. Conversely, it is hard to see that it should be acceptable to mutate mediation into arbitration and still call it mediation. The limits to flexibility are clearly overstepped in such a case, and the activity should be given a different name.[8]

As stated before, there ought to be some link between these assumptions, which are the basis of mediation, and the mediation activity itself – which requires that the mediator has some conscious presumptions about values. This means that evaluation may be contra-indicated in mediation which is based on the assumptions described in Chapter 2, since it is assumed that the parties know what is best for them, and in any case it is the parties who must live with the consequences of their actions. In certain situations reality testing can come dangerously close to being evaluation, but, as described in Chapter 9 when discussing neutrality, there is the decisive difference that both in their atti-

8. Likewise Kovach & Love, op cit.

tudes and in their questions, mediators leave the parties in control of the process.

On the other hand, there can be many reasons why there should also be limits to how much a mediator can require mediation to be transformative. If the parties are unwilling and if their focus is on getting an agreement, it is difficult to see how a mediator can demand that the parties should participate in an education process. Mediation should not be governed by the needs or the wishes of the mediator, but by the needs of the parties.

The parties must define how broad the mediation should be

For these reasons, the parties must define how broad the mediation should be. The mediator can naturally have a view that it would strengthen the process and perhaps, in the long run, be more meaningful for the parties if other interests were included in the process and, as suggested in this book for example, if conflict mediation were to be regarded as an opportunity for the parties to change their approaches towards more sustainable solutions, not just for their own sake but on the basis of a broader motivation. But if the parties are not prepared to broaden the scope, the mediator must bow to their wishes. Conversely, the mediator must be ready to consider the inclusion of additional needs and interests, if on the basis of experience the mediator knows that this will make the process more meaningful and satisfying for the parties, but it is entirely up to the parties to decide what they want included. The willingness of the mediator to consider and to be flexible is decisive for the quality of the mediation.

Despite great respect for the experience and analytical work which lies behind the mediation models described in Chapter 2, none of the mediation models otherwise described in this book fit with any of these models in their pure form. In fact, fitting mediation within one of these forms would put a mediator in a straightjacket so that the form of mediation would govern the conduct of the mediation, rather than it being governed by the parties and the mediator's interaction with them. In reflexive mediation, it is the contact with the parties and empathy with them that is decisive, and neither contact nor empathy can be reduced to a formula.

This means that, as stated above in Chapter 2, in the reflexive model the mediator has considerable freedom to use different methods, for example to help the parties discover their interests and needs, to use phases as the basic structure of the mediation, to aim at reaching an agreement (if it is clear this is what the parties want), to work with insight and feelings (if this is what the parties want) etc. All this is subject to the precondition that contact between the parties is established and that the values and assumptions referred to previously remain the guiding principles of the process.

The reflective practitioner

The freedom described above makes great demands on mediators, because true contact means that it is not possible, once and for all – or indeed at all – to consider oneself an expert. As pointed out by Riskin (and many others), mediators are generally trained in other professions before they become mediators, and they bring to mediation the habits, values and mind-sets of their original professions. Given the nature of much of this professional training, mediators will be likely to see themselves as experts, steeped in some specialised knowledge which they bring to bear in helping clients solve problems.

Therefore, the mediator must take on the role of the reflective practitioner, as suggested by Donald Schön. Schön has suggested that a traditional expert's self-worth depends upon them seeing themselves as confident, competent and self-assured. There is no room for uncertainty, for exploration or discovery. The idea of learning from unanticipated events has no place in the temperament of an expert.[9]

The reflective practitioner

In contrast, the reflective practitioner acknowledges that the disputants understand the conflict and its origin, dimensions, dangers, and opportunities better than anyone. The reflective practitioner is open to uncertainty, to explor-

9. See Donald A. Schön, *The Reflective Practitoner*, San Fransoisco 1987; and Michael Lang & Alison Taylor, *The making of a mediator*, San Fransisco, 2000.

ing the unknown and the surprising, to seeking out information from the parties and encouraging them to be active and engaged in the process. The reflective practitioner believes in the collaboration between the mediator and the disputants, and trusts the parties to bring their knowledge and skills to bear on the problem.

A party's relationship with an expert and a reflective practitioner will be distinctly different from each other, and because the parties may be conditioned to transact with the expert model of professional relationship, the new relationship may be challenging for them as well as for the mediator committed to the principles and methods of reflective practice.[10]

However, if the mediator wishes to remain faithful to the underlying assumptions described in this book, they will have no choice but to exercise reflective practice. Happily, partly because it opens up for new insights and provides so much deeper satisfaction, the gratifications obtained from this form of mediation, also for the mediator, far outweigh the problems.

Flexibility does *not* mean that 'anything goes'

It is important to re-emphasise that the freedom of the mediator and the flexibility do *not* mean that 'anything goes'. It is outside the bounds of mediation for a mediator to make proposals for a solution or to evaluate proposals made by the parties. It is also outside the bounds of mediation for a mediator to enter into therapeutic activities with the parties. And finally, it is outside the bounds of mediation for a mediator to use primarily separate meetings, as this makes dialogue impossible. These activities are outside the bounds of mediation simply because they are against the values and assumptions which are fundamental to mediation, primarily the presumption and respect for the fact that the parties are the experts in their own lives, and that there would therefore not be concordance between the ends and the means. On the other hand, it is not merely within the scope of mediation, but must be regarded as a natural consequence of the method for conducting media-

10. Lang & Taylor, op. cit., p. 145 et seq.

tion as described in this book, that by their manner of conducting mediation, a mediator will at least communicate to the parties that there are several ways to look at a chain of events, that there may be several different explanations for why a given conflict may have arisen, and that the essence of dialogue is to recognise and accept the explanation given by the other party, without necessarily agreeing with it.

When, they have been through this process, the parties will have learnt and digested these points, and they will have become empowered in a way which will be useful not only for finding a solution for the present conflict, but also for dealing with future conflicts, because they will learn that the respect and acknowledgement which they themselves want and expect is equally wanted and expected by others.

The reflexive model has been shown to be applicable to all kinds of conflicts; it is not limited to marital disputes, cases involving victims and offenders, or commercial cases. What matters is that the mediator should be faithful to the fundamental values and assumptions of mediation, and on this basis adapts the process to the needs of the parties. This is to treat the mediation process with the greatest degree of seriousness and the parties with the greatest degree of respect.

Compared with the 5 'pure' mediation models described above, the freedom which is characteristic of the reflexive model is also solidly based on Danish values as expressed by various Danish thinkers such as N.F.S. Grundtvig,[11] Søren Kierkegaard[12], K.E. Løgstrup[13] and Hal Koch, [14] all of whom are known and valued in the other Nordic countries.

11. 1783-1872, priest, author and founder of the Folk High Schools movement.
12. 1813-1855, theologist, philosopher and advocate of a religious form of existentialism.
13. 1905-81, theologist and historian of ideas.
14. 1904-63, theologist, educator and strong advocate for representative democracy based on dialogue.

II. Ethics

A set of ethical rules to guide

Regardless of which form of mediation is used, a mediator must have a set of ethical rules to guide their work. It is therefore usual for associations of mediators, as part of establishing themselves a professional group, to adopt a code of conduct. There are two reasons for this: the first is to inform the outside world and mediation practitioners about ethical considerations and to ensure that work is conducted in accordance with proper ethical standards; the second is to protect the reputation of the profession against the depredations of irresponsible practitioners.

However, a profession needs to do more than just establish a framework within which its practitioners should work. It must also be active in ensuring that there is a correlation between what it would like done and what in fact is done. In other words, mediators must know why they do what they do when conducting mediations. They must 'walk the talk'.

a. Standards for the professional conduct of mediators

The European Code of Conduct for Mediators

In mid-2004, the European Union adopted the European Code of Conduct for Mediators.[15] The greatest significance of the Code, which is at a general level, is presumably partly the fact that it is in itself a recognition that mediation has achieved a certain status in the various EU Member States, and partly its connection with the draft directive on certain aspects of mediation in civil and commercial matters (COM(2004) 718 final); Article 2(b) of the draft directive states that 'Mediator' shall mean 'any third party conducting a mediation, regardless of the denomination or profession of that third party in the Member State concerned and of the way the third party has been appointed or requested to conduct the mediation.' Both the Code of Conduct and the draft directive are included in annexes to this book.

15. See www.europa.eu.int/comm/justice_home/ejn/adr/adr_ec_code_cpnduct_en.htm. and Annex B of this book.

Paragraph 1.1 of the Code emphasises that mediators must be competent and knowledgeable in the process of mediation, but it does not specify the level of training or approval that is required. The paragraph merely uses expressions such as 'proper training' and 'continuous updating of ... education and practice in mediation skills'. Article 4 of the draft directive states that the Member States must 'promote and encourage the training of mediators', but even here nothing is stated about the extent and quality of training, merely that the Member States must promote 'effective quality control'.

Thus, we are not much wiser from reading the Community texts with regard to the requirements for mediators, apart from the fact that it is assumed that mediators can come from different professional backgrounds, a fact which, in relation to the sphere of the law, it is important to establish as there is a widespread tendency for the sphere of the law to monopolise mediation, and in the light of history this would presumably mean that in the long run mediation will be annexed by the judicial system, which would be the death of mediation.

In Denmark, where both advocates and judges who have received training in mediation can act as court-appointed mediators, a working group of court-appointed mediators has drawn up a set of ethical guidelines to apply to all advocates and judges who act as court-appointed mediators. All court-appointed mediators are nominated by *Domstolsstyrelsen* (the Judicial Appointments Council), though in the case of advocates following recommendation by *Advokatsamfundet* (the Danish Bar and Law Society), and the cooperation between advocates and judges in drawing up ethical guidelines is unique. See Annex C.

In addition to this, the Danish national association for mediators (*Foreningen for Mediation og Konfliktmægling*) has adopted a set of ethical rules which mediators subscribe to when becoming members of the association.[16] The association is open to all who are interested in mediation, and it

16. See Annex D.

thus makes no demands either as to the level of a person's education, their professional background or the extent of their mediation experience. This openness in accepting members applies equally to the other Nordic associations which have been established within the last 3 years in Finland, Iceland, Norway and Sweden.

In addition to this, there are ethical rules for specific professional sectors, such as Danish advocate mediators, ethical guidelines for conflict mediation in local government (public provision of mediation in family conflicts), and the agreement which the parties must sign before the start of court appointed mediation includes a description of the nature of mediation and the obligations of the mediator towards the parties.

USA

In the USA, where mediation activity is widespread, rules of conduct for mediators have been developed both at state and federal levels. Also, many associations of mediators linked with specific professions have developed their own professional rules of conduct, for example: the Association of Family and Conciliation Courts, the American Bar Association – Section of Family Law, the Society of Professionals in Dispute Resolution.[17] [18]

The Association for Conflict Resolution (ACR) appears to cover the widest variety of mediators from an international perspective. The Association's *Ethical Standards of Professional Responsibility* states that a mediator has 'a duty to the parties, to the professions, and to themselves'.

b. Professional ethics

ACR's *Ethical Standards*

The ACR's *Ethical Standards* state that mediators 'should be honest and unbiased, act in good faith, be diligent, and not seek to advance their own interests at the expense of their parties'. Furthermore, mediators 'must act fairly in dealing with the parties, have no personal interest in the terms of the settlement, show no bias towards individuals and insti-

17. See Moore, op. cit., p. 353.
18. See also, Frank Blechman, 'Ethics and Field Building: the Chicken and the Egg', *Conflict Resolution Quarterly*, Vol. 19, 2002, pp. 273-382.

tutions involved in the dispute, be reasonably available as requested by the parties, and be certain that the parties are informed of the process in which they are involved'.

Accordingly, some of the most important issues a mediator should be aware of are:

1. A duty to be and to remain impartial and neutral, as far as possible;
2. Ensuring that the parties understand and accept the process they are involved in, including the roles played both by themselves and the mediator in the process;
3. Being clear about the extent of and limits to confidentiality in mediation;
4. Initiating and carrying out the process within a reasonable time limit;
5. Ensuring that the parties regard any agreement entered into as their own.[19]

The following is highlighted from the ethical guidelines drawn up by the Danish court-appointed mediators:

At any point following the preliminary hearing of the parties, a court-appointed mediator may terminate the mediation, and must terminate the mediation if:

a. one of the parties so wishes; see point 4;
b. the court-appointed mediator judges that one of the parties is not capable of participating meaningfully, or is not able to take care of their own interests;
c. there is an imbalance of power between the parties which can have a negative effect on the mediation and it is not possible to correct for it;
d. the court-appointed mediator has knowledge of information which would make it unethical for them to continue the mediation;
e. the parties wish to enter into an agreement which would be criminal or otherwise be contrary to mandatory law;

19. See also Moore, p. 354.

f. it appears that the conflict is not suitable for court-based mediation;
g. it is judged that court-based mediation is no longer appropriate; or
h. the court-appointed mediator judges that, for other material reasons, it is inappropriate to continue the court-based mediation.

The rules are remarkable in that, for example, in their daily work judges cannot refuse to see a case through to its conclusion, even though they may wish to do so.

c. The mediator's personal ethical standards

In addition to the broad rules laid down by professional codes of conduct, mediators are bound by an in-built moral sense, a basic sense of values, which inevitably leads to certain actions. This moral sense will define which actions mediators think are right and which they think are wrong. This results in a mediation ethic. On the one hand there are professional ethics and the professional code of conduct; but, in practice, there is also a personal ethic.

Morality and ethics

'Ethics' may seem a passive term, a philosophical concept with principles for how mediators 'ought' to act or how they should behave towards one another. It is also an idea about right and wrong. By contrast, 'morality' can be seen as an active concept, telling us which of our actions are right or wrong in relation to our values or ethics.

For example, when mediators use the first person singular, in order to remain within their own territory and enable each party to have his or her own view of the truth, which is an important element in mediation, they work to clarify the boundaries between 'me' and 'you'. In other words, they try to get the parties to consider themselves as individuals. But this is only part of a mediator's ends and means. The ultimate goal is for the parties to find solutions that satisfy them both, and the way to do this is often to move the parties from their initial standpoints towards a recognition of their interests and needs and further to acknowledgment. In this way, the parties not only feel themselves to be separate individuals, but also independent elements who together form a partnership.

A reaction to western individualism

Modern mediation can be seen as a reaction to western individualism. Modern individualism means that each person is free to decide what *I* think is right and what *I* think is wrong. In reaction to this individualism, mediation demands that one should also ask what is good for the other party. One should not only allow, one should require that mediation gives space for *communal* values *and needs* to be put in the foreground, and the parties will then have the opportunity to decide whether these needs are also some of their concerns. Mediation is thus concerned with both personal freedom and personal limitations. In this way mediation will become part of a viable approach to conflicts as not only can it deal with the short-term satisfaction of the needs of individuals, but it can also include a balancing of interests so that a more long-term, sustainable, result can be achieved.

A meaningful life

Whether we like it or not, behind our work as mediators lie assumptions about what we mean by a 'good' life, understood as a *meaningful* life, not necessarily an easy, successful and rich life, but a life which is based on an *interested and responsible relationship* with its context. These include existential paradoxes which we cannot avoid confronting: life/death, freedom/dependence, free-will/absence of free-will, growing old/living in the present, seeking truth and never finding it, and the meaningless of life/finding one's own meaning, etc.

Seldom, if ever, is mediation directly based on questions of this kind, nor do the parties themselves broach such questions. But they lie behind many conflicts. In particular, for many younger mediators, circumstances relating to existential truths will seem to be beyond the scope of ordinary mediation. However, existential truths are precisely that – existential. For example, with problems of cooperation between a younger employee and an older employee, or conflicts relating to the passing of property from one generation to the next, even though superficially such conflicts seem to concern incompatibility of temperaments, they may contain elements of despondency about ageing, difficulties in letting go of one's life's work, anxiety about depending on a pension, anxiety about living up to the expectations of new colleagues etc. During mediation these circumstances and feelings can be brought out into the open, not with sentimentality, but with a respect which clarifies what is really at stake. Whether this should take place at a joint meeting or at separate meetings will depend on the actual situation, including, for example, the relations between the parties, the feeling of the meeting etc.

As a mediator, one will find that it gives some relief when existential truths are referred to directly. Naturally, mediators are part of a culture that has sublimated these existential truths, so we must get accustomed to recognising them and talking about them in a relaxed and natural manner. Experience shows that it is often a relief to the parties and helps the process when existential truths are referred to and are dealt with.

When the parties come to mediation, it is because they want help in finding 'a good solution'. If we know what is needed to live a meaningful life, why isn't mediation about persuading the parties to believe the same as us? It both is and isn't. This duality is the essence of mediation's ethics and system of values.

Mediators must help the parties to discover, because we believe that the process will lead to discovery of the connection between our individuality and our connectedness, and thereby to responsibility for both parts, not as a duty, but as a right which gives the parties the possibility of making choices which give them meaning.

The outcome of mediation is the choice of the parties

Mediators cannot give good advice, because that would absolve the parties from discovering for themselves their relations to the many questions and the actions which follow. As mediators we must often remind ourselves of the fundamental assumptions that each person is an expert on his own life, and that the aim is to arrive at a situation in which the parties can use their own resources to resolve their problem, so that both are satisfied. On the other hand, we cannot expect the parties to obtain great personal enlightenment during the mediation process. The outcome of mediation is the choice of the parties. If all they are interested in is getting an agreement, that must be respected. But mediators have a duty to give them choices and to ask questions, based on the fundamental values of mediation, and which give them the opportunity of addressing the paradoxes which lie behind the conflict.

III. Mediators' liability

The consideration of mediators' risks of civil liability is closely linked to the ethical guidelines for mediation and the comments on the basis for mediation and its practice.

Considering the number of books that have been written about mediation, it is remarkable how many of them say not a single word about the liability of mediators, but this is not to say that the topic has not received a lot of attention.

As described by Kimberlee Kovach, there are a number of legal bases on which allegations of malpractice can be made against a mediator. Of these, general negligence is the most important, followed naturally by breach of contract, fraud and breach of confidentiality.[20]

A random search of the internet in July 2011 gave a very large number of 'hits' for the term 'mediator liability'. Of course, it lies outside the scope of this study to consider all these, nevertheless the sheer number of hits illustrates that there is considerable interest in the subject. However, at the same time it must be noted that the number of court cases in this area is very small indeed. To date, not a single case has been brought with a claim against a mediator in any of the Nordic countries.

Robert A. Badgley, who has recently written a general description of mediators' liability in the article 'Mediator Liability: A Survey', February 2010,[21] concluded that with the growing number of mediations there is a growing

20. Kimberlee Kovach, *Mediation, Principles and Practice*, Ed. 3, 2004 pp. 458-465.
21. At: hk-mediation.com/Case/Mediator%20Liability%20Survey%202010.pdf

number of claims for liability, but that in most cases the claims are baseless. But, if one of the parties to a mediation is dissatisfied with the result or the process, a claim may well follow. This form of liability inevitably becomes more relevant the more the mediation involves making evaluations.

Several states in the USA have adopted rules on the immunity of mediators, though primarily in cases where the mediators are associated with the judicial system. For example, the US Justice Department has informed the administrators of the various mediation programmes that 'it generally will defend court-connected volunteer mediators for the U.S. District Court and Court of Appeals for the District of Columbia if they are sued for malpractice. The District of Columbia Superior Court has purchased group insurance to cover all of its mediators, who are volunteers (although they may be paid modest stipends).'[22]

As expressed by Kovach in 2000, the subject is nevertheless important: 'if immunity is absolute, or sufficiently broad, the consumer of mediation services will have no recourse for any damage resulting from participation in mediation. Since mediation is still a rather new field, essentially without regulations, rules or standardized procedures, there must be a way to guard against abuse of the process and the parties by the mediator.' [23]

In any case, in the EU, where mediation is still relatively new, Kovach's concerns are still relevant.

Surprisingly few attempts to attach legal liability to mediators

It has been noted that 'around the world [there have] been surprisingly few attempts to attach legal liability to mediators'. This is presumably due to the fact that mediators are (often) careful to ensure that the parties sign a declaration exempting them from liability. Such a declaration can be included either in the agreement for entering into mediation, or in the final mediated agreement itself. Under such a declaration, the parties will neither be bound by the advice of the mediator, nor by drafts for agreements drawn

22. www.caadrs.org/studies/liability.htm
23. Kimberlee Kovach, *Mediation, Principles and Practice*, 2000 p. 327.

up by the mediator, but will always obtain their own legal advice etc.

Moreover, some mediators include in the final agreement a statement that the agreement is entered into freely and not under any pressure, and that the parties have had prior consultation with any relevant experts, that the parties have read and have understood the text of the agreement, and that signing the agreement implies that the mediator is exempted from any liability arising from the conclusion of the agreement.

PART 2

A practical step by step description of mediation

CHAPTER 14

Before the meeting

The purpose of this phase is to decide if there is to be mediation, and to agree the necessary framework for participation in and payment for such mediation.

I. The initiative for mediation

The initiative for mediation can come from many quarters: 1) by direct application by one or more of the parties, 2) on the reference of a friend, colleague, employer etc., 3) by automatic referral from a public authority, and 4) on the initiative of the mediator.

Direct application by one or more of the parties is the most usual way to initiate mediation, and the least complicated for the mediator. If both parties contact the mediator, or if one of them does so by agreement with the other, then it is clear from the start that both parties are interested in mediation. The mere fact that both parties are interested in mediation indicates that, even if they are unable to resolve their conflict without help, they are at least able to agree to seek the help of a mediator, who can therefore proceed to the preliminary stages of the mediation process.

A provision in contract

Sometimes the parties to a business agreement include a provision in their contract to the effect that, if a dispute arises between them, they shall seek mediation before resorting to, e.g., the courts or arbitration. As a rule, the parties stick to the agreement and seek mediation, in which case there will be no problem. However, occasionally one of the parties will refuse to take part in mediation, in spite of the existence of a mediation clause. In these cases it is inappropriate and contrary to the basic principles of this form of mediation to force mediation on the party. Thus, as a rule, a disagreement about whether or not to go to mediation resolves itself. Equally, it seems inappropriate to enforce mediation proceedings via litigation.[1]

One of the parties contacts a mediator

If only one of the parties contacts a mediator, without the other party being involved or agreeing to mediation, the mediator must decide whether, and if so how, the other party should be contacted. The easiest thing would be to give the party who has made contact some written information about the mediation process etc., and encourage them to forward the material to the other party. If both parties then agree to request mediation, then one of them can contact the mediator again and the process can be initiated.

Another possibility is for the mediator to send the material to the other party together with a letter saying that the mediator will contact them by telephone in a few days. This gives the party time and space to consider whether they want to take part in mediation. When the mediator then contacts the party, the mediator must be careful not to seek to put pressure on, let alone force the party to participate in mediation. The mediator must also be ready to explain and answer questions about the advantages and disadvantages of the mediation process.[2]

Someone other than the parties takes the initiative

Sometimes, someone other than the parties takes the initiative for mediation. This can be the parties' employer, a trade union representative, or some other party who is not a party to the conflict, but can have an interest in it being resolved. In such a case, once the mediator has agreed to take on the case on the basis of existing information, it is best to encourage the parties to refer directly to the mediator, perhaps after studying some written material.

In certain situations the parties to a conflict will automatically be offered mediation when they have been in contact with some public authority. This book is not con-

1. There is one English case concerning the bringing of litigation in spite of a mediation clause in the contract between the parties. The court found that the parties were obliged to try mediation first, *Cable &Wireless* v *IBM United Kingdom Ltd* (2002) EWHC 2059.
2. See Moore: *The Mediation Process*, 1996, p. 83.

cerned with obligatory mediation, but such offers of mediation from a public authority will often include a possibility of refusing mediation if one of the parties so chooses.

Finally, the initiative for mediation can be taken by the mediator contacting the parties directly, for example, if the mediator becomes aware of an existing conflict via the media and believes it may be suitable for mediation. In these cases the mediator will typically send a letter to the parties and offer themselves as a mediator, assuming either that the parties are unaware of the mediation option, or for some reason have not overcome their doubts about it.

II. What kinds of conflict are suitable for mediation?

In principle, all kinds of conflict can be mediated

Both the parties and the mediator must consider whether the conflict in question is suitable for mediation, or whether some other form of dispute resolution would be better. In principle, all kinds of conflict can be mediated *if the parties wish it.* What matters is the attitude of the parties and their willingness to mediate. If the parties need a decision on a matter of principle, mediation is not suitable and formal court proceedings would be better.

Mediation is not suitable if the parties do not have a mandate to determine what the agreement shall be. This can be because some public authority is involved, and one or other of the parties is bound by mandatory regulations, or they may be subordinate to someone who has the power to decide and who does not wish to take part in mediation. In such cases the parties do not have full powers over the conflict and cannot make a binding agreement.

It is naturally also a precondition that the parties are able to take care of their own interests, and not prevented from doing so by some mental illness or suchlike.

If, before the first meeting, the mediator becomes aware of circumstances which make the conflict unsuitable for mediation, they must naturally inform the parties and withdraw from the case.

III. Consent to mediation

Since the motivation of the parties is decisive for a successful mediation, then regardless of how the mediation is initiated, the mediator must ensure that the parties understand the mediation process. At this stage it must be made clear that information given in connection with mediation is confidential for both parties and the mediator, and it must be emphasised that the mediation can only go ahead if both parties are willing to take part in person.

Mediation is initiated by the parties' employer

For example, if the mediation is initiated by the parties' employer, it must be made clear to the parties and to the employer, that the confidentiality of the mediation excludes the employer. The mediator may agree to tell the employer whether a mediation meeting has taken place and if it has resulted in an agreement. Further information about the mediation will not be given to the employer; in other words not even information about the content of the agreement itself will be given, unless of course the parties wish and agree otherwise. In such a case it is for the parties themselves to undertake to inform the employer about the content of the agreement. It is important for the parties to be told about such an agreement between a mediator and an employer, and agree to it.

In some cases the parties will sign a consent form, declaring that they understand the mediation process and their obligations of active participation, confidentiality, payment etc.

IV. What information should the mediator have?

The main rule is that it is a good idea for the mediator to talk to the parties before the first mediation meeting is agreed. This can be a short meeting with each of them in person, or a telephone call. The aim is for the mediator to make sure that the parties know what the mediation is about, and for them to ask any questions before deciding whether to take part. This contact is important for establishing the trust of the parties in the mediator and in the mediation process. It is therefore best for the mediator to make the initial contact themselves, and not to delegate the task. If the parties get a positive impression of how the case will be handled, this will help the germination of an agreement.

The initial contact

At the initial contact, the parties will often be tempted to tell the mediator as much as possible about the conflict. The mediator should try to prevent this. The mediator needs to know no more about the conflict than is necessary for deciding whether the conflict is suitable for mediation and, if so, who should take part in it. It can also be necessary to decide whether the parties need to bring written information about the factual circumstances to the first joint meeting. For example, where a conflict concerns a divorce, it can be appropriate for the parties to bring tax returns etc., when they have to agree the sharing of assets and the payment of maintenance (where the agreement need not stick to the practice of the courts), or it can be relevant to bring accounts when a partnership is to be dissolved.

The more the mediator knows about the nature of the conflict in advance, the more difficult it will be for the mediator to keep an open mind about how the conflict should be resolved. Similarly, the more that written material is used in a mediation, including written submissions from the parties, the greater will be the risk that the focus will be on the past, and the process will become more like a court case or traditional negotiation, rather than mediation. It is therefore recommended that the use of written material should be kept to a minimum, or if possible left until the end of the mediation or postponed to a later meeting, so that from the start of the mediation the parties are as free as possible to address the areas where they feel their interests are most infringed.[3]

3. For a different view see Moore, op. cit. p. 114 et seq.; and Anne Austbø & Geir Engebretsen, p. 66 about in-court mediation.

V. Who should take part in mediation?

As stated, the mediator also needs to have an overall view of the conflict in order to help the parties decide who should take part in the mediation process.

The concept of a 'party' to mediation

When a case is brought before the courts, it is relatively easy to determine who is a party to it. In order to be a plaintiff or a defendant, one must have legal interest in the case, according to the rules of procedure. The concept of a 'party' to mediation is not so straightforward. The mediator must discuss who should take part, together with those who have made the first approach. On the one hand, it is not necessary for the parties to have a legal interest in the case, but on the other hand it is not enough for a party to be merely interested in the outcome.

For example, if there is a dispute between an employer and an employee about whether the dismissal of the employee is justified or should be compensated, the legally interested parties are clearly the employer and the employee. However, if the case is referred for mediation, and it appears that the company is family owned, that the owner is the father-in-law of the dismissed son-in-law, and the mother-in-law is the accountant, it is not so clear who should take part in the mediation. Should it be the father-in-law and the son-in-law? Or should the mother-in-law and daughter also be involved, even though the daughter has no employed status?

Participation of some adviser

As a rule, the mediator can suggest the attendance of parties who are involved in the conflict on the basis of their central interest in the resolution of the conflict. If there is a conflict between groups of people, the mediator, together with the parties, must decide whether it would be helpful to appoint a representative. If the parties propose the participation of some adviser, for example a lawyer or a trade union representative, the mediator needs to be clear that the parties have authority to take decisions, will contribute positively to the climate of negotiation, and help the process in general.[4] It is for the parties to decide who should take part in the mediation, but obviously if the mediator thinks it is a bad idea, for example, for a trade union representative to take part, they can advise against it or ultimately decline to proceed with the case.[5] Often, both lawyers and trade union representatives will have a legally-oriented approach, and this can make it more difficult to achieve fruitful and flexible progress of the mediation.

If it is agreed that the parties may have advisers present, it will be a good idea for the mediator to speak with the advisers directly, to clarify the mediation procedure and their role in it.[6]

VI. Payment

The question of payment ought to be clarified before the start of the mediation.

In some cases mediation is offered without charge, for example, where it is publicly funded. In other cases the mediator will charge a fee which the parties pay. It is usual for the parties to share payment between them. If there is a written contract which the parties sign prior to mediation, it will usually state that the parties are to share the payment. Of course, there is nothing to prevent the parties agreeing to some other division of responsibility for payment during mediation. It is not unusual for some third party, e.g. an employer, to pay.

VII. Where and when?

Once the parties have agreed to take part in mediation, it is necessary to decide when and where it shall take place.

4. See Moore, *op. cit.*, p. 134 et seq.
5. As for the influence of cultural factors on who should take part in mediation, see below.
6. The reader is referred to Chapter 24 for further discussion of advisers.

This often depends on the kind of case and how much time is needed. The more personally involved the parties are, for example marital disputes, the more emotionally stressful it will be to take part in mediation. In such cases it is often best to set aside no more than three hours per day, with several meetings if necessary.

With business disputes it may be possible to set aside a whole day, in the hope of solving the problem in one sitting. In business disputes too, there are limits to the stamina both of the mediator and the parties. Some mediators like to start early in the morning and carry on late in order to reach an agreement. Agreements made through the exhaustion of the parties are seldom the best and will do little to repair relations between the parties, and since there can be a risk of a mediator having professionally liability for bad mediation, this practice is not recommended.[7]

Even if the parties succeed in reaching agreement at the first meeting, some mediators have a rule that it is best for the parties to 'sleep on it' to make sure that the agreement will stick. In other cases it may be clear in advance that there will be a need for several meetings. In these cases it is best to schedule the meetings from the start, so the momentum of the process can be maintained and there are no long gaps during which the parties can tire of the process and lose their enthusiasm etc.

Location neutral

The location of the meeting must be neutral. This means that it cannot take place at the home or office of one of the parties. It can take place in premises which the mediator occupies, or a meeting room can be rented at a hotel, or suchlike. Naturally, a mediation meeting can be held in a meeting room at the joint workplace of the parties, but it will usually be preferable for the parties to meet away from their usual surroundings and from the attentions of their colleagues, and will also often release them from their otherwise fixed roles.

7. As for the professional liability of mediators, see Chapter 13.

VIII. Physical preparations

Making the meeting room ready

The physical preparations consist of making the meeting room ready. It should be relaxing with friendly surroundings. There should be fresh air, facilities for tea and coffee, mineral water, fruit and fresh flowers. There should also be necessary equipment such as notepads and pencils, flip-over boards, marker pens, and so on. If there is access to word processing, the agreement can be written out on the spot; a copying machine can also be helpful.

The seating of the mediator and the parties in the meeting can be important for the communication between them. The physical set-up is an area in which the authority of the mediator can be expressed, perhaps only indirectly, so this is something the mediator should consider carefully.

The parties should be able to see each other and the mediator without straining their necks, and the mediator should be able to keep both parties in view, able to observe both, regardless of which is speaking. The parties should not sit too close to each other, as this can feel uncomfortable for parties who are in conflict with each other. If there are people present other than the parties, they should be placed furthest away from the mediator, so the seating signals that the main participants in the mediation are the parties themselves.

Mediators should also decide whether to have a table between themselves and the parties, or whether to work without a table. A table will often create a certain distance. On the other hand, some people find it too informal not to have a table. Mediators should experiment with different lay-outs, and be aware that it is the feelings of the mediator or their expectations of the feelings of the parties which matters.

If the mediator expects there to be a need for separate meetings during the mediation, rooms should be prepared for this. The optimal situation is to have separate rooms for joint meetings and individual meetings with the parties, but this is not absolutely necessary. What matters is that there should be scope for holding separate meetings, and ensuring their confidentiality.[8]

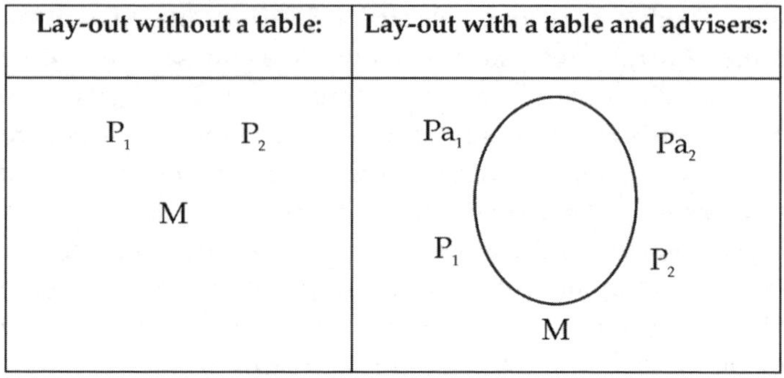

Figure 15. Seating for a mediation meeting

IX. Mental preparations

The mediator should also prepare mentally for the meeting. It is usually a good idea to arrive at least half an hour and up to a whole hour before the meeting, to ensure that the meeting room is in order, and to think through the mediation process. It is important for the mediator to be calm and relaxed, well rested, not hungry, dressed in clothes which are comfortable and suitable for the occasion etc. What each mediator feels is necessary for preparing for a meeting depends on the individual; many tend to underestimate this part of preparation and believe it is sufficient to have read any papers and arranged the practicalities. However, mediators should be aware of the importance of their role, and it can require a conscious effort to achieve the relaxed atmosphere and the focus which the parties and process deserve. Personal preparation ought to be part

8. The reader is referred to Chapter 16 for discussion of separate meetings.

of every mediation meeting, including successive meetings in the same mediation.

Apart from this, it is of course necessary to prepare for the substantive meeting; this will include studying any written materials, and less experienced mediators may have made notes for the preparatory talk which should be read through before the meeting, the procedure should be run through mentally, and thought given to how to start the meeting and perhaps which of the parties should be first to put their side of the argument.

X. One or more mediators?

The subject-matter complex

As a rule, mediators work singly. This is easier to arrange and does not cost as much as two mediators. However, in certain circumstances it can be appropriate to have two mediators. This can be because the subject-matter of the conflict can be complex, for example a company merger, so it can be agreed that the mediators can take it in turns to concentrate on the mediation process or to keep track of the facts. It may be because there is a need for special expertise, for example in a conflict concerning information technology, so one of the mediators may have the particular knowledge required. Or in the case of marital disputes, there can be a risk that one of the couple suspects there is an alliance between the one of the couple who is of the same sex as the mediator and the mediator, so two mediators, one of each sex, may be preferable. Finally, the mediator may be inexperienced and need the support of a colleague.

Co-mediation

Regardless of the reason, when mediators work together in co-mediation, they must have a clear agreement about how they will work together, before they start. It can be agreed that they will take in turns to chair the meeting and, for example, signal to the other when they want to say something. Another possibility is for there to be a principal mediator and an assistant mediator, which can make the process clearer, and has the advantage of giving the principal mediator someone to analyse the process during any breaks or afterwards, and enable the assistant to learn from the process.

If one is to work together with another mediator, it is important that the chemistry is right, otherwise it may not only result in confusion for the parties, it can be damaging for the process if the mediators talk across one another and ask questions which seem to be at cross-purposes. What matters is that both the mediators and the parties feel comfortable with the situation.

Checklist before a mediation meeting:

- Who should take part in the mediation?
- One or more mediators?
- What information should the mediator(s) have?
- Is a contract necessary?
- Who is going to pay for the mediation?
- Find a neutral location for the mediation

Before mediation is starting:
* Physical preparations are needed
* Mental preparations are needed

XI. Mediation in groups – multiparty mediation

This book primarily describes mediation between two or a few parties. Multiparty mediation often arises from a combination of separate meetings, joint meetings in which a whole group is gathered, and mediations which involve two or a few of the parties in a direct mediation meeting. In joint meetings the use of 'rounds' or 'dialogue circles' will often be appropriate. The ability, as well as the will, of the mediator to vary the process is thus essential to an even higher degree when several parties are involved in a conflict, just as it remains of the greatest importance that all the parties should agree to the method used in the proceedings. Much of what has been written, not least concerning assumptions and values, is therefore also applicable to mediations which involve several parties.[9]

However when one moves from working with individual parties or a few parties to working with conflicts with large groups, it is natural to consider the extent to which, as a mediator, one can use the same skills as previously, or whether one has to be aware of particular characteristics of large groups. The answer is not 'either/or' but 'both'. Participants in large groups are also, naturally, still individuals with the patterns of behaviour, norms etc. that are found in interpersonal conduct, and at the same time a mediator must be aware of the existence of additional dimensions.

Conflict Management Initiatives and the Conflict Information Consortium at the University of Colorado have identified the following further dimensions as being points for attention when moving from interpersonal conflicts to conflicts in large groups:[10]

- The number of interests and issues is often greater;
- More persons are interacting, both within each contending group and between the groups – so there are more variables and greater complexity of process;
- Decision-making is more cumbersome and problematic, both intra-party and inter-party;
- Cross-cultural tensions and misunderstandings add complexities and may roughen the road to consensus – mediators' sensitivities are imperative;
- Multi-party disputes place still greater demands on the process;
- It is often difficult for some parties to move away from their accustomed arenas of public contest, pressure tactics, media exploitation, etc. and into the quieter, non-public mediation chamber;
- In some cases mediators may need to take into account serious power imbalances between the parties; and

9. For international conflicts, which include multiple parties, see Chapter 12.
10. (copyright by 2000-2007).

– Assuring continuing compliance with an agreement may be more difficult.

The process will be more demanding on mediators in terms of:

a. overall demands on time;
b. the complexities of scheduling to accommodate everyone's needs (often in the evenings or at weekends);
c. mediators' energies, stamina, patience and creativity;
d. in addition it can be necessary to have additional agency staff, along with volunteers; and
e. the mediator has a greater responsibility to try to ensure representation of the views of all key interest groups or stakeholders.

This author fully agrees with the list and will not develop it further here.

CHAPTER 15

Stage 1: Opening – The first joint meeting

Confidence in the mediator and the mediation process

This chapter deals with the first mediation meeting at which all the parties and any advisers are present, together with the mediator. The parties will often be anxious and nervous, the advisers may be sceptical, and the mediator will be determined to ensure a good meeting for all participants. This is an important meeting which lays the foundation for the following mediation, and it can be said that the mediation starts from the first handshake.

The first stage in the mediation has a number of different purposes; it has to set the tone for the meeting, information must be given, confidence must be built up in the mediator and the mediation process, a constructive attitude must be established in the parties, and a final decision must be taken to proceed. For these reasons, already at this stage the mediator must be aware of what role the presence of power, whether from the mediator or between the parties, play in the mediation.

I. Creating a good atmosphere

Mediators must consider themselves as the host of the meeting, the person responsible for creating a good atmosphere. When the mediator adopts a positive attitude, is relaxed and gives an impression of competence, it is easier for the parties to relax, and this already creates a good basis for the work to follow. It is understandable and natural for the parties to be nervous, but they should preferably not be stressed. If the mediator has arranged for refreshments and flowers, this signals a relaxed atmosphere and that care has been taken for the comfort of the participants.

Even though the mediator may plan to hold separate meetings in the course of the mediation, the first meeting ought always to be a joint meeting. It is important for the parties to greet one another, even if with a certain reserve, and they should jointly receive the information which sets the framework for the mediation process. Normally the parties will consider it natural and positive to start with a joint meeting; starting with separate meetings is more likely to reinforce differences.

Questions can arise in the opening session which are not directly concerned with the content of the conflict. These can be about the extent of confidentiality or the possibility of consulting professional advisers. Answering such questions can mean that the mediation is already active, so it is important that both parties are present at this stage, and that they can observe the mediator's ability to deal with such questions and get a first impression of the possibility of reaching agreement with the other side.

Humour

If it feels natural, the mediator can use humour as a means of creating a positive atmosphere. Properly used, humour can deflect a tense situation when it is possible to laugh together. However, humour can also be a false friend; it can sometimes fall flat and seem clumsy, having the opposite of its intended effect, not least when there are cultural differences between those present. It is not possible to lay down guidelines on whether humour can be used or not. This must depend on the parties' and the mediator's reading of the situation. Charm can lighten the atmosphere just as well as humour, and it certainly works more frequently.

II. Welcome, seating and presentation

When the parties arrive, and their advisers if relevant, the mediator will of course welcome them in the manner of a host, typically with a handshake, telling them where they can hang their coats, where the toilets are etc. If there are advisers, it is important for the mediator not to pay more attention to them than to the parties. The conflict belongs to the parties, they have the principal roles in the mediation, so they must feel welcome and respected.

It is important for the parties to be actively involved in the mediation. In the meeting, the mediator will usually seat the parties closest to them and seat any advisers further away. This reinforces the view of the parties that it is they who have the central roles in the mediation, and strengthens the possibility that the discussion will take place primarily between the parties and the mediator, and only exceptionally include the advisers. Sometimes advisers automatically sit themselves closest to the mediator, even though the mediator may have asked them not to do so. This can naturally give rise to some tension in the room, which is probably best dealt with by the mediator quietly and calmly asking them to move, so that the parties can sit closest to the mediator. By this means the mediator clearly shows their authority, and the advisers, who have just as clearly demonstrated their desire to dominate the process, will have a reduced presence.

Information about the roles of the parties and the mediator

The mediator starts by welcoming everyone. The parties often know each other, so it will not be necessary for them to present themselves. Mediators ought to present themselves, and say a little about themselves and their background. This can lead naturally to giving information about the roles of the parties and the mediator. Quite often, parties who are in conflict will want the mediator to express a view about how the conflict can be resolved. It is essential for the mediator to establish from the start that this is the sole responsibility of the parties, and this can be emphasised by how they are seated. If there are advisers at the meeting, their roles and relationships to the parties should be explained.

If the mediator is a lawyer, they must make it clear that in this context they are acting as a mediator and not as a lawyer, so the parties must seek advice on legal questions from their own legal advisers. As a lawyer, it can be tempting to comment on the probable outcome of the conflict if it were to be dealt with by the courts, but this would be to step outside the role of mediator and could lead to loss of the trust of the parties. It is not merely inadvisable to make such comments, it is prohibited. The same applies to any other professional who acts as a mediator. The mediator must refrain from expressing a view as to how the case should be settled, and if, for example, there are disputed facts which can be established by an expert, the parties must be encouraged to obtain outside advice.

Right from the start the mediator must strive to introduce an atmosphere of dialogue. It will therefore be of wholly inappropriate for the mediator to start with a long monologue about the process of mediation, the rules of procedure etc., though it must be made clear that the mediator's role is not to propose solutions or express a view, and whatever the expectations of the parties, this is not open to debate.

III. Information about the mediation process, rules of conduct

Make the process as transparent and predictable as possible

Even though mediation has now been practised for a number of years, only very few people have taken part in a mediation more than once in their lives. This means that few people know what it is, and fewer still have tried it. Part of the initial uncertainty of the parties is due to the fact that they do not know what will happen. One should therefore make the process as transparent and predictable as possible, so the parties know what to expect and how they can contribute to make the process as easy as possible.

As early as possible, the mediator should relate what has taken place before the first joint meeting: who contacted the mediator, whom they have spoken to by telephone or in person, and what they know about the conflict at this point. It is reassuring for the parties to feel that they both have the same information, and that the mediator wants the process to be transparent.

The mediator should give a short description of what generally happens at a mediation meeting, how much time has been set aside for the meeting, the fact that further meetings can be held if needed, whether smoking is allowed, when there will be breaks or parties themselves can ask for breaks etc. The mediator's introduction not only gives the parties a better understanding of the process, it enables them to get to know the mediator, and hopefully gives them more optimism about the course of the mediation.

If the mediator thinks it is probable that separate meetings will be needed, information about this should be given in the introduction. Otherwise, there is a risk of creating unnecessary uncertainty and mistrust if suddenly, in the middle of the meeting, the mediator announces that they want to have discussions with each of the parties separately.

Authority to take decisions

If the conflict only concerns the two parties present, and no-one else is involved, clarification of their powers is not necessary. However, if, for example, the conflict is between two companies, and a representative from each is present, it will be necessary to establish at the start that they have authority to take decisions and that an eventual agreement will be approved. Even though the mediator may have had prior knowledge, the authority of the representative must be confirmed at the first meeting. There is nothing more frustrating for the mediator and one party if, after a good mediation, one believes that an agreement has been reached, only for the other party to say that the agreement must be approved by his superior or board of directors. However, if this is understood from the start, the parties can take this into account and carry on the mediation in this context.

Guidelines for the conduct of meetings

In some kinds of mediation, it is also in the initial phase that it is found appropriate to adopt some guidelines for the conduct of the meetings. Some mediators suggest that it is a good idea for the parties not to interrupt each other when talking about their conflict. However, such guidelines can often seem like rigid rules and can be inhibiting and give the parties the sense of a formal procedure. However, it can be hard to listen to the other party relate a course of events which seems totally different from the course of events one knows about oneself, and the temptation to interrupt can be great. If the mediator reassures the parties that each of them will have the opportunity to say what they need to say, then a guideline not to interrupt may be adopted later in the proceedings, if the parties so wish. The parties' need to interrupt one another can be a sign of their engagement in the process or the intensity which they feel, and this energy can help to push the case forward to find a creative solution. The mediator must make a concrete evaluation of whether it would be appropriate to discuss with the parties whether their interaction is seen as constructive and if so, what they think should be changed.

Confidentiality

Confidentiality both for the parties and for the mediator is an essential prerequisite for mediation and must be confirmed from the start. However, as stated in Chapter 8, confidentiality is not an easy concept and it can be the cause of much debate if the mediator adopts a style of dialogue from the start of not only giving information as objective truth but involves the parties in this explanation. It is essential for mediators to assure themselves that the parties fully understand what they have agreed to take part in. If exceptions are to be made to confidentiality, all parties must agree to them. Where there is mediation between two colleagues in a workplace, the employer may be interested in knowing how the mediation is going. If the mediator has agreed with the employer to notify when a meeting is held and whether an agreement has been made, the parties may be informed of this and accept it. It can be similar if a dispute is of public interest. It may be necessary for the parties to agree, before a meeting concludes, whether anything shall be said to the outside world, and if so what. Such an agreement means that there must be agreement from the start that confidentiality is absolute unless otherwise agreed. Agreement on this at an early stage in the mediation allows for a more optimistic approach to the following proceedings.

Note taking

It can sometimes be a good idea for the mediator to take notes during the meeting. However, it can be difficult to maintain eye contact with the parties, observe their body language etc. if one is too engaged in taking notes. As they become more experienced, the mediator will be comfortable with taking fewer notes (or none at all), mostly in the form of subject headings, so the meeting can carry on without interruption. Since there are to be no long minutes of meetings, the notes are only to help the mediator's memory. If relevant, the parties ought to be told that the mediator may make notes, but that these will be destroyed after the mediation, so that confidentiality is maintained both during and after the process.

In the reflexive model, in contrast to several other models of mediation, it is not regarded as acceptable, either in the first meeting or subsequently, to inform the parties about what may happen if they do not reach an agreement by means of the mediation. Such an approach has the risk of raising doubts about whether the conflict can be solved by mediation and it could be seen as a threat. Neither of these promotes a positive mediation process, so this is not recommended. If it appears later that the parties do not think that the mediation process is leading to a satisfactory result for them, whether in terms of a concrete result, greater insight, reconciliation or otherwise, then the mediator and the parties can discuss how, in these circumstances, the parties should relate to their conflict, possibly in the light of considering how the conflict might otherwise be resolved.

If it is customary for the parties to sign a contract, once they have been informed of the conditions for mediation, the contract will probably have been signed before the first joint meeting. If not, it will be natural to sign it in the joint meeting. This is also the latest date by which to clarify who is to pay the costs of the mediation, these normally being shared equally between the parties.

Not a monologue by the mediator

The parties ought to be involved in the introduction, so that it does not become a monologue by the mediator. It would be best for the parties to be included in a discussion of what rules of conduct they want if any, rather than be presented with a list read out by the mediator. The possible rules of conduct should be for the benefit of the parties and not to protect the mediator. Finally, the parties should be asked if they have any questions, and whether there are any points, in addition to those discussed, which they want clarified. If not, then the parties should confirm that they are ready to proceed to the discussion of their dispute which is the reason for the meeting, and the next stage of the mediation process can begin.

A summary of the relevant points for the mediator to consider at stage 1:

1. Presentation of the mediator, the parties and any others present.
2. Explanation of the mediation process and the roles of the participants.
3. What the mediator knows about the matter.
4. Confidentiality.
5. Joint meetings – separate meetings.
6. Practical information about breaks, refreshments etc.
7. Possible guidelines for conduct.
8. Note taking.
9. Clarification of financial matters, if not already clarified.
10. Signing the contract, if required.
11. Acceptance of moving to the next stage.

The order in which the information is presented is not decisive, and it need not all be presented at once. However, points such as confidentiality, the roles of the participants and – if the mediator thinks they are likely – the possibility of separate meetings should always be explained, as it will create confusion and uncertainty for subsequent proceedings if these matters are not established from the start

CHAPTER 16

Stage 2: The submissions of the parties and dialogue

Underlying needs and interests

Once the opening stage has been completed and the parties have agreed to proceed, they must each have a chance to give their view of the dispute. The *aims* at this stage of the proceedings are to uncover the various problems, to focus on the underlying needs and interests, to enable there to be some emotional relief for the parties and allow attention to be turned to the future.

If the mediator has not already said what he knows about the case in the introduction, now is the time to do so, and if this can be done so as to emphasise the relations between the parties, this will often help calm things from the start. For example, it can help if the mediator can say that he understands that the parties have had a trading relationship which has worked well for a number of years, but that now some problems have arisen, or that the parties have lived as man and wife and been able to cope with life's daily problems until recently etc.

Since, unlike in a court case, there are no fixed rules about who should speak first, the mediator can decide what is best or can leave it to the parties to decide for themselves. If the mediator chooses to decide, they can use various criteria for the decision; for example the mediator can allow the more tense of the parties to begin, or the one who made the first approach for mediation, or perhaps the party who, on the face of it, seems weaker. What the mediator decides and whether they explain the reasons for the decision to the parties will depend on the mediator and the circumstances of the case.

Even where the parties are accompanied by advisers, it is still preferable for the parties themselves to start by explaining in their own words how they view the dispute. The mediator can then ask the advisers if they have anything to add. The order can be different if the advisers are lawyers, and the reader is referred to Chapter 23 on this.

The first presentations by the parties can be made without interruption from the mediator. However, these presentations should preferably be short; between 5 and 10 minutes is usually enough. One should be aware that it can be very difficult for a party to listen to a presentation which differs totally from their perception. This means that it is best to get both parties involved at an early stage, so their respective views can be aired, and the parties can begin to listen to each other. If one of the parties talks for too long, it may be necessary for the mediator to ask them to draw their comments to a close so the other party can have a chance to say something. On the other hand, if both parties are experienced negotiators and used to making long speeches, it may be necessary to allow time for long presentations, and then the mediator can proceed to ask short and precise questions. The knack here is for the mediator both to control the process and to give the parties space to tell their stories.

Even if, in the first instance, the parties have an uninterrupted opportunity to give their side of the story of the conflict, the mediator's active engagement will soon be necessary in order to help promote dialogue. What information is given will depend to a great extent on how the mediator addresses the parties and what questions are asked. In other words, mediators must be conscious of the form of communication they use, and must be prepared not to keep their distance and not hide behind their professional role, but to engage different sides of themselves and their personalities.

The mediator's language must promote communication

The purpose of the communication or discussion which will hopefully develop is, in addition to clarifying the facts of the dispute, to obtain some insight into the feelings that lie behind the conflict, in order to be able to make orderly progress. It is therefore necessary for a mediator to learn to uncover the feelings of the parties and talk to them naturally. For example, in Denmark it will seldom be natural to ask: 'How are you feeling right now?' First, the word 'feel' is often used synonymously with the word 'think', so it would not be clear from the question whether the intention is to get the party to talk about their mood. Second, many would regard such a question as being too intrusive. Thus it is necessary to use language that encourages a party to open up. For example, expressions such as 'How was that from your point of view?', or 'What did that do for you?' will be formulations that will often encourage communication.[1]

It is important for the mediator to be able to observe both parties at the same time, and to note if the non-speaking party shows impatience. This party can indicate, by body language, facial expressions, fidgeting etc., that they find it difficult to listen to the other party give their side of the story. In this case, the mediator can turn to the impatient party and confirm that it will soon be their turn to speak, and perhaps encourage them to make notes of points they wants to be sure to remember when it is their turn. Such intervention by the mediator can often restore calm, because it involves some recognition of the party's impatience.

While the aim at this stage is to exchange information, it is not for the mediator to decide what is the truth. On the one hand, purely factual information should be established, for example, when a colleague has been at work or whether a contract has been signed, and on the other hand it should be shown that circumstances which appear to be the same are perceived differently, for example, that a colleague is 'always' absent from work, or that one party believes that the disputed point is covered by the contract while the other does not. One should be aware that the positions the parties adopt at the start of the mediation will be exaggerated. Positions are not the same as factual information. Positions are an expression of the parties' conclusions

1. See Lin Adrian, p. 49.

based on circumstances which each of them views as factual, seasoned with their own viewpoints and emotions.

Apart from clarifying facts and differing views, the aim of this stage is to enable the parties to hear each other's explanations. They should get some insight into the fact that they differ, and begin to see that their own facts and feelings are their own, and that the other has a different view of the facts and different feelings. In other words, there is a specific benefit in the parties hearing each other's presentations of their views. It gives a better understanding of the other person, and often gives a more realistic view of events and of expectations than if one only talks to one's lawyer or loyal friends, when sympathy distorts the picture.

The explanations given by the parties will sometimes slip into a discussion of proposals for a solution. Since it is probable that neither of the parties will have changed their view of the conflict at this point, it is too soon to make concrete proposals. This must wait for a later stage. However, as proposals for a solution are often an expression of a willingness to be constructive, the mediator ought to acknowledge this, and the proposals should be noted down for later discussion. If the parties express more abstract wishes such as 'I wish he would come to work at the same time as me in the mornings', this expresses a hope of working together and can contribute to a positive atmosphere at this stage.

Feeling of injury

When there is a conflict, there will always be some feeling of injury. When the parties present their view of the situation they will probably express emotions such as anger, hurt etc., and the mediator must be ready to deal with these emotions without being intimidated. Parties will often make accusations in their presentations, and when or if they address one another directly at this point, this will often take the form of reproach or argument. It can be useful for the parties to see how this form of communication is not constructive, and afterwards they may be more motivated to conduct an open dialogue. As described in Chapter 2, the feelings of the parties, in for example the problem-solving and cognitive mediation models, are regarded as being too disturbing for the process so that only if necessary is allowance made for so-called 'venting', i.e. allowing the parties to let off steam, possibly in separate meetings, or the mediator must act quickly to shift the focus of the parties to a more cognitive process. In the reflexive mediation process the feelings of the parties are considered to be an important part of a reality, and it is not the job of the mediator to remove or diminish them. It is clear that harsh exchanges of opinions between the parties are not constructive in the long run, and can sometimes have the appearance of a direct attack. There are unquestionably cultural differences in this, but it is often the task of the mediator to reflect the feelings of the party who expresses the strong feelings and to acknowledge their hurt. When the parties feel that they have received this acknowledgement from the mediator, it will often be possible for them to address the other party in a less upset or upsetting manner, and the other party will have been witness to the first party's hurt and the mediator's acknowledgement of it.

A challenge, especially for unexperienced mediators, is to speak about feelings in a language that is acceptable to the parties. As mentioned earlier direct talk about feelings in a Danish context is often inadvisable. On the other hand, if the mediator asks a party what they think about this or that, the response will often relate to their feelings so that their feelings will be addressed without the party feeling intimidated.

Sometimes parties begin to cry. Some mediators can feel uncomfortable about this. As a rule, it is a good idea to allow space for the person to cry but not to be affected by it too much oneself. Apart from being an expression of grief, crying can be a means of communication. The crying usually passes quite quickly; if not, one can suggest taking a short break, to allow the parties to gather themselves.

Empowerment

When both parties have given their views of the dispute, and have had some exchanges of views about it, the mediator should refer back to the various main points of the dispute, as the mediator sees them. The mediator will, of course, confirm with the parties that they agree with the mediator's view, and ask them to make corrections and additions as necessary. The next part of the discussion aims to get an insight into the needs and interests of each of the parties, and to enable the parties to get a better understanding of their own and the other party's role in the conflict. As was described in Chapter 10, the part of the process where each party's history and the setting for their motives is revealed is an important part of the empowerment which then enables each party to work actively to find a solution which meets the needs of them both.

I. How to reveal the underlying interests and needs of parties in conflict?

It is naturally essential for mediators to have the skill of active listening, as described in Chapter 6, in order to be able to conduct a proper mediation. In other words, the questions put by the mediator are prompted by her genuine inquisitiveness about the situation and her desire to help the parties find a solution, both factual and emotional. What is decisive is that the mediator should not have her own agenda, but on the contrary should demonstrate the flexibility to understand the thinking of the parties so that the conflict and its complexities can best be illustrated.

However, there are other things besides active listening that can help the mediation process. Here are some examples:

Allow the parties to look at their own part in the conflict

When parties seek mediation, they have reached a point in their conflict where neither feels able to find a way out, and they usually believe the conflict is kept alive by the obstinacy of the other. 'If *you* just did this or that, then *I* wouldn't have any conflict.' Each party explains his behaviour on the basis of the conduct of the other. An ancient technique, used in Tibet, is to allow the parties to *look at their own part* in the conflict. This can first be done once the mediation has made some progress, after the interests and needs have been revealed, as the parties should be able to feel that the most important factual and emotional circumstances on each side are being dealt with. If the parties see their own part in the conflict, this will typically produce some movement in the attitudes of the parties, and it will then be easier for them to see how each of them can contribute to a solution.

Another way is to use repetition, *asking one party to say what they have heard or understood from what the other party has just said.* This technique can be used when the parties have difficulty in hearing what the other says. The response will usually not accord with what was said originally, so there will be an opportunity to correct it. The person who is asked to repeat is forced to try to understand what has been said, without necessarily agreeing with it, and the person who originally said it has a chance to ensure that the other person has understood his intentions.[2] However, the use of this technique requires great sensitivity; if the timing is wrong, the parties will feel they are being talked down to.

Mediation in groups

Finally, one can suggest to the parties that they should not only speak in turn, but also listen in turn. In a mediation with many parties it may even be possible to use a form of token which is circulated, and which gives a party a right to speak when they have possession of the token, rotating the dialogue. The point is that it is easier to listen when one knows that one will have a turn to speak while the others listen. This method has been used successfully by this writer in highly sensitive situations, such as in mediations between different ethnic groups in the former Yugoslavia, immediately after the end of the war.

As described in Chapter 4, how one expresses oneself can either escalate or de-escalate the situation. Parties taking part in mediation will often express themselves in the second person. Time and again they will give the actions and words of the other party as the cause of the conflict, and express this in terms that blame the other person. It is important that, already during the submissions by the parties, the mediator should try to help the parties to *'stay in their own half of the playing field'*, using the first person and focusing more on their own needs, feelings, interests and

2. See Lin Adrian: *Konfliktløsning ved mediation*, Encore 2001, p. 53.

so on. The use of the second person, which involves the language of reproach, leads to the parties causing each other hurt, closing their minds etc. The use of the first person means that one cannot be angry, hurt or unhappy about something the other party has done, and it means that one takes responsibility for one's *reactions*. This is why changing the form of expression used is such an important part of the work of the mediator.

In mediation it is usual for the parties to say at the start what they hope to get out of the mediation. In other words, they formulate their demands clearly. The parties will certainly usually have no difficulty in saying why they think their demands are justified – because the other side has done this or that, or has not done something. In contrast, the parties seldom formulate what is at stake for them, i.e., the interests behind their demands.

Hidden agenda

There can be several reasons for the parties' lack of clarity. Often the parties are either not aware of their true interests, or they are too shy to reveal them, or they are aware of them but are reluctant to express them because they think they can make a better deal if they keep quiet about them. This last is their *hidden agenda*.

Communication techniques

The mediator has several techniques available for helping the parties reveal their interests. The mediator can ask why the party thinks it is important to obtain what they have demanded, what they intend to gain by it, how it will change their situation. By using communication techniques such as *active listening*, the mediator can get the parties to describe their reasons and background considerations in more detail. Active listening is discussed in detail in Chapter 6.

In general, if a party declines to talk about their background considerations and maintains their demands, the conflict is not suitable for mediation. Mediation presupposes that the parties are willing to work together towards a solution in which the needs and interests of both parties are met, as far as possible. If the parties are unwilling to reveal their needs and interests, they are probably not minded to take part in the process and it may be necessary to call a halt to the mediation.

The mediator acts as a role model

It is essential to get the parties to develop an understanding that interests are important, and then to understand each others interests. For this purpose, apart from using various communication skills, the mediator's genuine interest and inquisitiveness to understand the parties' views of the world can mean that the mediator acts as a role model, or the mediator can directly explain the differences between positions, interests and needs, and the aim of mediation to seek solutions which satisfy as many interests as possible.[3]

The mediator should not be shy of asking questions. In their first submissions the parties will probably touch on many different topics, which the mediator can follow up in questioning. If one trail does not lead anywhere, the mediator must just try another, as the parties should be able to indicate whether the question leads to a dead end or whether it is significant.

1. Power in mediation

Power and resources

As described in Chapter 10 there is power in every relationship, so this is also the case in mediation. Influencing the process inevitably means influencing its content. The mediator's activity should therefore be considered in the context of their duty to remain impartial and neutral. Even though mediators are in principle neutral in relation to the parties, and impartial with respect to the outcome of the mediation, in trying to establish a balance of power between the parties they become directly involved in pushing the parties towards making an agreement. As a mediator may not directly argue on behalf of a party, this can cause a dilemma for the mediator.

Different styles of mediation will deal with this dilemma differently. One school argues that the mediator has a duty to help find solutions which are reasonable and fair, and so should help empower the weaker party so they can obtain

3. See Moore, pp. 235-236.

a fair and reasonable agreement.[4] Another school of thought argues that mediators may do very little, if anything, to influence the power relations between the parties, partly because this would put their impartiality at risk, and partly because mediators, as in transformative mediation, find that it is only the parties themselves who can achieve their empowerment through the mediation process.[5]

It is up to the individual mediator to determine which approach to adopt, subject to the fundamental principles and values of mediation being maintained. However, it seems critically important to distinguish between a situation in which a mediator helps a party identify and organise their existing resources, and a situation in which the mediator becomes an advocate for a party and helps them generate new power and influence.

Whether they like it or not, mediators usually constitute a power in themselves, purely by virtue of their authority, knowledge, familiarity with the mediation process, experience, linguistic skill etc. A mediator does not have the power to produce a solution, such as the parties might hope for at the start of the mediation, as that is a power which only the parties themselves can exercise. Instead, the mediator has responsibility for using both their own powers and the powers of the parties in the service of the objectives of the disputants, and when possible to foster the empowerment of the parties.[6]

As the leader of the meeting and the person responsible for the process, the mediator has decisive influence on whether there is a balance of power in the mediation. In mediation, the powers of the parties are often eliminated by the process itself. The resources are what a party is assumed to have, regardless of their content; just as there are no fixed norms giving a predetermined outcome, so there

4. This view is championed, for example, by Susskind 1981 and Haynes 1981, and is the whole basis of agreement-focused and cognitive mediation.
5. See in its entirety Bush & Folger, *The Promise of Mediation*, USA, 2004.
6. See Haynes, 1989, Bush & Folger 1994 and 2004, as well as Lang & Taylor 2000.

are equally no fixed definitions of resources. By identifying interests and needs, these are converted into resources in the course of the mediation, and thereby become strengths, in the sense of being assets which are given significance on the basis of fairness and equality, which are the overriding aims of the mediation. Since fairness is also a standard which is established by the parties and agreed by negotiation, this definition of resources is not fictive, but is decisive for the success of the mediation. Thus, power derived from a party's higher position in the hierarchy is redefined in the mediation process from being associated with structural power to being personal. This is the process by which the problem of power in mediation often becomes more theoretical than practical.

A mediator has several ways of influencing the mutual power relations of the parties by:[7]

Controlling the mediation process

1. *Controlling the mediation process* itself, for example, by the choice of joint meetings or separate meetings. The problem of power is one of the major determinants for the use of separate meetings; see the section on this.

Controlling communications with and between the parties

2. *Controlling communications with and between the parties* by trying, among other things, to allow more or less equal time for the parties to speak. However, mediators should be aware that allowing precisely the same amount of time to each party can sometimes lead to inequality or unfairness in fact, and over-strict control requires a level of activity by the mediator which will often be incompatible with the respect for the parties which is one of the fundamental principles of this book. Reframing and relabeling, as well as preventing interruptions are other ways in which the mediator can control communication. The mediator can also reduce or prevent the effect of threats etc., either by ignoring them and persuading the threatened party to do the same, minimising them by rephrasing them as less threatening statements, or by advising the parties about the costs of

7. See e.g. Moore, 1996, p. 327 et seq.

making threats etc.[8] However, it should be borne in mind that all these techniques can be contra-indicated by consideration for respect for the parties' autonomy and by mediator's wish to limit her influence on the parties as well as on the substance. On this topic, refer to the relevant preceding sections.

Physical arrangements for the negotiations

3. The *physical arrangements for the negotiations*, ensuring that both parties can sit in comfort, see each other and the mediator, and that the mediator can be in contact with both parties simultaneously.

Timing

4. The *timing* of the negotiations, giving the mediator scope for determining the duration of meetings, intervening to build bridges between the parties when possible, holding breaks etc.

Exchanging information between the parties

5. *Exchanging information between the parties*. In a mediation there is a constant flow of information between the parties themselves and between the parties and the mediator. The mediator can influence how direct and confrontational the exchange of information should be.

Assistance from experts

6. *Assistance from experts*. Here too, the mediator can have a more or less direct role in proposing the involvement of expert assistance and in selecting an expert.

Exploiting the doubts of the parties

7. *Exploiting the doubts of the parties*. The mediator can have a significant influence on the process by confronting the parties with their doubts, whether in separate or joint meetings. Consideration of the consequences of not reaching agreement through mediation and developing a BATNA (Best Alternative To a Negotiated Agreement) are elements of this confrontation.

However, the most important elements in the mediation process for changing the balance of power are probably:

8. Moore, op. cit., p. 255.

8. *Uncovering the interests and needs of the parties,* and thereby shifting the focus from the traditional trappings of power, such as money, status, education etc. to more personal elements. If the parties are flexible and have insight into each other's needs and interests, then the power relations can be changed from an objectification of the other party to something more personal and subjective.

   Uncovering the interests and needs of the parties

   Example: In a nationwide newspaper a journalist depicted a homeless drug addict in an article about the social conditions of homeless drug addicts. The addict, who came from the provinces and whose parents were not aware of the conditions of his life in the big city, felt that his rights had been infringed by being exposed in this way. The newspaper had received a number of similar complaints and did not want there to be publicity about the complaints, so it instituted mediation proceedings between the drug addict and the journalist. The initial differences in power between the drug addict and the journalist were altered radically during the mediation process, as the addict experienced a dramatic feeling of empowerment by telling his story and being listened to.
9. *Terminating the mediation.* Finally, if the mediator finds there is no serious intention to take part in mediation by either or both of the parties, the mediator can terminate the mediation on the basis that there is insufficient cooperation to justify continuing.

   Terminating the mediation

2. How the mediator involves the question of justice

Since the parties presumably give an expression of the injury they feel, and which is the cause of the mediation, at a very early stage, already at this point there will be an indirect statement that they feel that the situation is unfair or unjust.

Mediators must be able to express what the parties mean by 'justice', and help them to think their ideas through so as to arrive at a solution. This means that discussions about reasonableness and justice can be a major part of the mediation process.

Different kinds of injustice

In the course of mediation the mediator can encourage the parties to describe different kinds of injustice they have experienced; disrespectful treatment, exclusion from social, professional or commercial intercourse; being the target of gossip etc. None of these is an injustice that is recognised by law. But if one expresses them as injustices, even if the other party rejects the idea that they are unfair, they will be presented as injustices which have been experienced, and the mediation then becomes a forum for a discussion on how injustices can be righted. The attempts of the parties and the mediator to clarify and resolve their opinions will be attempts to reach agreement about what they would see as a redress in this situation.[9]

The justice that is achieved in mediation is the justice which the parties themselves experience, articulate and express in their solution to the conflict. For the parties, the legal rules are just one of many factors in a range of norms and expectations which result in the experience of correct conduct, a fair process and a just solution. Justice in mediation can be described as being derived not through the operation of law, but through autonomy and self-determination.

Just as mediation makes it possible to deal with many different forms of injustice committed by another party, it also allows many different ways of compensating for or making good an injustice. These can be constructed so as to address directly what is felt to be unfair. This can be the removal of critical comments from a personal memoir, the giving of a sincere apology, removing the physical installations that were the cause of the problem, or by some other specific act. The redress consists both of the acknowledgement and the act performed, and is the result of better understanding achieved by the parties through dialogue. This is not a form of justice that is available through the normal justice system.

'An eye for an eye'

'An eye for an eye' is a form of revenge rooted in the Old Testament, meaning that an injury received should be

9. See Hyman & Love, *op. cit.*, p. 181.

answered by meting out a matching injury. But, as pointed out by Mahatma Ghandi, the doctrine of an eye for an eye makes the whole world blind.

In mediation, the discussion is focused on whether justice, or restoring the balance, can be achieved without blinding the other party. To this extent, discussions about justice can relate to the desire for revenge, even if revenge, as normally conceived, is not usually the outcome of mediation. It is more likely that the desire for revenge will be transformed either by recognising the wider context of the dispute, by the offender expressing regret and apologising, or by the offender making some significant reparation or paying compensation. By comparison, the reaction of the courts is often to teach the offender a lesson (i.e., revenge). Maybe the offender learns a lesson, but equally often, both parties learn about the uncertainty of litigation, the enormous costs involved, and the humiliation of being made to feel powerless, subject to the exercise of power by the public authorities.[10]

The parties' own ideas of justice

The outcome of mediation can never be predicted, as the parties have to create their own solution on the basis of their own understanding of the problem and their own needs. The measure of mediation is the extent to which any agreement is in accordance with the standards which the parties themselves define, and whether there is a balance of influence between the parties to the mediation. It is possible that, in their own way, the parties will arrive at a solution which is close to what a court would have decided if it had the same information and the same opportunities as the parties during the mediation process.[11] But this is not decisive. The parties can depart from legal norms and apply their own ideas of justice.

Gradually, as the parties make proposals, the question of distribution or sharing becomes important. The process allows for 'creating value' and optimising the individual and shared goals of the parties. Solutions can include: re-

10. See Hyman & Love, *op. cit.*, p. 167.
11. Hans Boserup & Susse Humle, p. 226.

storing harmony between the parties; increased understanding and improved relations; achieving better Pareto-optimality;[12] saving time, money, frustration and stress (these are injuries that are often added to the original injury, but which the legal system does not take into account); the opportunity for each party to tell their side of the story, etc.[13]

A mediator should be encouraged to set aside their immediate reaction about what is right or wrong and join the parties in finding solutions that are in accordance with their view of what is just. A non-judgemental approach by the mediator helps the parties engage in a critical assessment, in which they can formulate and understand their own values. Ultimately, the mediator acts as a catalyst for the parties to find a solution which they can live with and is in line with their own views of justice and fairness.

3. Separate meetings (Caucuses)

Pros and cons

Whether it is appropriate or justifiable to hold separate meetings in the context of mediation is the subject of ongoing debate. Broadly speaking, participants in this debate can be divided into two main groups: one group dismisses the holding of separate meetings on the grounds that the basic purpose of mediation is not merely for the parties to resolve their conflict, but also to re-establish relations between them. This is not thought possible unless the parties go through the whole process together so they obtain an insight into and understanding of each other's interests and needs. Separate meetings are also rejected on the grounds that it means that the mediator is the only person who has all the information, giving them too much influence and scope for manipulation.[14]

12. Pareto-optimality = obtaining the best possible result for each party, without harming the other party.
13. Hyman & Love, op. cit., give examples of several of these solutions at p. 186 et seq.
14. See, for example, C. Stevens: *Strategy in Collective Bargaining Negotiations*, New York, 1963; and O. Young, "Intermediaries: Additional Thoughts on Third Parties" in the *Journal of Conflict Resolution*, (1972) Vol. 16 No 1, pp. 51-65.

Against this, the other group emphasises the openness which a party can have towards the mediator, and the possibility for obtaining greater support and firmness in relation to the other party by having a meeting at which the other party is not present. This view also emphasises the creativity which the mediator can demonstrate both with regard to the process and its content. Some even argue that most conflicts would not be resolved without separate meetings, because they allow the mediator to contribute more creatively to the process.[15]

As a rule, joint meetings should be held

As stated previously the view of this writer is that, as a rule, joint meetings should be held and that separate meetings should only be used if there are specific reasons for them. However, there can be good reasons for holding separate meetings and should consider the advantages and disadvantages of separate meetings on a case-by-case basis.

These points are discussed below, and there is also a discussion of what mediators should watch out for if they choose to hold separate meetings.

4. Often mentioned reasons for use of separate meetings:

Hostile feelings between the parties

There may be hostile feelings between the parties because of the conflict, making it difficult for them to believe that the other party is making an honest attempt to resolve the conflict and perhaps instinctively making to the parties adopt entrenched positions. The possibility of considering the other party's interests, needs and proposals for a solution in a separate meeting with the mediator can help promote a positive attitude to the mediation process and increase the chances of a positive solution. Also, experience has shown that a party can be unwilling to reveal their views, arguments and offers in joint meetings, but that af-

15. See Moore 1989, p. 263 et seq.; J. Keltner, "Communications and the Labor-Management Mediation Process: Some Aspects and Hypotheses" in the *Journal of Communication*, (1965) Vol. 15 No 2, pp. 64-89, (in particular pp. 74-75); and W. Maggiolo: *Techniques of Mediation in Labor Disputes*, New York 1972, p. 53.

ter discussing them in a separate meeting, they may agree to these being made known to the other party.[16]

Sometimes the parties can be so emotionally involved in the conflict that it may harm the process if they express their feelings freely in a joint meeting. In a separate meeting the mediator can allow room for strong expressions of feelings without this harming the process. Correspondingly, a separate meeting may be helpful if one party is unable to respond to an emotional outburst by the other party. This does not mean that emotional outbursts in joint meetings cannot be constructive; sometimes they have a quasi-ritual purpose. Mediators must be aware of why they use separate meetings; they are not to be used because they feel uncomfortable with emotional outbursts, but because they believe they are best for the mediation process.

Clarification of misunderstandings and misinterpretations

It can also be appropriate to clarify misunderstandings and misinterpretations in separate meetings. However, such clarifications can also be used in a joint meeting to build a bridge between the parties, who can then get an understanding of different views of reality and the reasons behind those views. This is a benefit, which can be important for building relations between the parties, and may be lost if the clarification takes place in separate meetings, unless the mediator ensures that such insight is communicated at a joint meeting.

Reservations about putting forward a proposal

Separate meetings can also be used if the parties do not feel comfortable looking at different proposals for solutions in joint meetings. In joint meetings there is a risk that a proposal may be made prematurely, or it may reveal information about how one assesses one's BATNA (Best Alternative to a Negotiated Agreement), which one would rather keep to oneself.[17] A party may also have reservations about putting forward a proposal for a solution, for fear it may be considered a sign of weakness. Separate meetings give the parties the chance to discuss this with the media-

16. See Anne Austbø and Geir Engebretsen: *Mekling i Rettskonflikter*, 2003, pp. 92-98.
17. Moore, *op. cit.*, p. 262.

tor, who can help the party to assess whether the time is ripe for putting the proposal to the other party.

Finally, separate meetings can be used for: clarifying claims or interests; considering the other party's proposals for a solution; further developing one's BATNA; taking a needed break when joint meetings become too tiring; carrying out reality tests; revealing confidential information; educating an inexperienced party about the mediation and negotiation process; and preventing a party rejecting a proposal prematurely. Separate meetings can also be useful if the mediation has reached deadlock for one reason or another. However, these reasons for using separate meetings are most often mentioned in relation to the problem solving method, which is focusing on reaching an agreement, leaving the relationship between the parties aside, a price which as mentioned several times, this author is hesitant to pay.

Misunderstandings or disagreements between a party and their adviser

Misunderstandings or disagreements which may arise between a party and their adviser, for example their lawyer, is probably one of the areas in which the use of separate meetings is most justifiable. It can greatly weaken the position of a party if such disagreement is revealed in a joint meeting. Often, a lawyer will be more inclined to maintain a position than the party himself. Discussions in separate meetings can help clarify the party's interests, and lead to a softening of the position, to the benefit of the joint proceedings.[18]

It is true, though, that separate meetings can give the mediator the opportunity to be more supportive or more confrontational than is possible in joint meetings. In a joint meeting it can be difficult to confront a stubborn party with their share of responsibility for the conflict and with the risks of not making an agreement. In a joint meeting, confrontations of this kind can easily be seen as a weakness of the party. It is correspondingly difficult to emphasise the resources of a party in a joint meeting.

18. See Chapter 20.III.

Disadvantages in using of separate meetings

The mediator acquires great power with a risk of manipulation

However, also disadvantages in using of separate meetings should be mentioned. In such meetings, the parties are physically separated and prevented from communicating directly with each other. The main doubts about this are concerns about the position of the mediator, who becomes the only person with all the information communicated in the mediation process. The mediator thus acquires great power with a risk of manipulation. If the use of separate meetings is combined with the mediator's belief that it is right to make suggestions for a solution, or even merely to evaluate the suggestions of the parties or to present the other party's proposal as the mediator's own, then the mediation process is moving dangerously far from the basis of mediation which is that not only the conflict but also the solution must belong to the parties. The mediator will have surrendered their neutrality in relation to the solution to the conflict, and instead of a mediation, the process will instead have become a form of mini-arbitration.[19]

Separate meetings also prevent the parties seeing and hearing each other's feelings and reactions and will probably reduce their ability to understand one another. Consequently, the parties may not achieve the release and the will and capacity to find creative solutions, and the solution to the problem will seldom encompass the restoration of relations between the parties.

Information which trigger an ethical dilemma

Another problem of separate meetings is the risk that the mediator will become aware of information which will trigger an ethical dilemma. For example, in a case involving an employee and an employer it may become clear that the employee is pregnant but has not yet informed her employer of this, or in a divorce case a man may reveal that he has a hidden foreign bank account which he does not want to share with his wife. There is no simple answer to the question of how the mediator should deal with such a situation. Some mediators suggest that the mediator should state the limits to confidentiality in their opening remarks. For example, it is in accordance with the Model Standards

19. For the different kinds of mediation, see Chapter 2.

(1984) of the Association of Family and Conciliation Courts in America to disclose information about insufficient financial disclosure, abuse of children or the risk of physical assault.[20] Other mediators refuse to guarantee confidentiality in separate meetings.

II. Who, where and how

The mediator is the leader of the proceedings and naturally decides whether separate meetings should be held, even though the parties are of course free to ask for separate meetings. If the mediator expects to use separate meetings in the course of the proceedings, it is important that this possibility is referred to and possibly explained and discussed at the start of proceedings, otherwise it may cause needless worry and suspicion. It is difficult for the mediator to suggest holding separate meetings at a later stage, as this will often be interpreted by the parties as a sign that something is wrong, and so will not have a beneficial effect. At the start of proceedings the mediator can also refer to the possibility of the parties themselves suggesting holding separate meetings if they find this appropriate.

There are no rules for when it is best to hold separate meetings, which can, in principle, take place at any time. Moore suggests that separate meetings held early in the proceedings are primarily to enable heated emotions to cool, while separate meetings held in the middle phase of the process are typically focused on identifying interests and avoiding premature support for an agreement. Separate meetings held towards the end of proceedings will usually involve breaking a deadlock and developing new proposals.

The use of separate meetings can vary according to the nature of the case, and from mediator to mediator. However, there is a tendency for separate meetings to be used

20. See Moore, *op. cit.*, p. 326.

more in commercial mediations, and much less in e.g. marital conflicts.[21]

As a rule of thumb, one can consider using separate meetings if the explanations and clarifications of the parties begin to go round in circles with no sign of progress, provided that a substantive part of the submissions of the parties has been made. However, the parties will often be able to escape from the doldrums in joint meetings, and the mediator should not seize the first opportunity to split them up. If the parties become increasingly irritated with each other, it may be time to make a move, before their desire to participate evaporates.

Transition from the joint meeting

If separate meetings are decided on, the mediator must ensure that the transition from the joint meeting should be as smooth as possible. The mediator must decide which of the parties to speak with first. One can use the same kind of criteria as at the start of the mediation process, and consider whether either of the parties has been more reticent in giving information in the initial phase, in which case it would be more natural to start with the party who has played their cards closer to their chest. As with the initial submissions of the parties, there are no fixed rules for who should begin. The mediator must decide whether it should be the party who is more tense, the one who has asked for separate meetings, the one who initiated contact with the mediator, or the one who is calmer, who should begin. The mediator assesses the situation and decides.

Once the choice is made, it is important for both parties to have roughly the same amount of time in separate meetings with the mediator. The party who is left outside feels vulnerable, and the best way to overcome any suspicions of bias etc. is to treat the parties equally, as far as possible. The mediator should agree with each party how long the meetings will last. The duration will naturally depend on the situation, but if a meeting last more than 20 minutes to half an hour, it is reasonable for the other party to be given a

21. Moore, *op. cit.*, p. 321.

formal break so they can manage their time better.[22] Time can drag for the party who is sitting out the meeting, so it is a good idea if they can be given some task to do. For example, in a dispute about parental access to children, the mediator can ask a parent to investigate the different transport options and costs between the parents' homes, or ask them to consider their share of responsibility for the conflict.

When a mediator has asked an open question and obtained information about various circumstances from the first party, they should be careful that they do not, in another meeting, immediately allow the second party the opportunity to consider the circumstances the mediator has discussed with the first. Both parties have a right to approach the problem openly, otherwise it is probable that one will meet resistance from a party who feels neglected.

The mediator moves back and forth

It is best if there is a room where one party can wait in comfort while the mediator has a meeting with the other party, as well as a room for joint meetings. It is the mediator who should move back and forth between the parties, as this is more polite than showing the parties to the door in turns. It also ensures that the parties are truly apart in separate meetings, without being able to see or hear each other. This also gives the mediator a little time and space to think while moving from room to room. Even if the conditions are not ideal, the mediator must at least ensure that the parties really are kept separate in separate meetings.

III. Confidentiality in separate meetings

Information given in separate meetings is confidential in the same way as information given in joint meetings. In joint meetings the confidentiality applies to the outside world, and in separate meetings the confidentiality applies both to the outside world and to the other party.

22. Moore, *op. cit.*, p. 323.

It is precisely this confidentiality in relation to the other party which can promote greater openness in separate meetings. The party involved decides what shall be said to the other party, and before ending a separate meeting, the mediator must confirm what the party wants said. For example, the mediator can ask if there is anything which the party does not want passed on to the other party. This enables the party to specify what they do not want passed on, and gives mediators authority to use the information they think will help.[23] It is not uncommon for a party who finds it difficult to divulge information in a joint meeting, to find it less difficult once it has been discussed with the mediator in a separate meeting.

A mediator can say that they think that divulging certain information would probably help the progress of the mediation, but it is up to the party to decide whether to do so.

Confusion about the process and the role of the mediator

If, during a separate meeting, a party states how they would like the conflict resolved, but fears that a proposal might be perceived by the other party as a sign of weakness, some theorists suggest that the mediator should present the proposal as the mediator's own.[24] While this approach is a normal negotiating technique, it is difficult to reconcile this with the principles of mediation, which require that a mediator should not present proposals for solving the conflict, and it can cause confusion about the process and the role of the mediator.

It is not necessarily to be assumed that one party's proposal for a solution should immediately be given to the other party. Sometimes the mediator, with their overall perspective of the situation, will be best placed to assess whether the time is ripe for introducing the suggested solutions to the other party. However, this approach, which means that the mediator is not a mere bearer of messages, is open to the risk of manipulation. For this reason, the parties ought therefore at least to be informed of the media-

23. Moore, *op. cit.*, p. 324.
24. See, for example, Moore, *op. cit.*, p. 324.

tor's approach, so they do not have expectations of being presented with the other party's suggestions after the first separate meeting.

If the proceedings last a long time, and if there are several separate meetings, it can be difficult for the mediator to remember what information comes from whom, what information can be passed on and what is confidential. A mediator must develop a technique to deal with this. It is usual for the mediator to take notes in separate meetings so they can perhaps write the two different kinds of information in different coloured inks, or use two writing pads. Regardless of how they deal with it, it is essential for the trust in the mediator and the mediation process that the confidences of the parties are respected.

An ethical dilemma for the mediator

If, in a separate meeting, the first party gives the mediator information which the mediator believes is essential for the second party, but the first party does not want the information to be passed on, there will be an ethical dilemma for the mediator. The principle is clear: a mediator may not assist in making an agreement which the mediator knows to be based on incomplete or incorrect information.[25] One way out of this dilemma is for the mediator to confront the party who has given the information with the problem of keeping it secret. Another possibility is to ask, hypothetically, what the consequences would be for an agreement and what would happen if it were later discovered that the information had been withheld.

If the mediator finds that confidentiality is a bar to making an ethically acceptable agreement, they must terminate the mediation in a way which does not breach the confidentiality.[26]

25. Anne Austbø and Geir Engebretsen: *Mekling i Retskonflikter*, 2003.
26. See Anne Austbø and Geir Engebretsen: *Mekling i Retskonflikter*, 2003, p. 167.

IV. The transition from separate meetings to a joint meeting

The transition from separate meetings to joint meetings should be as smooth as possible. Before joint meetings are resumed, the mediator must consider carefully what to say about the separate meetings that have been held. For example, the first party may have expressed some regret which the mediator thinks the second party should hear directly from the first party. Or an offer may have been made which the mediator knows will be welcomed with surprise.

The mediator should discuss this with each party in the separate meetings and prepare them for what will happen when the parties meet again. The mediator also has to decide which party should speak first.

The final meeting should always be a joint meeting

The final meeting should always be a joint meeting. If, at this stage, the parties are not ready to meet, this is a clear signal to the mediator that the process has had little to do with mediation and that any agreement will have a weak foundation.

V. Manipulation and separate meetings

As the mediator is the only person who has all the information given during the mediation proceedings, and the parties will not have had the advantage of confronting each other face-to-face, when there are separate meetings there is considerable risk of manipulation and misuse of power. The scope for controlling, manipulating, suppressing or exaggerating information gives the mediator a unique position and therefore gives rise to heated debate between mediators, as has been referred to already.

There is a particular risk for manipulation if the mediator senses that it may not be possible to obtain an agreement between the parties, so they are tempted to put some pressure on the process or push the information so as to get an agreement. This is clearly unacceptable, and contrary to the professional ethics by which the mediator is bound.

It should be noted that, as they become more experienced, mediators who have been frequent users of separate meetings become more comfortable with the emotional outbursts of parties, and they often allow more and more of the mediation to take place in joint meetings. Of course, this is not the whole truth, as separate meetings can unquestionably play a positive, independent role, even for those whose starting position clearly favours joint meetings.

It is up to the individual mediator to decide whether and to what extent there should be separate meetings, subject to the code of conduct for mediators.

VI. Aids for the mediator

Almost inevitably, at times in the course of the mediation the distance between the parties will seem so great that it will seem impossible to find a solution. Not only the parties, but also the mediator can have a feeling of impotence and hopelessness. It is important for mediators to have some techniques by which they can maintain or regain calm and control. This involves remembering the elements described in the section on understanding conflicts:

The conflict ladder: The mediator knows that the conflict has become escalated, registers the level of the conflict, and knows that it will move up and down in the course of mediation.

The dimensions of a conflict: The mediator knows that, to begin with, the emphasis of the conflict is on persons and on values. In the course of mediation the emphasis will change to enable negotiation and agreement on various values which are understood and accepted.

Truth: The mediator knows that the parties look differently at their conflict, at its causes and at a possible solution. The mediator ensures that the differences are expressed and brought into the open.

Understanding v. agreement: The mediator knows that putting oneself in the shoes of the other party need not mean one agrees with their conclusions. This insight should be shared with the parties.

The use of flip-charts

The use of flip-charts: From time to time it can be helpful to use a flip-chart or board on which the positions, interests, needs and attitudes of the parties can be written as precisely and briefly as possible.

In general, the use of a flip-chart helps both the mediator and the parties to have an overview of the circumstances revealed in the mediation. But there are further advantages to using a flip-chart or board: *first*, it makes the interests and needs of each party visible, and confirms that their concerns are taken seriously. *Second*, it helps ensure that everyone in the room is talking about the same thing. When the mediator writes things down, they check with the parties whether they are using wording which is acceptable to them, and this makes it more of a joint project. To start with, only the positions of the parties can be written down, but as the parties see each others' attitudes written down, they will be engaged in finding the right words and investigating and understanding everything as well as possible. The parties will often identify a certain coincidence of interest, which will be encouraging. *Third*, in the course of the mediation, several pieces of flip-chart paper can be used, and these can be put up on the wall in series, so the parties can see visible evidence of development. The mere fact that the mediator moves from sitting face to face with the parties and stands up to write on the board can bring fresh impetus, and refresh the parties and the mediator, giving a feeling of movement both literally and metaphorically.

Sometimes, interests and needs can be revealed in a joint meeting, and sometimes it is better to do it in separate meetings, if this makes it easier for a party to be more trusting and open. This depends on the conflict and the wishes of the parties and, of course, the judgement and skills of the mediator.

This book reflects the basic view that the general rule should be that meetings should involve both parties and not just the first meeting, and that separate meetings should only be held if there is a specific reason for doing so. While the mediator is the leader of the process and the parties have control over the content and solution of the conflict, there is such a close link between the process and the content that mediators can hardly avoid influencing the content through their questioning and other actions. Therefore, if there is to be a correlation between the definition of mediation and the actual mediation process, the mediator's influence on the content should be as limited as possible. This can only be achieved by maintaining joint meetings as the default rule of the process.

Stage 2. The submissions of the parties and dialogue

There is a focus on:
Facts – what has taken place
Interests and needs – what lies behind the positions of the parties
Feelings
What must be recognised – what can be negotiated
Power and ideas of justice
The acceptance of different realities

Techniques:
Questioning
Summarising/rephrasing
Repetition
Silence
Validation
Ceding and controlling at the same time
Empowerment
Building bridges
Joint or separate meetings

CHAPTER 17

Stage 3: Defining the problem areas and setting the agenda

After completion of the phase in which the parties make their submissions, and when their needs and interests have been identified and their feelings are no longer an obstacle to progress, it is time to look forward, towards solutions. It is possible that the parties are not interested in solutions and are quite happy to have got a better understanding of their conflict, and this, of course, is entirely up to them. However, mostly the parties do want an agreement. Before moving on to generate suggestions for solutions, it must be clear to the mediator and to the parties about to what it is precisely that a solution shall be found, otherwise there is a risk that the following discussion will be about the aims of the process. The *aim* of this stage is thus for the parties and the mediator to have a shared view about what has been revealed about the conflict, so there can be agreement about the basis for the next part of the mediation process. Stage 3 thus represents a transitional phase between the stage of emotional release and information sharing and the forward-looking creative part of the process, and thus it is a natural extension of, for example, the double acknowledgement described in Chapter 6.

One or more headings

Experience shows that it is usually best to lay out the problem areas under one or more headings. These can be supplemented by sub-headings, and the cumulative solutions of these can constitute the solution to the main heading. The main heading is a kind of overall summary of the parties' conflict; it sets the scene. The sub-headings address the individual problems which the parties want solved. It is best to write the problem to be solved in the form of a question, as this naturally begs an answer.

In this part of the process, the mediator takes a more active role. The mediator knows the stages of the process and has an overview of what will happen later. The parties are not familiar with the process, few of them will have tried it before and certainly none will have tried it several times. Also, the parties are often, to a certain extent, still involved in the conflict, and lack perspective. The best starting point is therefore not to ask the parties how to word the headings to the problems. The parties will be confused, and this will not be a good basis for agreeing what the overall problem is. The mediator must take charge and try to summarise the points of conflict dealt with by the parties.

Short summary of the problems

The mediator starts with a short summary of the problems, the interests of the parties and the hopes they have expressed for the future. Then the mediator should say how they see the overall problem. If it is not clear to the mediator how the overall problem should best be described, it can be a good idea to take a short break, so they can study the flip-chart pages giving the parties' interests, needs etc. As a rule the mediator will have been prepared for this stage, and will be able to make a first proposal for a heading for the problem. It is important that the mediator constantly checks with the parties. The conflict is theirs, and they must live with the results of the mediation. If the parties comment on the mediator's suggestion, the mediator must be willing to amend it until the parties are satisfied. For this purpose the mediator merely plays a kind of secretarial role.

Examples of headings:

- How do we achieve good neighbourly relations?
- How can our divorce be arranged in the best way for both children and adults?
- How can we co-operate satisfactorily in future?
- How can we dissolve our partnership, while still ensuring that both can continue to make a decent living?

- Or, in the conflict over the cartoons of the prophet Mohammed: How can we contribute to a society with respect both for secular democratic and religious interests?

Sub-headings

These should be supplemented by sub-headings. In the example of neighbour disputes these can be on topics such as music and conflict resolution. In the divorce example, the sub-headings can include informing the outside world and co-existence, which may in turn concern the division of work and leisure time with the children, making space for leisure time without children etc. In the example of the Mohammed cartoons: How can we send a joint signal to the outside world about our future communications and conflict resolution mechanisms etc.?

If the headings are all at the same level, the parties and the mediator can easily lose perspective. Also, this may exclude possible solutions. If in the neighbour dispute one makes two headings which reflect the specific problems, they might be: 'When and how loud may music be played?', and 'How do we solve problems in future?'. In the example on co-operation, the headings might be: 'How should we share the work between us?', 'When and how should we exchange information?', 'By what criteria should we decide our days off?', or 'How can we make room for spending "constructive" time together?'. In the example of the Mohammed cartoons, the equally-weighted headings might be: 'What kinds of representation of the prophet Mohammed are acceptable?'[1], and 'How can we ensure respect for freedom of expression?'. This would mean that answers would only be given to the questions put. Other possible solutions, such as arranging a garden party together, agreeing to look after each other's dogs or mutual education in democracy and religion would not be

1. For example, in Norwegian schoolbooks used in religious education, for many years there have been pictures of the prophet Mohammed without any protests being raised, despite the general prohibition, by some Muslims, of making images of the prophet.

thought about. This becomes more likely under a more broadly framed main heading.

It is best to write the main headings and sub-headings on a board or flip-chart, so they are common to all and visible during the subsequent brainstorming. The headings should be written in ordinary language, with the parties' acceptance of both the content and the choice of words.

A decision about the order

Once the problem areas have been defined, a decision must be made about the order in which they should be dealt with. This forms a kind of agenda. It will usually be a good idea to work on the easiest points first, as this will gradually help to promote a positive atmosphere, making it easier to grasp the more complex issues later. However, there can be situations in which the solution to one problem is a necessary prerequisite for the solution of others. In such cases there is no way of avoiding dealing with that topic first. In a case concerning a father's access rights to his 12 year old daughter, over whom the mother had parental authority, it was impossible to deal with the extent of the father's access, which was what most concerned the parents, without establishing how the father should deal with the daughter's treatment for diabetes, which had hitherto been the mother's sole responsibility.

In any case, it is again the parties who decide what they find is most important for them to agree on first.

Stage 3: Defining the problem areas

- Summarise the problems and interests
- The mediator suggests headings and gets the parties acceptance of them
- The headings should be formulated as questions
- Consider whether the themes should be formulated as individual questions or as a broad heading with sub-headings
- Establish an order of priority, if there are several headings

CHAPTER 18

Stage 4: Generating possible solutions

I. Brainstorming

When, together with the mediator, the parties have written down the headings of the problems to be solved, it is time to move to the more creative phase. Suggestions for solutions must be generated, preferably as many as possible, so it will be possible to work with them in combinations which should take account of as many of the needs and interests of the parties as possible.

Brainstorming

The usual name for this is 'brainstorming', and the parties are often unaccustomed to it. In brainstorming the parties make suggestions for solutions free from criticism, and without judging whether the suggestions are realistic or not. The aim is to allow creativity to flourish. Experience shows that suggestions which are in themselves unrealistic can provoke other more realistic solutions which might not otherwise have surfaced, because the parties think too traditionally or rationally.

The mediators should make it clear to the parties that it is possible that something can now happen in the process which is entirely new and unusual, and even if the mediators have done so before, they should explain again what is to happen. It may be appropriate to make some changes to the arrangement of the room, or have some other kind of physical movement to signal the change. It may be a good idea to place the parties side by side in front of a flip-chart or board, so they feel involved in a joint project.

The first step in this process is for the parties to accept that there is a need to develop suggestions for alternative solutions. Often, parties enter into mediation with the view that there is one and only one solution to the conflict, and that the aim of mediation is to convince the other party of the correctness of their view. It is clear that this cannot form the basis of a mediated solution. Hopefully the parties will have become more conscious of their true needs in the course of the submissions phase, i.e., what they need rather than what they want.

This stage can often be very positive and even entertaining both for the parties and the mediator. While the earlier stages can be dominated by tension and pressure, this is a time to look forward, and it should be a relief for the parties. Nevertheless the mediator must be patient. Most people are not used to brainstorming, and it feels unnatural to start with. Some people may resist the idea of play involved in brainstorming, and it does not help to push too hard. If the resistance is simply due to lack of familiarity with the process, various techniques can be used to get things going. On the other hand, if the resistance is due to new problems surfacing which have not been dealt with at a previous stage, then there is nothing for it but to return to Stage 2 and work through the problems. It is important for the mediator then to make it clear to the parties that they are taking a step back in the process, as well as to make it clear when the brainstorming stage is reached again.

Lateral thinking

According to de Bono, brainstorming allows the parties to think differently, more slowly and in a less linear way. De Bono calls this 'lateral thinking', and he distinguishes it from normal vertical, logical, and sometimes too hasty thinking; lateral thinking is circular and often provoking. De Bono calls the analytical approach which most of us use virtually all the time 'vertical thinking', because it has a logical sequence from A to B to C to D and so on, and is based on experience and derived from existing and ordered knowledge. In other words, this way of thinking gives great certainty, but there is not much spark in it. On the other hand, lateral thinking includes seemingly irrelevant factors, jumps about, and accepts that one can follow a false trail and try new ways which can in the end lead to a good result.[1]

Vertical thinking

In order to have space to operate, lateral thinking should be done without criticism or classification. This must wait until afterwards, once enough suggestions have been generated. The mediator must be patient and give the parties time to get going. For many people lateral thinking is quite foreign, and for some its playful method is very attractive. Regardless of the approach, it is important to stress that lateral and vertical thinking supplement one another, as it would be impossible to get by in everyday life without vertical thinking, and the vertical approach must be used for assessing the various suggestions.

The most important thing for the parties to understand about lateral thinking is that, however they view a problem, it is only one out of an unknown number of possibilities.

Flip-chart

The mediator should write the ideas down on a board, flip-chart or overhead. This makes them visible for all parties, it can be encouraging and inspiring to see one's suggestions written down, and can prompt further suggestions. The suggestions should be written down in the order in which they are made. The mediator should not try to classify suggestions or indicate who made them, for example by dividing the board into sections for each party or using different coloured pens. If the originator of a suggestion is indicated, this can lead the parties competing to see who makes most suggestions, or they may be more critical towards the other party's suggestions when it comes to negotiating solutions. This is a time to bind in the parties as much as possible, and the experience is that a successful brainstorming session can result in the parties not remembering who made which suggestion, so they feel less inhibited when it comes to negotiating. The mediator ought also to emphasise that, just because one party has made a sug-

1. de Bono, *Lateral Thinking*, 1970; de Bono, *Teaching Thinking*, 1976; and de Bono, *de Bono's Thinking Course* 10, 1982.

gestion, it does not mean he 'owns' it or that he cannot subsequently reject the suggestion if he does not agree with it.

Extract the core meaning of a suggestion

All suggestions should be written down. Neither the parties nor the mediator should select the suggestions. Everything is allowed, though long suggestions should be made shorter, and vague suggestions made more specific. If a suggestion is very long, the mediator can try to extract its core meaning and check with the party that this is what they mean. Suggestions should preferably be written down in the words used and expressed as directly as possible. If a suggestion is unclear, the mediator can ask the parties to explain what they mean, and perhaps ask them to suggest some alternative wording. It is best if the suggestions are specific enough to prompt indicated actions. A suggestion that 'We should cooperate better in future' is too vague to be operational, and *in the negotiating phase* the parties should state more precisely how they see their suggestions working in practice. However, at this stage it is sufficient to note positive statements, without going into further details. If suggestions are expressed negatively, the mediator can ask whether it is possible to formulate them in a more positive forward-looking form. For example, 'John must not come to work too late in the morning' can be changed to 'John shall be ready for work at 9.00 a.m. each morning.'

The mediator should beware of commenting or giving the impression that they think some of the suggestions are better than others, for example by being more ready to write down some suggestions than others, or by verbal or non-verbal expressions seeming to praise some particular suggestion. During brainstorming, the primary role of the mediator is that of a scribe or secretary, and they should merely ensure that suggestions are made and that everyone concerned is clear about the meaning of what is written down.

Remember that the parties 'own' the conflict

There are differing views about whether, and if so how far, the mediator should contribute suggestions. It should be remembered that the parties 'own' the conflict and they should also 'own' the solution to it. This view is based on recognition of the fact that the parties have more information about their situation than the mediator, and the experience that parties are more likely to abide by suggested solutions they find for themselves, rather than those 'forced' on them or given to them. The role of the mediator gives them a certain authority and there is a risk that, if they suggest a solution, this will dominate the subsequent negotiations, possibly because it will be seen as being based on greater experience or suchlike. This can threaten the role of the mediator as an impartial leader of the process, and there is a risk that the mediator may be seduced by their own suggestion and become over-engaged in how the conflict is resolved.

On the other hand, if at the submissions stage the mediator has noted suggestions for solutions put forward by the parties which were not developed at that stage, they can remind the parties of them, and check to see if the ideas are still relevant. For example, a previously expressed wish to keep a particular customer may have been replaced by the possibility of getting a different and larger customer base. What matters is that the parties themselves make the suggestions.

If the mediator decides it is right to make a suggestion, they must at least ensure that they do not make just one suggestion but several, to indicate there are other possibilities, and to reduce the risk that the suggestion may bias later proceedings.

II. How to help the parties on their way

There are various techniques the mediator can use to get the parties to make suggestions.

When the interests and needs of the parties have been written on flip-chart pages which are hung up around the room, it can be a good idea to ask the parties to look at some of them and make suggestions based on them. They need not think they have to solve the whole problem at once; they can tackle it in bits which can later be linked together to make the whole. For example, one can ask: 'What do you think is the most important interest?', or 'What kind of solution would you like?'. Or it may be helpful to get a sense of the other party's interests and one can ask: 'What do you think Tom believes is most important? Is that something you agree with?'.

'I divide up the cake, you choose the portion'

One can also encourage the parties, in making their suggestions, not to think just about their own interests, but to try as far as possible to address the interests of others. On the basis of 'I divide up the cake, you choose the portion', there is often a desire to balance the suggestions.

Reflective questions

Hypothetical questions

One can ask reflective questions which get the parties to consider new possibilities. It is important that these should not be asked as if the mediator thinks some particular course is a good idea. They can be put as hypothetical questions such as: 'What if ...?', or 'Have you thought about ...?', or 'Is it possible that ...?'. It can be something as simple as 'What do you need so you can put this conflict behind you?'.

If the parties have previously co-operated, been colleagues, been married to each other or had some similar relationship, the mediator can ask if there have been times when the problem was not a problem. By asking this, the parties may recall something they have previously done which worked, and it is easier to continue or repeat something previously done than to start on something new. If the parties can recall other situations, it is important to identify specifically why there were not problems before, and what needs to be done to re-establish the situation.

Miracle question

One can also ask a so-called *miracle* question, about the future, where the parties are asked to imagine the situation in 6 months time when the problem has been solved. How will their everyday relations be?

Similarly to asking the miracle question, the parties can be asked to imagine that the problem is someone else's. They have been contacted by a good friend or a colleague. What advice would they give? Would this be a solution for their own problem?[2]

2. Anne Suzette Humle: *En samtale – to vindere*, Chapter 4.

Finally, one can ask the parties to think about the worst that could happen. And, what would be the first step away from the worst that could happen?

Some people believe that monetary claims do not allow scope for creative solutions. However, it is not so straightforward, even though it must be admitted that there are obstacles to creativity as long as one thinks along these lines. For example, payment can be made by instalments, or a guaranteed lesser sum now may be better than an uncertain bigger sum later etc. It is better to work on 'enlarging the pie' by including other interests than the purely monetary.

Single text procedure

One method which is sometimes used in negotiations is the 'single text procedure'.[3] This consists of first identifying all the parties' interests. Then, either one party or the mediator prepares a proposal for an agreement, taking the widest possible account of all interests. The proposal is treated as a draft agreement and is circulated between the parties, who make comments and suggestions for its revision. Each party should have the opportunity to amend the draft to bring it closer to their needs. Often, after several revisions, the resulting draft is acceptable to all parties. It is possible to use this approach in mediation between two or a few parties, but it cannot usually be recommended as this procedure would presumably only be necessary in such a small forum if it is not possible to establish sufficiently relaxed relations between the parties for creative brainstorming to work. On the other hand, this approach can be necessary in mediation between several parties, not least with international mediation.[4]

III. Separate meetings

The overwhelmingly usual practice is for the process of generating possible solutions to take place in joint meet-

3. Fisher & Ury: *Getting to Yes*, 1981.
4. Moore: *The Mediation Process*, p. 260.

ings, but it can – more usually in major commercial conflicts – take place in separate meetings. If the mediator has decided to carry on the proceedings in separate meetings, they must be careful to be equally open towards both parties, and not over-enthusiastic about a suggestion from one party, while asking the other party to express a view on it, thus shutting out the possibility of further suggestions for solutions being made. The mediator must remember that people generally do not like solutions to be forced on them, and most people welcome the opportunity to be constructive and to be able to make suggestions for solutions. Some mediators exploit this knowledge strategically by framing questions so the other party feels they have also contributed good ideas. However, this approach clearly has limits, and it involves a major risk of developing into manipulation.

If this stage of the proceedings is conducted in separate meetings, it can be a good idea to ask a party how they believe the other party will react to a suggestion, or ask them to think about the strengths and weaknesses of their suggestion.[5]

Stage 4: Generating possible solutions

Ideas must be allowed to flow freely.
The parties should be allowed, uninhibitedly, to generate as many (untraditional) suggestions as possible.
The suggestions should be written on a board or a flip-chart.

Aids:
Encourage the parties
See the conflict from the outside
Give the parties time to get going
Reflective questions
'Miracle' questions

5. See also Chapter 16 on separate meetings.

CHAPTER 19

Stage 5: Negotiating the agreement

I. Introduction

When the parties have made enough suggestions, it will be time to bring this creative phase of the process to an end and move to a more concrete phase. The parties must now assess the suggestions and possibly combine them. They should think both vertically and laterally in this phase, as their critical sense and realism must be combined with their creativity. The aim of this stage is for the parties to move closer to each other so they can negotiate a solution which is both realistic and meets the interests of both parties to the greatest possible extent.

It is best for the parties to prioritise their interests so there can be give and take without the parties feeling they have sacrificed a significant interest. This is a realistic scenario and often arises, for example, in conflicts about cooperation at work where it can be mutually beneficial to clarify expectations of work input, communication, experience exchange etc.

However, it is not always so easy, as the interests of the parties can in fact compete with each other. For example, both parties can be not only interested in, but absolutely dependent on, the right of access to a particular plot of land or source of water. One of the tasks of the mediator at this stage can therefore be to help the parties adjust their expectations so they are reasonable in relation to their interests and needs and what they think they can reasonably get out of the mediation. This often requires creativity by the mediator, combined with patience and hard work.

When working with the parties to get them to consider suggested solutions and gradually to move towards each other, the mediator can encourage the parties to:

- Bear in mind their interests and needs;
- Consider how suggestions already made could be developed to satisfy these interests and needs;
- If there are problems in reaching agreement, think about the best alternative solution to agreement through mediation;
- Begin to modify, integrate and combine different suggestions with a view to getting an agreement;[1] and
- Re-emphasise both their shared and conflicting interests.

Point 1: For the parties to be satisfied with the final agreement, it must address their interests to some extent. Therefore, it is helpful for the mediator to remind the parties of their interests and needs at this point, and to re-emphasise both their shared and conflicting interests. This reflection will often be helped if the parties consider not only their own interests and needs, but also the interests and needs of the other party, trying to see them in relation to each other and adopting a slightly longer perspective than the short-term satisfaction of needs.

Even if the mediator has written the interests on a board or a flip-chart, so the parties have their previous work before them, this point should not be omitted, as it reinforces the focus of the parties during negotiations and helps them to proceed more smoothly.

Group the suggestions by topic.

Point 2: The parties may need help to get an overview of the suggestions. They may need time to look at them, and to ask questions for clarification. If there are not too many suggestions, it may be a good idea to review them one at a time, giving the parties a chance to state the advantages

1. See for example Moore, p. 269.

and disadvantages of each, thus pointing out the need for creativity in the further development of the suggestions.

If there are a lot of suggestions, it can be a good idea to group them by topic. The mediator can do this by linking suggestions which seem to belong together, or by colour-coding them. It is the mediator who controls the pen, but it is the parties who help and must accept the suggestions. It is important for the parties to have a chance to comment on the suggestions and on the mediator's proposals for grouping them. The mediator may need a little time to gather their thoughts, so it may be best to take a short break between the brainstorming stage and this stage. It may also be best to discard suggestions which are clearly not acceptable. However, the mediator should not do this on their own initiative; so as not to hurt the feelings of the person who made the suggestion, or give the impression of having too close an interest in the result of the mediation, this should be done at the proposal of one of the parties.

Point 3: By this stage of the mediation, the parties will already have invested time and effort which will be wasted if they cannot reach an acceptable agreement; this can be an incentive in itself. The parties must assess how well their interests will be accommodated by a suggestion or a combination of suggestions developed jointly.

Point 4: As stated, at this stage the parties must be helped to relate to the advantages and disadvantages of the various possible solutions, and to negotiate with each other about them so that both parties are as satisfied as possible. The creativity of the parties, their cooperativeness and the degree to which they seek a solution will be decisive for this process. The aim is to reach agreement, and this should be as concrete and operational as possible.

II. Aids for the mediator in the negotiating phase

It is important for the mediator to be aware of how a case can be tackled and to have a conscious aim in their choice of technique.

a. Start with the easiest – and change

As an overwhelming rule, negotiations will be easier if the mediator ensures that the parties start by negotiating on the issues which are easiest to agree on. This may be because their priorities differ so they can give and take and each gets what they value more highly while giving up something they value less, or it can be that the problem itself is not so knotty.

This bargaining process, known as 'log rolling', presumes that the true interests and needs of the parties have been made known, so it is possible to clarify their relative importance. The priorities of the parties will often differ and the mediator will be able to help them give up what they can do without and take what they need.[2]

Just as it is easiest for the parties to suggest solutions to problems on which they stand closest together, it is also advisable to negotiate on the issues on which it is easiest to agree. Once the parties have solved some problems, they will have established a joint platform from which it will be easier to tackle more complex problems.

b. Look at the agreement as a whole

As far as possible, the mediator should help the parties to look at the agreement as a whole, and not to negotiate endlessly about less important points. This will promote greater flexibility during the negotiations, with the possibility of revisiting parts of the agreement should it prove too difficult to reach overall agreement. This approach involves the risk that agreement which may already have been provisionally reached on some points may unravel, but if the mediator summarises how far the parties have progressed, and emphasises the agreement already achieved, this will make it more difficult for the parties put it all at risk. This flexibility would not exist if every point were definitively agreed.

2. See Moore, p. 253.

c. Distinguish between the person and the argument

Although the mediation is in its later stages, the parties may still be personally antagonistic towards each other. This has a negative effect on willingness to negotiate, so the mediator must continue to help the parties focus on the issues and not on the person of the other party.

d. Summarising, breaks, focus on the future

If the parties get bogged down, then as well as summarising the progress made, it can be a good idea to take a break. The parties may need time to reflect on the advantages or disadvantages on their own, call a friend, lawyer or colleague etc. When the mediator suggests taking a break, they can leave the parties free to use the time as they will, or give them a 'working break', perhaps asking them to look into the tax effect of making some payment, or considering which of their interests is most important or which they may be most willing to give up.

Even though mediation is primarily forward looking and it is not its job to decide who is right and who is wrong, and even though the parties may have accepted this from the start, there is nevertheless a risk that even at this late stage, they will try to start a new discussion about what happened in the past. The past is obviously relevant for understanding why the parties come to mediation, but this understanding should already have been established by this stage. The mediator should try to get the parties to focus on how the parties want to shape the future.

e. Help the parties consider the best alternative

For the parties to be satisfied with an agreement they must be able to get a better result by mediation than they could by any other means. The mediator must therefore help the parties consider what the best alternative would be to an agreement obtained by mediation.[3] It is not enough merely to consider some specific pecuniary amount in this assess-

3. See BATNA (Best Alternative to a Negotiated Agreement) and WATNA (Worst Alternative to a Negotiated Agreement) in Chapter 7.

ment; there can be many other relevant factors which have a bearing on the satisfaction of the parties such as timing, the stress of possible litigation, or destroying a good relationship. For example, one should not discount the satisfaction of the parties from the feeling that they have conducted themselves properly or have been more generous than they originally intended. The parties should thus evaluate the costs in the broadest terms (personal as well as financial) when assessing a given outcome.

f. Reality testing

During the negotiations, the mediator must adopt the role of devil's advocate, putting all the questions they can think of to test whether an agreement the parties intend to make will be practical, legal and can be made to work.

In its final form, the agreement must be as concrete as possible; it must clearly state who shall do what, and when etc. With such reality testing it will become clear whether, for example, the parties are about to make an agreement which will impose obligations on someone who is not present at the meeting. Perhaps the parties to a conflict may agree that their manager should convene a meeting to tackle problems affecting the department. In such a case the mediator must step in and remind the parties that their agreement cannot impose obligations on others, though they can agree to act together to encourage the manager to do certain things.[4]

With reality testing the mediator asks questions but must refrain from giving the answers. The tone of voice used for the questions is important, so the parties do not regard the questions as threats. Responsibility both for the conflict and its solution is and remains that of the parties. If there is any question which the parties cannot answer themselves, perhaps because they do not have the technical or legal knowledge, the mediator should encourage the parties to seek information elsewhere.

4. See also Lin Adrian, p. 71.

Naturally, the mediator must not consciously encourage the parties to enter into an agreement which would be illegal. [Fortunately, in Danish private law there are few rules which are mandatory, i.e., which prohibit or require certain actions.] If the mediator is in doubt, they should ask the parties to take legal advice. The reader is also referred to Chapter 13 on ethics.

g. 'Point of despair'

The negotiating phase is both stressful and difficult. At this stage, when they have already made quite a lot of progress, the parties often feel unable to get over the final hurdles. Negotiations can reach deadlock and there is a risk that gains already made may be lost.

Even though, in principle, a mediator has no interest in whether a mediation succeeds, mediators are also people, and it gives them satisfaction when a mediation goes well. This means there is a risk that the mediator may want to move the process forward in order to get a result. There are good reasons why this stage is known as the 'point of despair'; some psychological mechanism seems to come into play so the parties often have to go through this phase before agreement can finally be reached. The mediator's knowledge of the process, including awareness of this phase, can help them resist the temptation to interfere or put pressure on the parties, and help the mediator to remain patient. Instead, the mediator should consider taking a break, summarising, reminding the parties of the BATNA (Best Alternative to a Negotiated Agreement) or WATNA (Worst Alternative to a Negotiated Agreement) etc.

Another effect of this is that the parties become so delighted at having obtained a result that they want to finish the mediation before an agreement has been properly worked through. The mediator must ensure that important considerations are not omitted, and that neither the parties nor the mediator succumb to the temptation to end their work before it is properly finished.

h. Moderating high expectations

Sometimes the parties are unwilling to accept that the mediation has reached the negotiating phase where not only can they make demands but must also make concessions in order to satisfy the other party. Their expectations may be too high and they may make unrealistic demands. The mediator must confront the party concerned with questions aimed at getting them to reflect on the basis for such demands, such as:

- If you were in the shoes of the other party, would you accept your own proposal?
- Do you think your suggestion is reasonable? And if so, why?
- Are you in a position to impose your demand?

If the party in question does not see any reason to moderate their demands on the basis of such questions, mediators should remind both the parties, and themselves, that an agreement by mediation is not always the best solution, and that even if mediation does not result in an agreement, at least it usually clarifies the situation for the parties. Whether these questions should be put in a joint meeting or in separate meetings depends on the actual situation.

i. Parties in deadlock

The parties may reach the point where neither of them will make a further move. The mediator can ask each, perhaps in separate meetings, whether they are willing to surrender apparent opportunities by insisting on their demands. If the parties say no to this, the mediator must assume that they do not want to risk the collapse of the mediation process, and they want to be more flexible, in spite of everything. The question of what is needed to satisfy the parties is replaced by the question of how little they are prepared to accept.

However, it is possible that there really is no scope for negotiation, and that the interests of the parties conflict in a way which does not allow for a mutually satisfactory solution. The best the mediator can do is to encourage the parties to think about their best or worst alternatives to a negotiated settlement (BATNA or WATNA). Here, the mediator ought to ask the parties, in joint or separate meetings, what possible procedural alternatives they have. The parties should be helped to consider factors such as time, costs (both personal and financial), the relations between the parties, the chances of succeeding in any litigation, the balance of power between them and so on. The aim is not to get the parties to agree by wielding threats, but to get them to look at the reality of their situation. For this reason, the reality testing should always be carried out in the form of asking questions and not by the mediator telling the parties how the mediator assesses the situation. If there is a need for more information before a party can answer various questions, the mediator must not be tempted to answer the questions, but encourage the party to investigate the issue themselves, possibly by discussing it with an expert before the next mediation meeting. A careful and realistic evaluation of the alternatives will often bring the parties back to the negotiating table with renewed determination to achieve a mutually satisfactory agreement.[5]

j. Single text procedure

If more than two parties are involved in a mediation, and if the parties have experience of drafting agreements, then as stated in Chapter xxx it is not unusual for either the mediator or one of the parties to prepare a draft agreement which can be the basis of negotiations. This can be circulated to the parties for suggestions for corrections or amendments. The draft then incorporates the suggested amendments, and is circulated again until the parties agree to a final wording. This process, known as the 'single text procedure', can save time and is used almost exclusively in connection with commercial mediations.[6]

5. See also Lax & Sibenius, 1985; and Moore, p. 278.
6. See Fisher & Ury, *Getting to Yes*; Gylling, 2000, p. 140; and Moore, p. 260.

k. Legal concerns

There is considerable debate among mediators about the role of legal concerns in mediation, and, if the mediator is a lawyer, whether they ought to advise the parties about the legal consequences of their agreement.[7]

The problem is probably best solved by always giving the parties the opportunity to discuss the draft agreement with others, including their legal advisers, before signing it. If the agreement contains matters which the mediator knows have legal consequences, then the parties should be positively encouraged to consult a lawyer. This applies whether or not the mediator is a lawyer; even if the mediator is a lawyer, they ought not to wear their 'lawyer's hat' during mediation and should refrain from making legal judgements. A lawyer-mediator who does not maintain this distinction between the two roles will risk losing the confidence of the parties in the long run. However, the mediator can draw attention to purely factual matters, whether legal or not, for example, that a separated spouse cannot prevent the other spouse who has parental authority over their joint child from moving. But the mediator must be careful and should at least refrain from making a direct evaluation of the parties' suggestions.

It is vitally important for the parties to be sufficiently aware of the law by which any agreement would be assessed. For example, if during mediation a woman accepts a smaller share of the marital property than she would have got if the rules on the division of property were followed, it is presumably right that she should know this, so she can assess whether the agreement contains sufficient other advantages for her, and can decide whether the mediation agreement is still best for her. Regardless of whether the mediator is a lawyer or not, they should guard against the possibility of the parties subsequently getting information about their legal rights which could make them regret having made the mediation agreement. In such situations, the mediator should encourage the parties to

7. See Hans Boserup, p. 65.

consult a lawyer (or other professional expert) and get their comments on the draft agreement, so the parties will be better qualified to judge whether they want to enter into the mediation agreement. The agreement will unquestionably be more satisfactory and enduring if, in spite of knowing that it would presumably be possible, for example, to obtain greater financial benefits via litigation, a party nevertheless prefers a mediation agreement for other reasons, such as maintaining good relations. Apart from consideration for the interests of the parties, a mediator who is legally qualified can risk being liable to pay damages for giving bad advice.[8]

Stage 5: Negotiating the agreement

If there are a lot of suggestions, group the ideas by topic – with the agreement of the parties Help the parties to look at the proposals in relation to the interests and needs revealed Review and clarify the proposals The parties assess the proposals – often starting where there is the greatest agreement Create an atmosphere of give and take Summarise along the way Subject proposals which are adopted to a test of reality Encourage the parties to consult a lawyer or other professional expert, if appropriate.

8. As for the professional liability for mediators see Chapter 13.

CHAPTER 20

Stage 6: The agreement must be checked and approved

Evaluation of the reality and neutrality of the parties' proposals

Some mediators think it is acceptable for them to evaluate the parties' proposals for solutions. Others think it is even acceptable for mediators to make their own suggestions. It has been made clear that this is not the view of this author.

It is clear that it is unrealistic to expect that a mediator will never have an opinion about how best to resolve a dispute. One way for a mediator to deal with their view of a case without putting their neutrality at risk is to ask questions of one or both of the parties, giving them the opportunity to consider the consequences of a proposed solution. These questions would aim to get the parties to consider the realistic implementation of an agreement, both in relation to themselves and the outside world. For example, a mediator could ask the parties to assess their chances of success in litigation. In a dispute between neighbours about a right of way of one party over the land of the other, a party may be more willing to make an agreement if they realise that, in order to prove this right, they will have to call 40 local residents as witnesses.

When a mediator tests the reality of proposals, it is important that they ask truly open questions, so the party can consider the questions freely and perhaps have the opportunity to seek advice. Whether or not the mediator is a lawyer, they must resist the temptation to say what they think about a case, even if asked. They must merely ask questions and let the parties find the answers, if necessary by asking a lawyer outside the mediation. Questions must never appear to be threats. The difference between open questions and threats often lies in the tone of voice.

The purpose of such questions is solely to give the parties the possibility of a more extended degree of reflection on the viability and durability of the potential agreement from the perspective of their own reality, and not from the perspective of some general yardstick or the mediator's personal view of such a yardstick.

I. Formalising the agreement

Ensure that the agreement can be made effective

In the final stage of the mediation process, the agreement must be defined and formalised. The mediator should go through the agreement with the parties point by point, to ensure that any doubtful meanings are clarified. The aim at this stage is to ensure that the agreement can be made effective, and to reinforce the unity achieved by some formality.

As a rule of thumb, the agreement should be so clear and well-defined that merely by reading it through, a third party would be able to see who is to do what, when, where, how, and how much. An agreement between two colleagues to the effect that 'we should co-operate better in future' should define in more detail how this should work in practice. For example, it could be agreed to hold a meeting once a week to discuss matters of common interest. This should be defined in greater detail; perhaps that the meeting should be held every Monday morning between 9 and 10 o'clock in the meeting room. This avoids doubt about who should convene the meeting, in whose office it should be held etc. If it becomes clear that the agreement is too restrictive, because relations between the parties become more relaxed, there is nothing to prevent them jointly relaxing the terms of the agreement.

The parties themselves decide how to define the individual points in the agreement, but it is within the remit of the mediator to make the parties aware that it would be a good idea to agree on certain points. If the parties think this is unnecessary, that is a matter for them.

Information to outsiders

Regardless of whether the parties have discussed the question of confidentiality towards the outside world in the first stage of mediation, at this stage the mediator ought to discuss with the parties whether they will inform any outsiders about what they have agreed, and if so how. For example, if there have been difficulties working together, there will usually be others in the workplace who are aware of the conflict and aware that the parties have taken part in mediation, so the parties may need to decide what information will be given to colleagues and how it should be communicated. Openness about the agreement can help to get the outside world to back it up. For example, the parties in a neighbour dispute may want the local council to take certain steps. In a case between a victim and a perpetrator, openness about the agreement may encourage the hopes of the perpetrator that the court will take it into account and reduce the penalty imposed. The mediator must act as the leader of the negotiation proceedings, and help the parties to agree. There will seldom be grounds for informing colleagues about the details of the proceedings, and a statement that 'we have taken part in mediation and have agreed to strengthen our cooperation in future' will usually be enough. It can be a good idea to include this kind of thing as part of the final agreement.

The natural cycle of conflict

Even though the mediation is so nearly finished that one believes the end is in sight, new problems, not previously been touched on, can nevertheless turn up. The parties may again feel despair; they are tired and cannot wait to end the proceedings. This makes demands on the optimism of the mediator, who must show the parties how far they have come, how little remains to be dealt with, and encourage them to clear the last hurdle. The 'point of despair' is also relevant at this stage, and the mediator's awareness of the natural cycle of conflict with alternating exhaustion and stimulation can be reassuring for the parties and for the mediator.[1]

1. See Chapter 4 on the cycle of conflict.

Agreement for a limited period

Sometimes it can be difficult for the parties to reach agreement because they cannot envisage its consequences. It is important to consider, for example, whether any arrangement for making payment is realistic in relation to the finances of the party; whether an arrangement for access to children fits in with the children's schooling and the parents' work commitments; and whether an agreement between colleagues to keep each other informed can fit in with the daily pressures of work. All this is part of testing the reality of an agreement. Even though these things have been discussed, the parties can feel that, while the agreement may look good in theory, it may be different in practice. In such cases it may be a good idea to make the agreement for a limited period, for example 6 months, perhaps in connection with holding another meeting with the mediator to make an interim assessment of how things are going. Restricting the period of the agreement can give the parties the confidence to give the agreement a try, knowing that it will be possible to adjust the agreement on the basis of experience within the foreseeable future.

In many conflicts the parties have a continuing relationship with each other, such as neighbours, colleagues, former spouses, business relations etc. Even if the mediation leads to a solution in the specific conflict, it is probable that relations between the parties will be sensitive in the immediate future. The mediator should encourage the parties to consider how to prevent future conflicts between them. This may be by deciding that they will refer directly to each other if there is a problem, not involving other colleagues, neighbours or children in the dispute, or it may be by agreeing to make early contact with the mediator or some other third party for help.

If the parties have not already consulted an outside party on the content of the agreement, the time to do it is now. If the parties have professional advisers, whether a lawyer, technical specialist or some other adviser, it may be appropriate for the advisers to be present during the finalisation of the agreement, so that anything which is not clear can be dealt with on the spot. Their attendance will make it easier for the advisers to understand why the parties have reached the agreement they have.

II. Writing down the agreement

Declarations of intent

A mediation agreement is not necessarily enforceable by law. Some mediation agreements are primarily declarations of intent, describing the problem and how the parties think it best to solve it in general terms. In such cases the basis of the agreement is purely the parties' sense of moral obligation.[2] As expressed by Boserup & Humle: 'the glue which holds a mediation agreement together is the goodwill of the parties, and this is an alternative to legal obligations.'

To reinforce the parties' sense of moral obligation, the agreement should be written down.

Some parties may find this unnecessary, which is naturally their choice, but the mediator should encourage them to formalise even minor points in the agreement, partly because it has a positive effect to see the points of the agreement in writing, and partly because it shows that the parties take their tasks seriously. If the agreement is in writing, this also allows the mediation process to end with a signature and the handing over of the agreement; it also enables the parties to renew or revise the agreement if necessary.

Some mediators think it best to write down the agreement themselves. Others are wary of incurring any liability by writing down the agreement and leave this to the parties or their legal advisers.[3] Whichever the case, the agreement should be written in clear language and, as far as possible, without legal or other special terminology. If the mediator has used flip-charts during the brainstorming session and the first part of the negotiations, it is relatively easy to formulate the agreement so as to include transcripts of the flip-charts. The mediator can withdraw to write out a

2. See Hans Boserup & Susse Humle, p. 71.
3. See Boserup, op. cit., p. 74.

clean copy of the agreement while the parties take a break, or the mediator can give the notes to the parties or their lawyers for them to write out the agreement. If the agreement is not written down until after the meeting, it can be sent to the parties who can confirm their consent by telephone, and it can then be circulated for signature.

However, this approach deprives the parties of the symbolic act of signing the agreement together, so it is not the best option.

The parties ought also to be encouraged to consider whether they think there is a need to agree on a renegotiation clause. It is, of course, possible to include a clause in the agreement that in the event of breach of the agreement can be enforced by public authorities if the agreement is otherwise enforceable (e.g. in the case of the payment of monetary amounts), but this does not seem to be in harmony with the concept of mediation.

III. The good agreement

Even though the mediator does not determine the content of the agreement, they are, as far as possible, a guarantor that the agreement will satisfy the parties. As a guide for themselves, mediators ought to assess, and possibly check with the parties, whether the mediation process gives procedural, psychological and substantive satisfaction. The mediation process should, in itself, help achieve all three kinds of satisfaction.

Procedural satisfaction

Procedural satisfaction is generally achieved by the direct participation of the parties in the mediation process. If each party has been actively engaged, and if the mediator has ensured that each has had the opportunity to speak and has said what they will, has received attention and recognition, and has felt that they have been able to present their case without being put under pressure, then most parties will be satisfied. Even in mediations where there is no final agreement, it has been shown that the parties can be satisfied with the process itself.

Psychological satisfaction

Psychological satisfaction will usually be obtained if the parties have not only had a chance to put their cases, but also had an opportunity to express their anger, frustration, disappointment, unhappiness etc. Thus the mediation process is structured to give an opportunity for feelings to be expressed. By actively listening, the mediator can let the parties know that they have been heard and hopefully the parties will also have listened to and acknowledged each other and had a meaningful dialogue. In contrast to litigation procedure, for example, the mediation process should in itself help give psychological satisfaction, within certain limits. Psychological satisfaction can be obtained even if the mediation does not result in an agreement.

Substantial satisfaction

The agreement itself belongs to the parties, not to the mediator. Nevertheless, the mediator should actively work to get an agreement which is *substantively* satisfactory, not by dictating some specific content to the parties, but by helping them examine whether, as far as possible, what has previously been discussed and proposed is included in the agreement.[4]

The mediator can check the following questions:

- Does the agreement address the needs and interests of the parties as far as possible?
- Is the agreement based on a choice between proposals or a combination of several proposals for a solution?
- Is the agreement balanced, i.e., do both parties have equal responsibility for making the agreement work
- Does the agreement clearly state who shall do what?
- Can both parties fulfil their obligations under the agreement?
- Will the agreement resolve the conflict and can it hold in the long run?

If both parties have procedural, psychological and substantive satisfaction, it is highly likely that they will fulfil their obligations under the agreement.

4. See Kimberley Kovach, 2004, pp. 329-341.

Formal requirements for an agreement

Even though there are often no great formal requirements for an agreement, it ought to contain certain standard elements:

The agreement should start by stating the names of those involved in the mediation, and a summary of what the agreement is about. This can be used as a check to see that the agreement does not impose obligations on those who are not party to the mediation.

Next, the agreement should contain the parties' joint formulation of the problem, see Stage 3, and perhaps also the intentions of the parties for the solution. Then the various ingredients of the solution should be stated, and it is important that these are expressed positively.

IV. The conclusion of the mediation

When the agreement has been written down and each point discussed, perhaps with the parties' advisers, the parties should have a further opportunity to read through the agreement at leisure. The agreement should then be signed and copies made so both can have a copy of it. Under the principle of confidentiality, which often means that the mediator does not keep a record or notes, the mediator need not have a copy of the agreement, unless this is the wish of the parties with a view to some later resumption of the mediation.

Signing and exchange of the agreement

The signing and exchange of the agreement is an important moment and must not be hurried. It is here that the parties finally acknowledge their obligations and draw a line under their previous conflict. The closing of the mediation ought thus to be seen as symbolic of putting aside the dispute, and should be confirmed ritually in the form of a handshake, a glass of wine or whatever is most appropriate in the circumstances.

Some mediators prefer to allow the parties time to think before signing the agreement. It is also possible that the parties themselves may want to 'sleep on it' before giving final approval. In this case, another meeting should be arranged as soon as possible, so the agreement can be completed and the ritual performed.

Stage 6: The agreement is checked and approved

The agreement is checked. The agreement is written down. Solutions are described and defined. There may be time for reflection, possibly referring it to professional advisers. Consider what would happen if the parties do not comply with the agreement. Agree what should be said about the agreement to outsiders. The parties approve the agreement and sign it. Conclude with some ritual such as a handshake, or similar.

CHAPTER 21

After the meeting

I. Implementation

When mediation ends with an agreement, it is naturally intended that it should be implemented in practice. In principle, the parties themselves are responsible for complying with the agreement, and the mediator has no role in this.

However, the mediator may have agreed with the parties' employer to inform him if an agreement is made. The mediator must accordingly give notice of an agreement being made, while respecting the confidentiality which is the basis of the parties' trust in the mediator and the mediation process.

Follow-up with the parties

Sometimes agreements are made for a limited period, or an agreement can provide for some follow-up with the parties. The follow-up can either be in a meeting or by the mediator telephoning each of the parties, as the parties may wish.

A follow-up meeting can either be requested by the parties or suggested by the mediator. Agreeing to a follow-up meeting is not the same as limiting the duration of the agreement itself, though it has some similarities with this. However, it can be a comfort for the parties to know that there may be scope for adjusting the agreement, especially after a long conflict. Of course, if necessary the parties can always go back to the mediator and agree on new mediation proceedings, though this may be difficult. At the final mediation meeting it may be suitable to schedule a follow-up meeting for 2 to 3 months ahead. For example, if there are problems of co-operation between two work colleagues, or conflicts between parents over parental access, this period will give the parties enough time to try to make the agreement work, while giving them the reassurance that a difficult agreement need not continue indefinitely.

However, mediators should be careful not to find themselves acting as nannies for the parties; agreeing to have a later meeting should not be seen as a comfort zone by the parties. In each case the mediator must decide whether it is appropriate to take on this role. The mediator is not under any obligation to follow up on agreements made.

The agreement is conditional

The parties can also make the agreement conditional, for example, on the approval of their lawyers or their spouses. In this case, the agreement is valid and binding once the lawyers or spouses have given their approval. In most cases where the agreement is conditional, the mediator will suggest that the parties should confirm to the mediator that the outside parties approve the agreement. Otherwise it will be unsatisfactory for the mediator not to know whether an agreement they have been involved in is final or not. When the mediator is told that the agreement is final, their role is ended, unless it is agreed that they should communicate the acceptance between the parties. This can be done by telephone, or by sending the agreement with an annotation that the condition has been satisfied and that the agreement is thus final.

Happily, evaluation reports show that most mediation agreements are complied with voluntarily.[1] If the parties do not stick to an agreement, there are often no immediate sanctions, unless the parties have agreed to include sanctions as part of the agreement. However, agreements will often be unenforceable through the courts, as they only amount to declarations of intent, for example about how

1. See, for example the evaluation of the Norwegian Mediation and Reconciliation Service prepared by Statskonsult, *Agenda Utredning og Utvikling* 1996, p. 130, which states that 97% of all agreements are complied with. An evaluation of conflict mediation in the Copenhagen area made in 1999 (prepared by CASA with Lone Illum Christiansen and Claus Syberg Henriksen) shows that, in the period of the study, agreements were kept to in 73% of the cases. In 27% of cases the agreements had been revisited, but it was not possible to see from the study whether the cases were re-opened, or whether there were merely follow-up meetings.

the parties believe good neighbourliness or good cooperation at work should be reflected. To this it can be added that it does seem to be contrary to the nature of mediation, and its voluntariness, that a mediation agreement should have to be enforced by some external power.

The mediator may have offered the parties the possibility of referring back to them if need be. If so, the mediator must assess whether they are willing to take up the case again, or whether they think it would be pointless.

If mediators find that either one or both of the parties do not keep to the agreement, it is important that they do not take this personally and blame themselves for the agreement not being good enough, or for not having done something differently, etc. The mediator must always remember that it is the parties' conflict and it is their agreement. It is up to them to comply with the agreement, and they must take the consequences of not complying with it. If mediators become too involved, they risk losing their neutrality.

II. The mediator's own post-mediation conduct

Conflict resolution can be both stressful and emotionally draining, also for the mediator. No two mediations are the same, and there is no such thing as a perfect mediator. Even if, in principle, the mediator has no interest in the outcome of the mediation, mediators get personal satisfaction when the parties reach an agreement which clearly indicates that both are satisfied and have got more from the process than they might have hoped. Conversely, a mediator can have regrets and doubts about their abilities when a mediation fails to produce an agreement.

A professional supervision group

A mediator may need to discuss a completed mediation with a good colleague, both so as to order their thoughts about it, and to give vent to frustration or exaltation. However experienced one is, it is always possible to learn something new. It is recommended that a mediator should make provisions for this by joining a professional supervision group which meets regularly.

CHAPTER 22

The parties do not keep to the agreement

When the parties make an agreement, they must decide what they should do if either or both of them do not keep to the agreement.

Conditions for the performance of the agreement

Unless lawyers are involved in drafting the agreement, as representatives of the parties, as consultants or as the mediator, the conditions for the performance of the agreement will seldom be a matter to which the parties pay much attention. The parties will often be happy just to have reached agreement, and will not be inclined to refer to, or even think of, the possibility that the agreement may not be kept to. It will normally be the job of the mediator to encourage the parties to consider this issue.

According to the theory, parties who take part in making an agreement should have such a sense of ownership of it that they will largely comply with it voluntarily – the idea being that the best guarantee of compliance with the agreement is the goodwill of the parties.[1] This is confirmed by American studies.[2] Nevertheless, it can be a good idea for the agreement to include provisions on what should happen if the parties are unable to keep to it, especially if it is to operate over a longer period. Apart from the response to a breach of the agreement, the parties could also discuss what they would consider to be a significant breach of the agreement. However, this can be a sensitive area, as focus-

1. See Hans Boserup, *Mediationsprocessen*, p. 75.
2. Janice A. Roehl & Royer F. Cook, 'Mediation in Interpersonal Disputes: Effectiveness and Limitations', in Kenneth Kressel & Dean G. Pruitt (eds.), *Mediation Research*, San Francisco, 1989, pp. 43-45.

sing on potential difficulties with the agreement can undermine the goodwill between the parties, and put at risk the success of the mediation process before it is finalised. It is for the mediators to decide whether to introduce this issue at the end of the mediation.

Oral agreements are valid in Danish law

As a rule, oral agreements are valid in Danish law, as is the case in many other countries. If the parties decide not to put their agreement in writing, it cannot be assumed that the agreement is less valid than it would have been. However, the problem with an oral agreement is that it can be difficult to prove afterwards what the content of the agreement is. Opinions and recollections can vary widely between the parties so it is almost always better to put the agreement in writing. It is up to each mediator to be aware of the legal status of oral agreements in their country.

A re-negotiation clause

Regardless of whether the agreement is oral or written, one way of making its implementation easier is to make it for a limited period, as discussed above. Before the expiry of the agreed period, the parties must agree to a new mediation meeting at which the agreement will be evaluated and perhaps amended in the light of experience. The chances of subsequent compliance with the agreement should thereby be increased. Another possibility is for the parties to agree expressly to resort to mediation again if a conflict arises. This can be done in the form of a re-negotiation clause, but it can also be written in everyday language. These measures can apply regardless of what the agreement is about – in other words, whether the parties have agreed to the payment of a sum of money, performance of some task, or if there is merely a declaration of intent by which the parties undertake to have weekly meetings etc.

The agreement can become enforceable

A third possibility is for the parties to agree that the agreement should be enforceable by a bailiff's order, which is a possibility in many EU Member States, even though it is in far from all Member States that this has yet been tried.[3]

3. For an overview of this, see CEDR: *The EU Mediation Atlas, Practice and Regulations*, UK, 2004.

However, mediation agreements do not often contain such provisions, presumably because this could signal dissatisfaction with the result and perhaps the mediation process.

Since mediation is relatively new in many countries, many of the circumstances surrounding the legal status of mediation agreements, mediators etc. have still not been clarified. It is not possible, in a book such as this, to give a comprehensive overview of the legal situation in the different countries, so each mediator is encouraged to become acquainted with the specific circumstances that apply in their country. The conditions described here only apply to the situation in Denmark, but it is hoped that this description can stimulate others to investigate the legal situation in their own countries.

Reference is also made to the Centre for Effective Dispute Resolution's (CEDR) comparative tables concerning limitation and enforceability in court-annexed mediation.[4] However it should be noticed that the legal situation of mediation is developing rapidly in some countries. It is planned that, in the course of 2011 and 2012, further surveys will be published of the legal status of mediation in the various EU Member States, to which reference is made, when they are available.

In Denmark, if the parties want an agreement to be enforceable by a bailiff it must be put in writing. It must contain a provision on forcible execution which satisfies the provisions of § 478.1.4) of the Danish Law on civil procedure. According to this provision, it must be clear from the agreement that it can be enforced, who has entitlements and who has obligations, and that the agreement contains a claim which can be forcibly executed, so that, for example, if there is a claim for money, payment was due at the time of entering into the agreement. This means that claims for specific performance or mere declarations of intent cannot be enforced by a bailiff.

Finally, in Denmark the parties can decide that the agreement is to be treated as a judicial settlement, i.e., that

4. CEDR 2004, op. cit.

it shall be entered in a court register of decisions. This possibility exists under § 478.1.2) of the Danish Law on civil procedure when mediation takes place within the administration of the court, i.e., when a writ has been issued. One can assume that most of the agreements entered into in future in connection with court-based mediation will have the character of a judicial settlement[5]. In contrast to a non-judicial mediation agreement (or in contrast to a mediation agreement which has an enforcement clause but is not entered in a court register), a judicial settlement can be enforced, even if the claim was not outstanding at the time of entering into the agreement. However, mere declarations of intent will not be enforceable, even if they are entered in a court register. But a bailiff can, for example, enforce an agreement for parental access to children if the parties have chosen to have their agreement be treated as a contact order, and if it is clear from the agreement what the claim is and who is covered by it. Obviously, a contact order enforced by a bailiff has entirely lost the character of a mediation agreement and the voluntariness which is the primary element of mediation.

In Denmark a non-judicial settlement can also be entered in the court register and thus achieve the status of a judicial settlement, see § 270.1 of the Danish Law on civil procedure, and can therefore also be enforced, even if, for example, a claim for money is not yet due.

5. Refer to Postscript for an overview of mediation in the Nordic countries.

CHAPTER 23

Problematic mediations

Some mediations do not go as smoothly as the parties and the mediator would like. Sometimes difficulties are encountered along the way which can make the participants lose heart. Occasionally a mediation has to end without a result, with no agreement and with the parties seeming to have learnt nothing. The frustrations generated by failed mediations can be considerable for the parties, for their advisers if they have them, and for the mediator. The aim of this chapter is to make the mediator mentally prepared to spot difficult situations in good time, and pass on some tips which can help prevent such difficulties turning into greater frustration.[1]

I. Characteristics of mediations which do not result in agreement

Typical characteristics of mediations which end without agreement

In the evaluations of the Norwegian judicial mediation experiment, there was reference to the typical characteristics of mediations which end without agreement. However, it is probably best not to draw too firm conclusions from the research, as one can assume that parties, advisers and me-

1. This chapter draws on research into judicial mediation in Norway undertaken by the sociologist Roald Knoff, published under the title, *Raskere? Billigere? Vennligere?*, Rapport fra Justisdepartementet 2000, Supplement to NOU 2001:32; it is also based on Anne Austbø & Geir Engebretsen's book *Mekling i Rettskonflikter, Rettsmekling, mekling ved advokater og mekling i forliksrådene og konfliktrådene*, Oslo 2003; and Lin Adrian's book *Konfliktløsning ved Mediation*, Copenhagen 2001; as well as the author's own experience.

diators view a mediation process which results in an agreement in a more positive light than a mediation process which does not have a positive outcome. Also, some of the characteristics will presumably have greater weight in judicial mediation than in mediation outside the judicial system. Nevertheless, the following is an attempt to analyse the factors which contribute to mediations failing, regardless of the regime within which the mediation takes place.

a. Lack of motivation

Most mediators will have found that parties who do not themselves pay for the mediation can sometimes lack the necessary motivation to participate actively. This is regardless of whether the costs are paid by an employer, a public authority or by some other means, for example, a legal aid system, through social security, or by an insurance company or some other means.

Value for money

It is understandable that parties who decide to go in for mediation, even though this involves expense for themselves or someone they feel responsible to, have a relatively high motivation to get value for money. On the other hand, if the parties do not have this sense of responsibility, they lack the financial incentive to get involved. Their only motivation will be the investment of their personal feelings and their time, and this is not always enough. In psychotherapy, it is quite normal for clients whose therapy is paid for them to lack sufficient motivation. It seems that there are comparable problems in mediation. It appears from the Norwegian evaluations of judicial mediation that considerations such as procedural risks and the fear of incurring the costs of the case play only a very small role in mediations where the expenses are largely covered by insurance arrangements.

Other factors that can work against the mediation process include parties being so sure of their cases that they do not doubt that in the event of litigation they would win. For example, a lawyer may have recommended mediation, but the party can be so convinced they are in the right that they are disinclined to be flexible or to listen to their lawyer. Also, if a party is not concerned about the conflict becoming known to the public, as would be the case with litigation, the scope for mediation can be very restricted. Finally, the parties can be basically uninterested in whether relations with the other party are improved or maintained, and in such cases, very little co-operative spirit can be expected.

b. The absence of the real decision-maker

People acting as representatives

As a rule, it is only when mediation takes place between people acting as representatives, for example for a group of employees, or a company etc., that there can be a problem that the person concerned does not have authority to enter into a final agreement. This is naturally frustrating, as the mediation can have proceeded on the basis that both the parties present have full decision-making authority. It can be extremely annoying for the mediator and for the other party if it suddenly appears that a party does not have the necessary authority. As a mediator, one should immediately encourage the representative to contact those who do have sufficient authority, usually the managing director, to get approval for the proposed solution. However, that manager will not have been involved in the process and not have had insight into how the problem appears to the other side, nor will they have seen how both sides have shifted their positions during the proceedings. This means that when the representative proposes a solution which may be a long way from the starting point, the manager may have difficulty in understanding the reasons for it, and may refuse approval.

This problem ought not to arise often and it should be possible to avoid it, as the mediator ought always to start the proceedings by checking that those present have the authority to decide. If this is not the case, the mediator ought to consider whether the mediation should go ahead under the circumstances, perhaps discussing this in a joint meeting so that everyone knows the conditions of the mediation.

There can be a similar though less common problem if, for example, the mediation is between two neighbours, and it has been decided not to involve the spouses of the parties present, as it is decided to mediate between the two original disputants. In such cases there can be a need to discuss a proposed solution at home before agreeing. This question is connected with the considerations which lie behind the definition of a party to mediation, see Chapter 14.

c. Negative atmosphere

There is no doubt that it is vitally important for a successful mediation for there to be a positive atmosphere. The atmosphere is often a reflection of trust in the mediator having the necessary personal and professional qualities and their ability to show empathy and understanding for the situation of the parties. The atmosphere is also decisive for the ability of the parties to be active and creative in proposing solutions.

Some mediations are just impossible

Naturally, a negative atmosphere can be due to the inadequate efforts of the mediator, or they may just be having 'a bad day'. However, it is also important that mediators do not to take failed mediations personally, or take upon themselves the responsibility for failure. A mediator should always be aware that the conflict and its solution are the responsibility of the parties, and if it is not possible to motivate the parties to move from a view that the conflict is the sole responsibility of the other party, with only one pre-determined solution, then there is little the mediator can do. Some mediations are just impossible.

d. Unpopular agreements

The Norwegian research into judicial mediations shows that, while a mediation can result in an agreement, the parties can be highly dissatisfied with it. The reasons for this can lie at either end of a spectrum; on the one hand a party can be so convinced they are in the right that an agreement which is a compromise is seen as unjust, as the result of horse-trading, because the mediator was biased or the case was taken over by the lawyers, so the agreement was out of the party's hands. At the other end of the spectrum there may be dissatisfaction because the party needed more than clarification of the elements of the case, and expected more openness and a greater opportunity to speak with the other party than the process allowed.

The way to avoid these difficulties is for the mediator to be highly aware of the communication, and always to remember that the parties are responsible for the agreement. It is not enough for the mediator to leave responsibility for information and drawing the parties into the process to lawyers or other advisers. As a specialist in mediation, it is the responsibility of the mediator to manage the process and to ensure that the parties are the principal actors throughout the proceedings. It is probable that the risk of pitfalls of this kind is greatest when the mediator feels pressure from the outside world, for example from professional colleagues or supervisory authorities, to appear effective.

II. Tips for tackling difficult situations

A party does not turn up to a meeting

Sometimes, without warning, a party does not turn up to a meeting; this is more likely when the party is not him or herself responsible for paying for the mediation. Since most people coming to a mediation meeting will be a bit tense, this non-attendance will understandably cause a lot of frustration for the other party, who has come to the meeting prepared for mediation.

As soon as it is apparent that a party is not coming to the meeting, the mediator should telephone to the absentee, if possible. There can be valid reasons for the absence: illness, a traffic accident, etc. It is important for the mediator to find out the reason, to see if it is worth arranging a new meeting. Any new meeting should be agreed after discussing it with the party who is present, as it is the parties who decide whether to take part in a mediation.

The mediator should naturally welcome the party who does turn up, but should be careful not to start talking about the dispute which is the subject of mediation, even if the party wants to do so. The mediation should start as a joint meeting, and this rule should not be set aside and risk damaging the process.

If the meeting is void, the question of payment is something the individual mediator must decide. However, it is recommended that a claim for payment should be maintained unless there are exceptional circumstances, as otherwise there will be loss of respect for the mediation and possibly for the mediator.

One of the parties turns up with an adviser

Another problem which can arise with mediation is that one of the parties turns up with an adviser, without having agreed this beforehand. Since it is essential for both parties to agree who takes part in a mediation, the presence of advisers must be discussed with both parties. The problem can be settled in several ways: the adviser takes part in the meeting; a new meeting is arranged to which both parties bring advisers; the adviser waits outside the room while the mediation takes place; or in the last resort that the mediation is cancelled. In any case, the mediator as well as the other party must agree to the participation of the adviser in the meeting.

If it is accepted that advisers shall take part in the meeting, there can be a problem about the extent of their participation. Even though the mediator may have discussed the roles of each participant prior to the meeting, an adviser may find it difficult to accept an unobtrusive role. If an adviser interrupts too much, the mediator may have to suggest taking a break and discreetly remind the adviser that it is the parties that have the leading roles. It will not usually be appropriate to give such a reminder in an open meeting. If the adviser finds it difficult to accept this role, it can be agreed that they should wait outside the meeting room during the proceedings. The art is to make use of the resource of advisers, so they feel their role is acknowledged, while not dispossessing the parties of their ownership of the mediation.

The parties are sceptical about the appropriateness of mediation

A mediator may sometimes find that the parties are sceptical about the appropriateness of mediation, or accuse the mediator of bias. According to the advice on how to tackle conflicts in Chapter 4 in such cases the mediator should be open to the concerns of the parties and listen to their objections. It is important for the mediator not to react by trying to defend either themselves or the process, as this may provoke further resistance. The mediator can remind the parties that participation in mediation is voluntary, that they can leave whenever they choose if they feel uncertain, and that it is quite usual to start with some reservations about the process, but that experience shows that most mediations result in agreements. Finally, the mediator can offer to retire from the case and find another mediator.

One of the parties gets up and leaves

It can be a rather unpleasant experience if, in the middle of the process, one of the parties suddenly gets up and leaves. Since mediation is voluntary, the mediator cannot prevent a party from breaking off discussions. If possible, the mediator should ask the party to sit down, either in a joint or a separate meeting, and explain briefly why they want to leave the mediation. Once they have been given space to express their opinions and feelings, such a party will often decide, after all, to continue with the mediation, but if not, the mediation should be stopped.

A mediation reaches a deadlock

Finally, there can be countless reasons why a mediation reaches a deadlock. The mediators' job is to ask themselves what will give the parties enough hope to continue the process.

Instruction in understanding conflicts

Even though for some mediators it can seem strange and 'off the agenda' so to speak, at this stage, if not before, it can be beneficial for the mediation process for the mediator to give the parties some instruction in understanding conflicts. For example, the mediator can suggest briefly describing to the parties the conflict ladder and the dimensions of a conflict[2]. It is often a relief for the parties to distance themselves a little from their own conflict, and see it in a wider perspective. Sometimes, knowing about conflicts in general helps the parties see that, despite its unique character, their own conflict has points of similarity with countless other conflicts, some of which have been resolved. It also helps each party to see their own part in the conflict and not just the other party's. This can help the motivation to resume work on the conflict.

2. See Chapter 4 on this.

Emphasise the responsibility of the parties for the conflict

In order to emphasise the responsibility of the parties for the conflict, the mediator can directly ask the parties how they think it would be best to proceed. The mediator can also suggest taking a break, which can give the parties and the mediator an opportunity to weigh up the situation. Perhaps the mediator can use the break to discuss the situation with a colleague, and obtain ideas and energy to carry the process forward. Finally, the mediator can take separate meetings with each of the parties, and with greater openness it may be possible for ideas to emerge as to how the mediation can move forward.

CHAPTER 24

Lawyers and other professional advisers in mediations

I. Clarification of roles

There can be good reasons why people other than the parties themselves should take part in a mediation. Quite often, in legally defined conflicts these people will be lawyers, but they can also be trade union officials, accountants, social workers, technical experts, therapists and suchlike. What is common for the involvement of all professional advisers is that their roles in the mediation must be made clear so that they, the parties and the mediator can act accordingly.

Expectation that the adviser can help the party

For the parties, the reason for the presence of an adviser in the mediation will usually be an expectation that the adviser can help the party. This can be because the adviser has special knowledge of some particular topic, or because they are an experienced negotiator, or the adviser may be sufficiently distanced from conflict to be able to avoid becoming emotionally involved in it. Whatever the case, the reason for the participation of advisers in the mediation will be an expectation that the party will feel stronger and more secure if the adviser takes part.

For the adviser, taking part in mediation may be a bit unusual, perhaps because the practice of mediation in some countries is still not so widespread, or because the adviser – at least in Scandinavia – may play a more subordinate role than the one they are used to. If the adviser is a lawyer, they must understand that they must prepare for the case differently than they would do for a court case. They should act more as an adviser than as one who fights a case on behalf of a client. Even in larger commercial cases it will often be the parties themselves who conduct the case and explain how the conflict appears from their point of view. If the case is complex, the lawyer's task will therefore consist of studying the case thoroughly, making a summary of the case in everyday language, and then to be present to support and advise the party during the mediation proceedings. However, there are those who believe that lawyers should not be present at the mediation meeting, but merely act behind the scenes as sparring partners and supporters for the parties during the breaks etc.

It is primarily when an adviser is a lawyer or a trade union official that there is the greatest risk that the adviser will take on an active role, and that both the party and the adviser will think that the adviser should do the talking.

It should be part of the task of a lawyer to explain the mediation process to the party, not least the court mediation process in which communication between the court and the parties is often via the parties' lawyers. Since mediation in some countries is still a relatively recent phenomenon, and not all lawyers have experience of it, the lawyer's information about mediation may not be so detailed, as yet. In any case, this is a rather unaccustomed role for most lawyers, who will need to find their feet. Just like most of those who are new to mediation, they need to learn that the best results are far from always defined within a framework of winners and losers, and they will need to impress this on their clients.

Establishing fruitful cooperation

From the mediator's point of view, the participation of advisers can either make the mediation easier or more complex. Experience suggests that in the worst cases, lawyers can be wholly destructive to the mediation process, while in the best cases they can be catalysts enabling a dispute to be settled which would otherwise appear to be insoluble. Establishing fruitful cooperation with the advisers is thus a high priority for the mediator.

Mediators can sometimes regard it as advantageous for the mediation process if advisers participate.

For example, in a case involving a male manager and two female colleagues, the female mediator encouraged the manager to bring with him a male adviser in order to prevent the manager feeling under unnecessarily pressure by virtue of being the only man taking part in the mediation. After initially rejecting the need for this, the manager nevertheless decided to bring a male adviser who unquestionably had a positive effect on the balance of the mediation process.

Prior to the mediation, the mediator should contact any advisers, to ensure that they know about the mediation process and are prepared to adopt the role which the mediator thinks appropriate. It is probably best for this contact to be made by telephone, as written material seldom gives the same level of understanding as a telephone conversation between mediator and adviser. Advisers will often have a less prominent role, as this will be most in accordance with the aims of the mediation and the basic idea that, since the parties 'own' the conflict they should also be responsible for its resolution. In the conversation with the advisers, the mediator must ensure that they are willing to play less prominent roles and that the parties are willing to participate actively in the mediation, even though their advisers are present. Even though judges do not normally talk about a case with the lawyers before the first hearing, in connection with the recently introduced court mediation Danish judges have, with great success, adopted the practice of telephoning to the lawyers who are to participate on the mediation in order to ensure that the lawyers understand the mediation process and accept that they must play a less prominent role in it.

However, there can be situations in which a party needs a larger measure of support during the mediation, and in such cases the mediator must naturally arrange to accommodate the adviser. If a party finds it difficult to participate actively in the mediation and needs a measure of support from an adviser, the mediator must consider whether mediation is in fact the right forum for dealing with the conflict.

Restate the roles of each of the participants

Even though, prior to the mediation, an adviser has accepted that they must play a less prominent role, the mediator should be alert to the fact that it can be difficult for an advisor to be present at a meeting without doing something. The role will be unfamiliar, and lawyers in particular will feel that they ought to do something to justify their attendance fee. If the adviser is a lawyer, they will have informed the party about the mediation process, but until lawyers themselves have more experience of mediations, the information given to the parties will probably not be detailed. It is therefore necessary for the mediator in the first joint meeting to restate the roles of each of the participants in the opening of the mediation. A legal adviser may be more relaxed if the party hears from the mediator's own mouth that the lawyer should play an unobtrusive role, and the mediator will have confirmed that each party is ready to participate actively in the mediation.

It can be a good idea for the mediator to ask the parties to speak first and afterwards to refer to the advisers to ask if they have anything to add. However, in commercial conflicts there is a tendency to allow a legal adviser to put the initial case. There is a risk that a lawyer's presentation of the case may seem like the opening phase of a court case; it will be detailed, focus on legal and technical questions, take a long time etc., and this is seldom good either for the process or the parties' perception that they are the leading players in the conflict. It is therefore better for the parties themselves to explain how they see things, quite possibly after taking the advice of their adviser or lawyer and bearing in mind that it is the other party, and not the mediator, they must convince. There will otherwise be a risk of the proceedings being too similar to arbitration proceedings, and thus not living up to the principles of mediation.

There is a particular problem for the mediator when the adviser's role is that of an interpreter. Ideally, an interpreter should be a neutral person, and the mediator should emphasise that the translation should be as accurate and precise as possible. Usually the mediator will not understand the language into which the proceedings are translated, and will not be able to judge the quality of the translation. In such a situation the mediator should be especially alert to tone of voice, mimicry and body language, which may be impossible to translate, but which are nevertheless important elements of communication.[1]

II. Conflicts of interest

Conflict of interest between the party and the adviser

When there is an adviser at a mediation, there is always a risk of there being a conflict of interest between the party and the adviser. It may be that the party would like to make an agreement, but the lawyer would like the case to go to court, either because they may earn a larger fee or because they would feel more sure of the law; or a trade union representative may regard an agreement made by the parties unacceptable, because it is contrary to the policy of the union. It is, of course, equally possible that a lawyer will encourage a party to make an agreement because they consider the case hopeless, while the client may obstinately insist on litigation.

Naturally, conflicts of interest are an extremely sensitive area. However, it is important that such conflicts of interest should be brought out into the open when the mediator becomes aware of them. In these situations it can therefore be appropriate for the mediator to propose a separate meeting, either with the party and their adviser together or separately, in which the conflicts of interest are clarified and future conduct discussed. Again, it must always be remembered that it is the parties' conflict and they should not only have control over it, but responsibility for how it is resolved. In the final analysis, it is the parties who have to live with the consequences. The task of the mediator is therefore to help the parties to subject their attitudes and decisions to a reality test, and if necessary to ensure that the influence of the advisers is subordinated to the parties' own opinions.

1. See also Kimberley Kovach, 2004, pp. 55 and 167.

III. 'Professional brotherhood'

The mediator should acknowledge the skills of the advisers, and be ready to make use of them in the course of the mediation. For example, when the time comes, a mediator can encourage the lawyers to cooperate in writing down the agreement of the parties. However, there is a risk that the agreement may be formulated in more legalistic terminology than is intended by the parties, so it may not always be an advantage.[2]

'Professional brotherhood'

If the mediator makes a lot of use of the professional skills of advisers, the mediator should be aware of the risk that the parties may feel there is some sort of 'professional brotherhood' between the mediator and the lawyers, and that they have been side-lined. As described in Chapter 22 this is an experience which has been emphasised by parties who have been dissatisfied with mediation.

2. In a recently completed PhD thesis on judicial mediation, in connection with which Lin Adrian interviewed parties about their understanding of the mediation agreements which they had themselves entered into, but which had been put into 'proper form' by lawyers, often the parties did not understand what the legal terms in their own agreements meant.

POSTSCRIPT

Mediation in the Nordic countries – past, present and future

While there may be differences between the individual countries, today in the Nordic region it is possible to find mediation in civil conflicts – both in connection with and independently from the judicial system, in conflicts between criminals and their victims, in family conflicts, school conflicts, workplace conflicts, and neighbourhood conflicts. Nordic countries have also acted as mediators in various international conflicts.

Today, both its historical roots and its various links with the judicial system prompt one to look afresh at conflict mediation with both positive and critical eyes. In a Danish Regulation of 10 July 1795 (Fr. 1795) a general rule was adopted that 'all civil cases in general' should be subject to mediation. For this purpose special conciliation commissioners were appointed to carry out the mediation.

These conciliation commissioners were appointed first in Denmark, and then in Norway and Iceland, but they were never appointed in Sweden or Finland.

The ideas that were current at the time of the French Revolution, about the state and its citizens, were the inspiration for the Danish legislation of the 1790s, including Fr. 1795.[1] Central elements of the reforms of the 1790s were considerations for the security of citizens and the demand

1. Ditlev Tamm, 'Den danske "Constitution" og den franske revolution', *UfR* 1989B, pp. 449-460.

for justice, which were largely based on the principles expressed in the French Declaration of the Rights of Man.

Fr. 1795 was aimed at either avoiding judicial proceedings, or – where they could not be avoided – ensuring their rapid processing. In the preamble to Fr. 1795, it was stated that the king wished to see unnecessary and costly litigation between subjects prevented, and the arrangements for conciliation were to be put into operation immediately. The main motive for the creation of this new institution was that the handling of civil cases had become a great burden for the lower courts. Therefore one category of proceeding was to be removed from the regular judicial processes, to be decided instead by local commissioners.

Apart from considerations of cost and effectiveness, the state also had an interest in having satisfied and contented citizens. The reason for there being so much litigation was laid at the door of incompetent lawyers who misled their clients into going to court.

Altogether, Fr. 1795 made a strong appeal to the subjects' goodwill and understanding, and it fitted in nicely with the fact that the king did not want to grant litigants *beneficium paupertatis* or *beneficium gratuiti*[2] for litigation before he had been assured of the claimants' readiness to reach a conciliated solution through negotiation. The same thinking was followed in the fees paid to the commissioners; they were to receive no fee if they were unsuccessful in achieving conciliation in a case.

At the same time, it was a fundamental idea of those who were behind the establishment of the conciliation commissioners that a party should not be forced to attend conciliation negotiations, so that throughout, the conciliation should be based on voluntariness.[3]

2. *Beneficium paupertatis* and *beneficium gratuiti* are kinds of legal aid, referring to either the indigence of the party or the nature of the case as a determinant for granting aid.
3. The draft for the regulation on the conciliation commissioners was prepared by Christian Colbjørnsen, who occupied a central position at court in the years 1788-1804, holding the office of Procurator General, the official who drew up proposals for new laws and

The aim was the establishment of peace between citizens, meaning peace throughout society and not just the settlement of individual disputes. The institution of the conciliation commissioners was part of a paternalistic and even authoritarian care for individual citizens.[4] This Danish arrangement was distinguished from the arrangements in other countries (England and France) by placing conciliation negotiations with a body which was entirely outside the court system. Another feature of the conciliation authority was that it was devolved to a non-legal body that was sometimes entirely without legal knowledge. Instead, priority was given to local knowledge and the ability of lay people to solve conflicts, as well as the right of the parties to have some influence over their own conflicts.

Throughout the 1800s the conciliation commissioners influenced local society in Denmark, Iceland Norway, and they were important in promoting the democratic handling of problems. The commissioners primarily dealt with civil cases, but the boundaries between civil cases, and cases on defamation, debt, marriage and violence were not clear cut. The principle of using lay people prevailed in the commissions; lawyers were denied access to mediation, both as mediators and as representatives of the parties. In Norway, lawyers were not even allowed near the place where mediation was taking place. To be a mediator was a civil duty, unpaid, though there might be some payment if the mediation was successful. The parties had a duty to attend (but not to agree on a settlement), and mediation took place behind closed doors. The aim was a peaceful solution, and not necessarily a solution in accordance with the prevailing law.

The work of the conciliation commissioners developed differently in Denmark, Iceland and Norway. In Denmark they kept strictly to mediation and at no time were the commissioners given judicial authority. Mediation in Denmark was pushed more and more towards the legal

who was in general the government's legal adviser. See Ditlev Tamm op.cit.

regime as lawyers, in particular, questioned the commissioners' lack of legal skills. The background to the proposal for the abolition of the system of conciliation commissioners which was put forward in 1899 was that, among other things, it was found that the conduct of mediation behind closed doors, where mediators put persuasive pressure on the parties, and the prohibition of the presentation of evidence were out of date and in conflict with the principle of openness which should be associated with the exercise of judicial authority. Slowly but surely there was a movement away from paternalism, both between the state and the citizen and between citizens, and towards a more rights-oriented treatment of civil disputes. In 1932 compulsory mediation was done away with, and in 1952 the institution of the conciliation commissioners was abolished at the same time as conciliation in civil cases was finally brought under the courts as part of a wider reform of civil litigation. It was not expected that there would be any cost savings from abolishing the conciliation commissioners and referring all conciliation to the courts. The main reason for this lay in the view that there would be better qualified and more effective handling of disputes by courts using expert legal knowledge.

In Iceland the number of cases increased after the Second World War, but the conciliation commissioners were abolished in 1981 and conciliation was transferred to an officer of the district court. Since then the number of conciliation cases has fallen to almost nothing.

In Norway, conciliation boards still exist but in a different form, as they were given judicial authority in cases involving debt in 1869, and in 1915 they were given general judicial authority. Conciliators are no longer chosen by the people but are appointed by local government authorities and today conciliators are placed together with police authorities. The Norwegian conciliation boards are a strange mixture of mediator and court; they are not generally regarded as being part of the modern mediation movement and today the future of the institution is uncertain.

Today, in the whole of the Nordic region (i.e., Denmark, Finland, Iceland, Norway and Sweden) there are arrangements for instituting meetings between criminals and victims in minor criminal cases. The arrangements differ a little in detail, so that in Denmark a meeting between a criminal and a victim is a supplement to criminal proceedings, whereas in Norway it is an alternative. In all countries such a meeting is voluntary, and so it can only take place if both the criminal and the victim are interested in meeting.

As for civil cases, in Denmark, Finland and Norway there is a possibility of court mediation if the parties so wish. Here too the arrangements are not identical, but in these three countries judges act as mediators. What is peculiar to Denmark is that advocates can be mediators on an equal footing with judges in court-appointed mediation, and are publicly financed in carrying out such tasks. In Iceland and Sweden, discussions about the introduction of court-appointed mediation are ongoing, but such a system has not yet been put in place.

As for mediation in cases involving families, this has been established in all the Nordic countries, though here too with minor differences. For example, family mediation in Denmark is always voluntary whereas in Norway it is compulsory when there are children in the family.

The extent of training differs widely in the Nordic countries where there is court-appointed mediation. For example, in Denmark training has had a high priority from the start; if a judge or advocate wants to be a court-appointed mediator there is a requirement for seven days intensive training with subsequent supervision at least once per year. In Norway all judges have a right to act as mediators, without prior training. There is obviously a high risk that mediation activity that is conducted by a judge who does not have training in mediation will appear to be like the ordinary administration of the law, merely behind closed doors, with the possibility of separate meetings, and without the right of appeal.

Conflict as Property

It is worth learning the lessons of the experience of the conciliation commissioners. Despite the starting point of there being respect for the common sense of the layman, over a relatively short period there was increasing professionalisation and gradual channelling into the legal system, with the consequent disempowerment of individual citizens' ability to solve their conflicts. This is a warning, as the Norwegian sociologist and criminologist Nils Christie has persuasively written in his article 'Conflict as Property', where he describes how experts in modern society 'steal' conflicts from the people. This is highly topical in connection with modern mediation.

Mediators are experts on the process of mediation, but not on the substantive matters in a dispute. This means that the task of the mediator is to help the parties gain sufficient insight so they can make better qualified decisions, but not to provide them with substantive knowledge. Mediation gives the parties the possibility of addressing questions they have not previously thought about, and getting new information and insights, whether about themselves, the other party's situation, background etc., or information given by an expert who is consulted. But a solution can only be found if each party balances their own needs against the needs of the other. Responsibility for the outcome of the conflict rests on the parties themselves, and they must take account of their responsibilities towards others and of their own needs.

Sometimes, the challenge for the mediator is to avoid being persuaded to depart from this position by parties who want to abdicate their responsibilities, appeal to the mediator's authority and ask them to propose a solution, or express an opinion on the strengths and weaknesses of the case. Mediators must avoid deceiving themselves into thinking they know better. This temptation, to which all can succumb, must be held in check by education and continuing supervision.

But mediator education is a two-edged sword. The key features of mediation are the mediator's leadership qualities, combined with attentiveness and empathy. But professional methods and the precedents from a growing number of previous cases can mean that mediators become case-oriented advisers. There is probably a natural limit to how busy mediators can be before they become 'expert mediators' with their core values becoming diluted under the pressure of lack of time and resources.

The mediation which was established in the Nordic countries as a result of the Regulation on conciliation commissioners in 1795 was primarily intended to act as an alternative to the courts. To start with, the conciliation commissioners functioned well, but they were gradually absorbed by the judicial system until they vanished or lost their purpose in the course of the 1900s. After some years the need arose again for an alternative to the courts, and a Law on arbitration was adopted (in Denmark in 1972), according to which decisions made by arbitrators chosen by the parties should not be overturned by the courts.

The idea was that arbitration should be less formal, cheaper and quicker than the courts. And so it was to start with, but today we seldom consider arbitration to be a proper alternative to the courts, as arbitration is often neither quicker, cheaper nor less formal than the courts. The decisions are often of a purely legal character, so that today the greatest benefit of arbitration is that it can take place behind closed doors, allowing the parties to air conflicts or commercial secrets away from the openness to public scrutiny which is required by the courts.

After this, a need arose for an alternative to arbitration, as well as an alternative to the courts. This time the alternative is conflict mediation which has many similarities with the mediation that was undertaken by the conciliation commissioners from 1795. However, there is yet again a risk that conflict mediation can become distorted so as to become a matter for experts.

Annexes

Annex A

Commision of The European Communities
Brussels, 22.10.2004
COM(2004) 718 final
2004/0251 (COD)

Proposal for a
DIRECTIVE OF THE EUROPEAN PARLIAMENT AND OF THE COUNCIL
on certain aspects of mediation in civil and commercial matters {SEC(2004) 1314}
(presented by the Commission)

EXPLANATORY MEMORANDUM

1. Scope and objectives of the proposal

1.1. Objective

1.1.1.Ensuring better access to justice

Better access to justice is one of the key objectives of the EU's policy to establish an area of freedom, security and justice, where individuals and businesses should not be prevented or discouraged from exercising their rights by the incompatibility or complexity of legal and administrative systems in the Member States. The concept of access to justice should, in this context, include promoting access to adequate dispute resolution processes for individuals and business, and not just access to the judicial system.

The proposed directive contributes to this objective by facilitating access to dispute resolution through two types of provisions: first, provisions that aim at ensuring a sound relationship between mediation and judicial proceedings, by establishing minimum common rules in the Community on a number of key aspects of civil procedure. Secondly, by providing the necessary tools for the courts of the Member States to actively promote the use of mediation, without nevertheless making mediation compulsory or subject to specific sanctions.

Provisions touching the mediation process or the appointment or accreditation of mediators have been excluded from the proposed directive. Having regard to the reactions to the Green paper of 2002 and current developments at national level, it is not clear that legislation is the preferred policy option as regards this type of provision. While excluding regulatory measures concerning the mediation procedure itself from this proposal the Commission has instead sought to encourage self-regulatory initiatives and is seeking to continue to do so through the proposed directive also.

In the consultations on the preliminary draft of this proposal most respondents endorsed the overall approach of the draft concerning the issues covered as well as the issues excluded from it. Compared to the preliminary draft certain changes, mainly of a technical nature, have been made to specific provisions and are further explained in the annex.

1.1.2. A sound relationship between mediation and civil proceedings

What have been retained for this proposal are essentially matters which cannot be adequately addressed through market-based solutions. This concerns notably civil procedural rules which may impact on the use of mediation as well as on its effectiveness. The interaction between mediation and traditional civil proceedings can take place at several occasions, for example:

- The parties consider use of mediation immediately after the dispute has arisen, as an alternative to launching civil proceedings; if the parties do chose to use mediation and fail to reach a settlement agreement, civil proceedings are launched after the termination of the mediation;

- If a settlement agreement is reached through mediation, one of the parties may fail to honour the agreement, calling for civil proceedings to be launched anyway;
- The parties launch civil proceedings immediately after the dispute has arisen, without having (yet) considered the possibility of mediation.

At present the interaction between mediation and civil proceedings presents a number of uncertain elements, due to the absence of or discrepancies between national procedural laws, elements which make themselves known with particular force in situations involving cross-border elements. Even if mediation may be the most suitable form of dispute resolution in a given case the parties may therefore opt for traditional civil proceedings in view of these uncertainties. A stable and predictable legal framework should contribute to putting mediation on an equal footing with judicial proceedings where factors related to the specific dispute play the most significant role for the parties in determining their choice of dispute resolution method. Such a framework should also help to preserve the possibility for the parties to solve their dispute through judicial proceedings even if mediation is attempted.

1.1.3. Promoting the use of mediation

The value of increasing the use of mediation rests principally in the advantages of the dispute resolution mechanism itself: a quicker, simpler and more cost-efficient way to solve disputes, which allows for taking into account a wider range of interests of the parties, with a greater chance of reaching an agreement which will be voluntarily respected, and which preserves an amicable and sustainable relationship between them. The Commission believes that mediation holds an untapped potential as a dispute resolution method and as a means of providing access to justice for individuals and business.

The role of the Community in directly promoting mediation is however by necessity limited and the only concrete measure to promote mediation contained in the proposal is the obligation for Member States to allow courts to suggest mediation to the parties. Ensuring a sound relationship between mediation and judicial proceedings will however indirectly contribute to promoting mediation also.

The pursuit of the objectives of this proposal can not take in place in isolation without regard to the very provision of mediation services. The question of quality of mediation services must therefore be addressed together with, and as a function of, the other provisions of the proposed directive which must operate with a sufficient level of mutual trust between the Member States in cross-border situations.

1.1.4. The relationship with the organisation of the judicial systems of the Member States

One of the often quoted benefits of mediation is that its increased use can offload pressure on the court system, thereby reducing what are often long delays in case-handling and possibly allowing for savings of public resources. As the proposed directive seeks to promote the use of mediation, it could indeed have a positive impact in this sense. This is however not pursued as an independent objective, for several reasons. First, the organisation of the judicial system is the sole competence of the Member States. Secondly, and most importantly, mediation has a value in itself as a dispute resolution method, to which citizens and business should have easy access and which deserves to be promoted independently of its value in offloading pressure on the court system. The Commission does not see mediation as an alternative to court proceedings; it is rather one of several dispute resolution methods available in a modern society and which may be the most suited for some, but certainly not all, disputes. Moreover, it should be stressed that the availability of ADRs in general can not in any way detract from the obligation of Member States to maintain an effective and fair legal system that meets the requirements of the European Convention of Human Rights, which forms one of the central pillars of a democratic society.

1.1.5. Impact assessment

A preliminary impact assessment of this proposal was carried out in the context of the Commission's annual policy strategy for 2004. The proposal has not been selected for an extended impact assessment. The proposed directive aims at increasing the use of mediation in the EU, which will have beneficial economic effects by lowering transaction costs for individuals and business, through a quicker and more cost-efficient resolution of disputes. Mediation can also contribute to more sustainable economic and social trends in preserving the relationship between the parties after the dispute has been solved, in contrast to the often disruptive effects of solving a dispute through an adjudicatory process. The consultation process and other preparatory steps are described in the annex. In terms of alternative policy options the proposed directive contains mainly rules on civil procedure, and the results can not be achieved using another policy instrument.

1.2. Legal basis

The objective and content of this proposed directive fall squarely within the scope of Article 65 TEC since it concerns civil procedural rules, where the provision on quality and training in Article 4 is ancillary to the other provisions. The proposed directive is necessary for the proper functioning of the internal market in view of the need to ensure access to dispute resolution mechanisms for individuals and business exercising the four freedoms and in view of the need to ensure the freedom to provide and to receive mediation services.

As has been stressed in the description of the objectives of the proposal the need for Community action in this field stems from the need to ensure legal certainty throughout the duration of a dispute regardless of the presence of cross-border elements at one stage or another. To ensure a coherent legal framework it is therefore necessary to address key aspects of the whole chain of possible events that can follow after the dispute has arisen, having regard to any possible scenario (success/failure of the mediation, settlement agreement followed by both parties or not, etc).

In the context of ADR the impact of cross-border elements is potentially greater than when considering measures relating to civil proceedings in isolation, since it is necessary to have regard to relevant factors at the time of the mediation as well as at the time of any subsequent civil proceedings, including the circumstance that these factors may change in the meantime. For example, cross-border elements may come from the domicile or place of business of one or both of the parties, the place of the mediation, or the place of the competent court. The agreement to mediate may in itself be governed by a different law than that which governs the original legal or contractual relationship between the parties, and an ensuing settlement agreement may be governed by the law of yet another third country. The settlement agreement may have to be enforced in yet another Member State depending on, for example, the location of the debtor's assets at the time when enforcement is sought.

However, it would not be feasible to restrict the scope of the proposal so as to *only* aim at removing obstacles created by cross-border elements or to ease the resolution of only those disputes displaying a cross-border element, however defined.

In assessing the suitability of mediation as a dispute resolution method for a given dispute, cross-border elements make up for only one of several relevant circumstances to be taken into account. Other circumstances include the nature of the dispute and the merits of the case as well as factors related to costs, delay and prospects of success. Promoting mediation in relation to those disputes that display a cross-border element only would therefore be arbitrary and create a risk of discriminatory effects, since the courts would suggest mediation to some parties only depending on their place of residence. A restriction of this type will undoubtedly entail a substantial reduction in the practical impact of the proposed directive also. Making the applicability of the civil procedural rules contained in the proposed directive subject to the presence of cross-border elements would rather lead to increased legal uncertainty. Alternatively such a restriction in scope may leave the applicability of the directive in the hands of the parties, who could introduce cross-border elements through their choice of mediator or court for the dispute in order to benefit from the rules laid down by the directive.

The proposed directive will form an important part of the legal framework for mediation services in the Community, as concerns the freedom to provide services in another Member State as well as the freedom to receive services. A limitation in scope to cross-border situations would lead to the creation of two parallel legal regimes, possibly even different standards as concern the provision and receipt of mediation services, with a risk of discriminatory effects for users as well as providers of mediation services. Such effects run counter to the principles of the internal market as well as the efforts of the Community to simplify the regulatory framework for individuals and business.

In conclusion the Commission considers that introducing an explicit condition of cross-border implications would invalidate the objectives of the proposed directive and be counterproductive to the proper functioning of the internal market. The directive must therefore apply to all situations regardless of the presence of cross-border elements at the time of the mediation or at the time of the judicial proceedings.

1.3. Subsidiarity and proportionality

In view of the need for legal certainty and predictability in situations involving the relationship between mediation and civil proceedings in situations displaying a cross-border element and the need to ensure the proper functioning of the internal market for the provision of and receipt of mediation services the objectives of this proposal cannot be sufficiently accomplished by the Member States. Measures taken at Community level will be more effective compared to individual initiatives taken by each Member State, for reasons of coherence and reasons of providing certain basic uniform rules applicable in cross-border situations as well as in domestic cases.

The provisions of the proposal are strictly limited to what is necessary to reach the objectives. A directive has been chosen as the most appropriate instrument since the provisions are designed to achieve certain specific objectives while leaving the means for how to reach those objectives to Member States' discretion. The proposal also confines itself to issues which can only be solved through legislation while inversely issues where market-based solutions are feasible have been excluded from the scope.

2. Background to the proposal, consultation with interested parties, and comments on main provisions

The staff working paper annexed to this proposal provides further information on these issues.

Annex B

European Code of Conduct for Mediators

1. COMPETENCE AND APPOINTMENT OF MEDIATORS

1.1. Competence

Mediators shall be competent and knowledgeable in the process of mediation. Relevant factors shall include proper training and continuous updating of their education and practice in mediation skills, having regard to any relevant standards or accreditation schemes.

1.2. Appointment

The mediator will confer with the parties regarding suitable dates on which the mediation may take place. The mediator shall satisfy him/herself as to his/her background and competence to conduct the mediation before accepting the appointment and, upon request, disclose information concerning his/her background and experience to the parties.

1.3. Advertising/promotion of the mediator's services

Mediators may promote their practice, in a professional, truthful and dignified way.

2. INDEPENDENCE AND IMPARTIALITY

2.1. Independence and neutrality

The mediator must not act, or, having started to do so, continue to act, before having disclosed any circumstances that may, or may be seen to, affect his or her independence or conflict of interests. The duty to disclose is a continuing obligation throughout the process.

Such circumstances shall include:

- any personal or business relationship with one of the parties,
- any financial or other interest, direct or indirect, in the outcome of the mediation, or

- the mediator, or a member of his or her firm, having acted in any capacity other than mediator for one of the parties.

In such cases the mediator may only accept or continue the mediation provided that he/she is certain of being able to carry out the mediation with full independence and neutrality in order to guarantee full impartiality and that the parties explicitly consent.

2.2. Impartiality
The mediator shall at all times act, and endeavour to be seen to act, with impartiality towards the parties and be committed to serve all parties equally with respect to the process of mediation.

3. THE MEDIATION AGREEMENT, PROCESS, SETTLEMENT AND FEES

3.1. Procedure
The mediator shall satisfy himself/herself that the parties to the mediation understand the characteristics of the mediation process and the role of the mediator and the parties in it.

The mediator shall in particular ensure that prior to commencement of the mediation the parties have understood and expressly agreed the terms and conditions of the mediation agreement including in particular any applicable provisions relating to obligations of confidentiality on the mediator and on the parties.

The mediation agreement shall, upon request of the parties, be drawn up in writing.

The mediator shall conduct the proceedings in an appropriate manner, taking into account the circumstances of the case, including possible power imbalances and the rule of law, any wishes the parties may express and the need for a prompt settlement of the dispute. The parties shall be free to agree with the mediator, by reference to a set of rules or otherwise, on the manner in which the mediation is to be conducted.

The mediator, if he/she deems it useful, may hear the parties separately.

3.2. Fairness of the process
The mediator shall ensure that all parties have adequate opportunities to be involved in the process.

The mediator if appropriate shall inform the parties, and may terminate the mediation, if:

- a settlement is being reached that for the mediator appears unenforceable or illegal, having regard to the circumstances of the case and the competence of the mediator for making such an assessment, or
- the mediator considers that continuing the mediation is unlikely to result in a settlement.

3.3. The end of the process
The mediator shall take all appropriate measures to ensure that any understanding is reached by all parties through knowing and informed consent, and that all parties understand the terms of the agreement.

The parties may withdraw from the mediation at any time without giving any justification.

The mediator may, upon request of the parties and within the limits of his or her competence, inform the parties as to how they may formalise the agreement and as to the possibilities for making the agreement enforceable.

3.4. Fees
Where not already provided, the mediator must always supply the parties with complete information on the mode of remuneration which he intends to apply. He/she shall not accept a mediation before the principles of his/her remuneration have been accepted by all parties concerned.

4. CONFIDENTIALITY

The mediator shall keep confidential all information, arising out of or in connection with the mediation, including the fact that the mediation is to take place or has taken place, unless compelled by law or public policy grounds. Any information disclosed in confidence to mediators by one of the parties shall not be disclosed to the other parties without permission or unless compelled by law.

Annex C

New ethical rules for court-appointed mediators (in Denmark)

A working group of court-appointed mediators in Denmark has drawn up a set of ethical guidelines to apply to all advocates and judges who act as court-appointed mediators.

Definition of court-appointed mediation

Court-appointed mediation is a voluntary system for resolving conflicts in which, by means of a structured process, one or more neutral court-appointed mediators helps the parties themselves to find a solution to their conflict that is satisfactory for them. The process of court-appointed mediation is arranged in cooperation with the parties. The court-appointed mediator does not provide any legal advice and takes no decisions in connection with the mediation. What takes place in the course of the mediation remains confidential.

Court-appointed mediation takes place within the framework of Chapter 27 of the Law on the administration of justice. In addition to this, the following guidelines apply:

Court-appointed mediators

Court-appointed mediators are impartial and neutral persons who, in meetings with the parties, help the parties to find for themselves a satisfactory solution to their conflict.

The role of a court-appointed mediator is to lead the mediation process without deciding on the conflict. Court-appointed mediators support the parties in examining the conflict, including the interests and needs that lie behind the conflict. Court-appointed mediators also support the parties in working towards, developing and examining the parties' own proposals for a solution.

Court-appointed mediators have a duty to help ensure that the mediation is carried out within a reasonable time and is properly conducted.

It is a clear principle that court-appointed mediators should be reticent about making proposals for solutions or pointing out the strengths and weaknesses of the parties' arguments. Court-appointed mediators can do so, exceptionally, if the parties so request and if the mediator finds that it is appropriate and reasonable to do so. Even if a court-appointed mediator is a judge or advocate, in mediation he or she only acts as a court-appointed mediator.

If a court-appointed mediator is an advocate, the mediator may not advertise for his or her firm in connection with a mediation. This does not prevent the use of the firm's name in connection with correspondence or the use of the firm's facilities in connection with the mediation.

Court-appointed mediators must have undergone a relevant course of training as a mediator, such as the court-appointed mediator training of *Domstolsstyrelsen* (the Judicial Appointments Council) or the mediator training of *Advokatsamfundet* (the Danish Bar and Law Society). Court-appointed mediators must also take steps to keep their skills up-to-date.

Neutrality and impartiality

Court-appointed mediators must act neutrally, both in relation to the parties and in relation to the conflict. Among other things, this means that a court-appointed mediator must not favour one party more than the other.

Court-appointed mediators must inform the parties of any circumstances that might affect the neutrality of the mediator, even if the mediator does not believe that their neutrality is affected.

If, in the course of the process, a court-appointed mediator can no longer act neutrally, the mediator must inform the parties of this and withdraw from the mediation. The same applies if one of the parties believes that the mediator is not neutral. Court-appointed mediators must help the parties appoint another court-appointed mediator, if the parties so wish.

Voluntariness

Participation in court-appointed mediation is voluntary, and the mediator must ensure that the parties are informed of this. Any party may, at any time, break off the mediation.

Prior to the start of the mediation process, a court-appointed mediator must make sure that all participants in the mediation have received information about the process and consent to it. For this purpose the mediator may use a written agreement about the mediation, which the parties consent to before the start of the mediation. Such an agreement must be formulated in accordance with the terms of the Law on the administration of justice, and of these guidelines.

Duty of confidentiality

Court-appointed mediators have a duty of confidentiality with regard to all information that is produced in the course of the mediation; see Section 277 of the Law on the administration of justice.

In principle, court-appointed mediators do not have a duty to give evidence in any subsequent litigation proceedings; see Section 170 of the Law on the administration of justice.

If a court-appointed mediator holds separate meetings with the parties, he or she must agree with the parties whether what takes place in such separate meetings is to be kept confidential from the other party.

In addition, the rules in Section 277 of the Law on the administration of justice, on the duty of confidentiality and secrecy, apply to all parties and other persons who participate in a mediation process.

The participants in the process

The parties to the litigation participate in person in the court-appointed mediation process. These parties are the primary actors in mediation, also when the parties' advocates and/or advisers participate in the mediation.

If the parties are not identical with the parties to the conflict, the parties can involve in the mediation the other person or persons who have direct knowledge of the conflict.

The parties are entitled, at any time, to use advisers in connection with the mediation process.

Termination of the mediation process

At any point following the preliminary hearing of the parties, a court-appointed mediator may terminate the mediation, and must terminate the mediation if:

a. one of the parties so wishes; see point 4;
b. the court-appointed mediator judges that one of the parties is not capable of participating meaningfully, or is not able to take care of their own interests;
c. there is an imbalance of power between the parties which can have a negative effect on the mediation and it is not possible to correct for it;
d. the court-appointed mediator has knowledge of information which would make it unethical for them to continue the mediation;
e. the parties wish to enter into an agreement which would be criminal or otherwise be contrary to mandatory law;
f. it appears that the conflict is not suitable for court-based mediation;
g. it is judged that court-based mediation is no longer appropriate; or
h. the court-appointed mediator judges that, for other material reasons, it is inappropriate to continue the court-based mediation.

Annex D

Advisory Ethical Guidelines for the Danish Association for Mediation and Conflict Resolution adopted at the Association's annual general meeting on 30 March 2005.

Introduction

These Ethical Guidelines have been developed from a desire to create a set of ethical rules which all those who work professionally with mediation and conflict resolution, as well as organisations that offer mediation and conflict resolution, can work with as a minimum standard. The Guidelines are an expression of the professional aims of the Association. Everyone, members and non-members alike, is welcome to adopt these Guidelines and to make them the basis of their own practice.

Those mediators who are listed on the Association's website are obliged to follow these Guidelines.

'Mediation' and 'conflict resolution' are used synonymously in these Guidelines.

1. Definition of mediation

'Mediation' is a method by which conflicts can be resolved, in which one or more neutral third parties help conflicting parties to find their own way towards a satisfactory solution by using a structured process. The mediator takes no decisions about a case. Mediation is voluntary and confidential.

2. The mediator

The mediator's role is to lead the process, without deciding about the case and without taking the side of one or other of the parties. The mediator supports the parties in developing and examining their own proposals for a solution. When a person offers their services as a mediator, that person should act in the capacity of a mediator and not in the character of the profession which that person might otherwise practice.

In order to practice as a mediator, a person must have successfully completed a course of training in methods of conflict resolution, and must keep their professional skills up to date.

3. Neutrality

A mediator must maintain neutral conduct, both in relation to the parties and to the case. This means that a mediator must not favour one party over another, may not promote their own ideas for a solution, and may not have a personal interest in the outcome of the case.

A mediator must inform the parties of any circumstances which, in the view of the parties, could influence the mediator's neutrality, even if the mediator does not him or herself believe that their neutrality will be affected. The parties to a case should be informed about how the mediator has been introduced to the case, and about the mediator's organisational connections or employment.

If in the course of the proceedings the mediator is unable to maintain neutrality, he or she must inform the parties of this and withdraw from the case. If the parties so wish, the mediator should help them to find another mediator.

After the conclusion of the mediation, the mediator may not undertake to give individual advice to a party about a matter associated with the conflict dealt with in the mediation.

4. Voluntariness

The parties to a conflict participate in the mediation process voluntarily, and any party can withdraw from the process at any time.

5. Consent

Prior to the start of mediation, all the participants in the mediation process must be informed about the process and must consent to participate. As the process is voluntary from start to finish, this consent can be withdrawn at any stage. For young persons under the age of 18, the consent of those with parental authority over such persons is required, unless there are special rules on this in the area concerned.

6. Duty of confidentiality

Mediators have a duty of confidentiality. This duty of confidentiality covers both the initial contact and what happens during, between and after mediation meetings. If the parties agree, this duty of confidentiality can be relaxed in whole or in part.

If a mediator holds separate meetings with the parties, the mediator must agree with the party concerned whether what takes place in separate meetings shall be confidential or not.

In addition to this, the general rules of Danish law with regard to the duty of confidentiality, the duty to provide information, and the duty to act as a witness.

7. Payment

If the parties themselves pay for the mediation, the expenses shall be divided equally between them unless some other method of allocation is agreed.

There must be agreement about payment before the start of mediation.

The mediator's fee may not be made dependant on whether the conflict is resolved, nor may it be based on a percentage of the value of the result.

8. Participants in the process

The parties to a conflict participate in the process in person. If one of the parties wishes to be accompanied by one or more persons, the other party or other parties must consent to this. If agreement cannot be reached on this question, the mediation cannot be proceeded with. Agreements about the presence of accompanying persons must be made before the start of the meeting.

The parties are the primary actors in the mediation, even when they are accompanied.

9. External advice

The parties are free to seek advice before, during and after the mediation meeting.

The mediator can, at any time, encourage the parties to obtain relevant information with a view to improving the basis of a decision, if this is necessary to enable the parties to discuss the conflict on a qualified basis.

The mediator can encourage the parties to seek advice prior to entering into an agreement, if there is a real risk that the parties cannot themselves foresee the consequences of the agreement.

10. The agreement

An agreement between the parties can either be in writing or oral. The mediator can write the agreement down if the parties wish, but this can also be left to the parties themselves or to others.

Mediators shall ensure that the parties understand the content of the agreement they enter into.

The acceptance of an agreement can be made conditional on the approval of others, or upon the expiry of time for reflection.

11. Termination of mediation

The mediator shall terminate the mediation if

- the parties request it,
- the mediator judges that one of the parties is not able to participate meaningfully, or is unable to take care of their own interests,
- there is an imbalance of power between the parties which affects the mediation negatively and which cannot be redressed,
- it is felt that the mediation does not serve its stated purpose,
- the parties want to enter into an agreement which the mediator believes to be criminal, damaging to a third party, or serves the interests of one of the parties in a wholly unacceptable way,
- the conflict appears to be unsuitable for mediation, or
- for some other important reason, the mediator judges that it is inappropriate to continue with the mediation.

As far as possible, the mediator shall inform the parties why the mediation is terminated.

Litterature

Adrian, Lin, *Konfliktløsning ved Mediation (Conflict Resolution by Midation)*, Encore, Copenhagen 2001.

Adrian, Lin, *Mellem retssag og Rundbordssamtale. Retsmægling i teori og praksis (Between Mediation in Court and Round Table talk)*, unpublished Ph.D. thesis, Copenhagen 2011.

Allred, Keith G., *Anger and retaliation in Conflict, The Role of Attribution*, in The Handbook of Conflict Resolution, Morton Deutsch (ed.), Sam Fransisco 2000, s. 236-255.

Arendt, Hannah, *The Human Condition*, New York 1958.

Assefa, Hizkias, *Nairobi Peace Initiative, Renconciliation and Healing*, Nov. 1995.

Aubert, Vilhelm, *Løsning av konflikter i par og trekant (resolving conflicts in couples and triangles)*, Tidsskrift for Samfunnsforskning, s. 89-102 1961.

Aubert, Vilhelm, *Competition and Dissensus: Two Types of Conflict and of Conflict Resolution, The Journal of Conflict Resolution, Vol. VII no 1*, 1963.

Aubert, Vilhelm, *Rettens Sociale Funksjon (The social function of law), Oslo 1976.*

Aurbach, J., *Justice without Law, Resolving Disputes without Lawyers*, New York 1983.

Austbø, Anne and Engebretsen, Geir, *Mekling i Rettskonflikter, Rettsmekling, mekling ved advokater og mekling i forliksrådene og konfliktrådene*, Oslo 2003.

Azar, E. *Protracted International Conflicts: ten propositions*, in Azar and Burton: International Conflict Resolution: Theory and Practice, 1986.

Bagger, Tuk and Deleuran, Pia, *Retsmægling – om advokaten som bisidder og partsrepræsentant (Mediation in court - the lawyer as professional advisor and representative)* in Advokaten 82. årg. nr. 7/8.

Balvig, Flemming and Vestergaard, Jørn (ed.), »*Med lov* ...«, *Retsvidenskabelige betragtninger, festskrift til Vagn Greve*, Copenhagen 1998.

Barnard, C.I., *Functions and Pathology of Status Systems in Formal Organizations*, in Whyte (ed.) Industry and Society, New York 1946.

Bateson, Gregory, *Steps to an ecology of mind*, New York, 1972.

Bercovitch, Jacob, *Mediation in International Conflict, An overview of Theory, A review of Practice*, in Zartman and Rasmussen (ed), *Peacemaking in International Conflict*, 1997.

Berkowitz, L., *Aggression, It's Causes, Consequences and Contract*, New York 1993.

Berliner, Peter, *Konflitkløsning*, Copenhagen 1999.

Berliner, Peter, *Vold og Trusler på arbejdet (Violence and threats at the work place)*, Copenhagen 2000.

Bertelsen, Jes, *Et essay on frihed (An Essay about Freedom)*, Rosinante, 2010.

Birke, Richard and Teitz, Louise Ellen, *US Mediation in the Twenty-first Century, The Path that brought America to Uniform Laws and Mediation in Cyberspace*, in Alexander (ed.), Global Trends in Mediation, Köln, 2003.

Blechman, Frank, *Ethics and Field Building, the Chicken and the Egg*, in Conflict Resolution Quaterly, vol. 19, 2002.

Boraine, Alexander and Levy, Janet, *The Healing of a Nation*, in Justice in Transition, Cape Town, 1995.

Boserup, Hans and Humle, Susse, *Mediationsprocessen*, Copenhagen 2001.

Boserup, Hans, »*Advanced techniques and dilemmas in mediation, The issue of autonomy and social control in particular*«, www.mediator.dk.

Boulding, Kenneth, *Three Faces of Power*, Californien, 1989.

Braiker, H.B. and Kelley, H.H., *Conflict in the development of close relationships*, in Social exchange in developing relationships, ed. R.L. Burgess and T.L. Huston, New York, 1979.

Brown, H. and Marriott, A., *ADR Principles and Practice*, London 1993.

Buber, Martin, *I and Thou*, Touchstone 1996.

Burton, John W., *Conflict Human Needs Theory*, New York 1990.

Bush, Robert and Folger, Joseph (ed.) *Designing Mediation, Approaches to Training and Practice within a Transformative Framework*, Inst. for the Study of Conflict Transformation, Hofstra University School of Law, New York 2001.

Bush. Robert and Folger, Joseph, *The Promise of Mediation, Responding to Conflict Through Empowerment and Recognition*, San Francisco, 1994 and 2. ed. 2005.

Buzan, Barry, Wæver, Ole and Wilde, Jaap de, *Security: A new Framework for Analysis*, Boulder 1997.

Christiansen, Lone Illum and Henriksen, Claus Syberg, *Evaluering af konfliktmægling i statsamter* udført af CASA, Center for Alternativ Samfundsanalyse, april 1999, www.casa-analyse.dk.

Christie, Nils, *Conflict as Property*, The British Journal of Criminology (1) 1977, 1-15.

Clausen, Steen, *Kompendium 2000, Mægling gennem dialog (Mediation through dialogue)*, Center for Konfliktløsning, 2001.

Clausewitz, Carl von, *On War, 1831/1976,* trans.et ed. M. Howard, M. Paret and P. Paret, Princeton.
Coleman, Peter T., *Power and Conflict,* in Morton Deutsch, *The Handbook of Conflict Resolution,* San Francisco 2000.
Creighton, J., *Communications,* Tulsa, Oklahoma, 1972.
Curle, Adam, *Tools for Transformation,* Worcester 1990.
Curle, Adam, *Another Way, Positive Response to contemporary violence,* Oxford, 1995.
De Bono, Edward, *Lateral Thinking,* New York 1970.
De Bono, Edward, *Teaching Thinking,* New York 1976.
Deuntzer, J.H., *Om Forligsmægling i Civile Sager,* 3. oplag, Copenhagen 1898.
Deutsch, Morton, *The Handbook of Conflict Resolution,* San Francisco 2000.
Deutsch, Morton, *The Resolution of Conflict, Constructive and Destructive Processes,* New York 1973.
Diamond, Louise and John McDonald, *Multi-Track Diplomacy,* Connecticut 1996.
Dombernowsky, Lotte, *Lensbesidderen som amtmand,* Copenhagen 1983.
Doyle, M., *Advising on ADR, The Essential Guide to Appropriate Resolution, Advice Services Alliance,* 2000.
Druckman, Daniel, *Negotiating in the International Context* in Zartmann and Rasmussen (ed.) *Peacemaking in International Conflict,* Washington 1997/2001.
Druckman, David, *Negotiating in International Conflict,* in Zartmann e.u. *Peacemailing in International Conflict, Methods and Techniques,* Washington, 2001.
Dullum, Jane, *Konfliktrådene,* Institut for Kriminologi, University of Oslo, sept. 1996.
Dworkin, Joan, Jacob, Lynn and Scott, Elisabeth, *The Boundaries Between Mediation and Therapy,* Ethical Dilemmas, Mediation Quaterly vol. 9 no. 2, 1991.
Enderud, Harald, *Konfliktbeslutninger, I og II, Tre perspektiver på konfliktorganisering, Gylling* 1987.
Engebretsen, Geir, *Mekling som konfliktløsning, 6 år med rettsmekling ved norske domstole (Mediation as conflict resolution. 6 years with mediation in the Norwegian courts),* upubl. Nedre Romerike, oktober 2003.
Espersen, Ole, Harhoff, Frederik and Spiermann, Ole, *Folkeret (International Law),* Copenhagen 2002.
Evaluering af den norske konfliktrådsordning, udarbejdet af Statskonsult, Agenda Utredning og Utvikling 1996.
Falk, Bent, *Kærlighedens Pris (The price of love),* Frederiksberg. 2002.
Foucault, M., *Le Pouvoir, comment s'xerce-t-il?,* Chicago 1982.
Fisch-Thomsen, B., *Om ændring af de gældende Forligsregler i borgerlige Sager,* in Juristen 1948, s. 25.

Fisher, R. and W. Ury, *Få ja når du forhandler (Getting to Yes)*, Gylling 2000.

Fisher, R. and W. Ury, *Getting to Yes*, New York 1981.

Fisher, R., *Negotiating Power, Getting and Using Influence*, American Behavioral Scientist, Vol. 22. No. 2. Nov/Dec. 1983.

Fisher, Simon et.o., *Working With Conflict*, London 2000.

Fledelius, Karsten, *Forsoningens Hemmelighed (The secret of reconciliation)*, in *På vej til Grazz*, Copenhagen 1997, s. 29-33.

Foighel, Isi, Gammeltoft-Hansen, Hans and Zahle, Henrik (ed.) *Ret som teknik, kunst og videnskab (Law as technique, art and science)*, Copenhagen 1999.

Folger, Antes, *Tranforming Conflict Interactions in the Workplace*, Hofstra Labor and Employment Journal, vol. 18, no. 2, 2001.

Folger, Joseph, *Transformative Mediation, Fulfilling the Promise*, Institute for the Study of Conflict Transformation, inc., Hofstra University School of Law, NY 11549, 2000.

Folger.J, Scott P. and Stutman R., *Working through Conflict*, Allyn and Bacon 2009.

Follett, Mary Parker, *Power*, in Fox and Urwick (ed), *Dynamic Administration, The Collected Papers of Mary Parker Follett*, London 1973.

Fong, Larry, *Consultation in Mediation for Lawyers, Asking Questions of a Difference that make a Diferrence*, paper presented at Master i Konfliktmægling, University of Copenhagen, November 2003.

Fong, Larry, *Milan Mediation Model*, paper på Master i Konfliktmægling, University of Copenhagen 21-22, november 2003.

Friis-Hansen, J.V., *Nogle Bemærkninger om Forligskommissionerne uden for København*, UfR 1927B s. 110-111.

Galtung, John and Carl G. Jacobsen, *Searching for Peace, The Road to Transcend*, Virginia 2000.

Galtung, John, *Conflict Transformation by Peaceful Means*, www.transcend.org.

Galtung, Johan, *Cultural Violence* in Journal of Peace Research, Vol. 27. no. 3. 1990.

Galtung, Johan and Næss, Arne, *Gandhis politiske etik (The political ethics of Gandhi)*, Oslo 1995.

Gamborg, Helen, *Det usynlige i helbredelse, (The invisible in Healing)* Viborg 1991.

Gammelgaard, Judy, *Mellem mennesker – træk af indfølingens psykologi (Between humans – elements of the psychology of empathy)*, Copenhagen 2000.

Genn, Hazel, *Contemporary experience of mediation in England and Wales, report to the European Commission for the efficiency of justice (CEPEJ)*, september 2003.

Gifford, D., *Legal Negotiation, Theory and Application*, St. Paul, Minnesota 1989.

Gjellsvik, Øistein, *Konflikt, megling og legitimitet – en sociologisk undersøgelse av rettsmekling som alternativ domstolsbehandling i sivile tvister (Conflict, mediation and legitimity)*, Oslo 2000.

Glasl, Freedrich, *Konfliktmanagement – Ein Handbuch für Führungskräfte, Beratterinnen und Berater,* Stuttgart 1999.

Goldberg, Rachel M, *How our Worldview Shape our Practice,* in Conflict Resolution Quaterly, Vol 26, No4, p 409 et seq., 2009.

Goleman, Daniel, *Working with emotional intelligence,* Bantam 1998.

Goleman, Daniel, *Emotional Intelligence*, Bantam, 1995.

Gomard, B., *Civilprocessen*, 4. udg., Copenhagen 1994.

Gomard, B., *Civilprocessen*, 5. udg., Copenhagen 2000.

Gordon, T., *Leadership Effectiveness Training*, New York 1978.

Hagerup, G.F., *Forelæsning over den norske Civilproces I-II,* Kristiania 1895-99.

Hammarskjöld, Dag, *The International Civil Servant in Law and in Fact,* speech quoted in W.Foote, (ed), *The Servant of Peace, A Selection of the Speeches and Statements of Dag Hamamrskjöld,* London 1962.

Hammerich, Else and Vestergaard, Bjarne, *Mindfull Conflict Resolution*, Dharamsala, 2001.

Hammerich, El. and Frydensberg, K., *Konflikt og Kontakt (Conflict and Contact)*, Hovedland 2009.

Hansen, Karl Ole, *Nogle Tanker om Forligsmægling m.m.,* in Sagførerbladet 1947, s. 149-150.

Hareide, Dag, *Conflict Mediation,* Nordic Forum for Mediation and Conflict Management (forthcoming 2007).

Harrington, Christine and Merry, Sally Engle: *Ideological Production: The Making of Community Mediation,* Law and Soc.Rev. Vol. 22, No 4, 1988.

Harrington, Christine, *Shadow Justice, The Ideology and Institutionalization of Alternatives to Court*, London 1985.

Hartwig, Ernest, *Om frivillige Forligs og Vekslers Eksigibilitet*, in Juristen 1939, s. 318-322.

Haynes, John, *Mediating Divorce, A Casebook of Strategies for Successful family Negotiations*, San Francisco 1989.

Haynes, John and Gretchen L., *Mediating Divorce,* San Francisco 1989.

Haynes, J, Haynes G., and Fong, L. *Mediation*, Amazon, 2004.

Heilesen, C.C., *Om Forligsmægling i borgerlige Sager (Compromise in Court in Civil Cases)*, UfR 1920B, s. 65-68.

Hildebrandt, S. and Stubberup, H, *Bæredygtig ledelse (Sustainable Leadership)*, Gyldendal Business 2010.

Hostrup, Hanne, *Gestaltterapi*, Copenhagen 1999.

Hume, Cameron A, *A Diplomat's View*, in Zartman 1997.

Humle, Anne Suzette, *En samtale – To vindere* (*One dialogue – two winners*), Albertslund 1993.

Hurwitz, Stephan, *Tvistemaal*, 1. udg., Copenhagen 1941.

Hurwitz, Stephan, *Tvistemål*, 3. udg., Copenhagen 1965.

Hyman, Jonathan M. and Love, Lela P., *If Portia Were A Mediator, An Inquiry Into Justice In Mediation*, Clinical Law Review, Vol. 9, no. 1, 2002.

IDEA (UNDP), *Democratic Dialogue – a Handbook for Practitoners*, New York 2006.

Jakobsson, Ann-Sofi and Øberg, Jan, *Konfliktløsning*, Lund 1994.

Jelvard, Johan, *Om Forligskommissionernes Eksistensberettigelse*, in UfR 1945B, s. 94-96.

Kaye, J.S, *New York State Court Alternative Dispute Re4solution Project, State of New York, Unified Court System, Court Referred ADR in NY State*, Final Report of the Chief Judge's New York State Court Alternative Dispute Resolution Project, 1996.

Kelman, Herbert *Social-Psychological Dimensions in International Conflict*, in Zartman and Rasmussen (ed). *Peacemaking in International Conflict*, Washington 1997.

Keltner, J., *Communications and the Labor-Management Mediation Process, Some Aspects and Hypotheses*, Journal of Communication, 1965, 15(2) s. 64-89.

Kemp, Peter, *Den nye Verdensorden (The new World Order)*, 2007.

Kennedy, Gavin, *How to Negotiate and Win*, London 1982.

Keshavjee, M.M. and Whatling, T., *Reflective Learnings from the training programmes of the Ismaili Muslim conciliation and arbitration boards, globally*, 2005.

Kimmel, Paul R., *Culture and Conflict* in Morton Deutsch, The handbook of Conflict Resolution.

Kirschenbaum, Howard and Henderson, Valerie Land (ed.), *The Carl Rogers Reader*, Constable & Co, London 1989.

Kleiboer, Marieko, *The Multiple Realities of International Mediation*, London 1998.

Kolb, Deborah, *How existing Procedures Shape Alternatives. The Case of Grievance Mediation*, 1989 Journ. Disp. Resol.

Kovach, Kimberlee K., *Mediation, Principles and Practice, sec.ed. Minnesota 2000 and 3. ed. 2004.*

Kovach, Kimberlee K. and Lela P. Love, *Mapping Mediation, The Risk of Riskin's Grid, 3 Harv. Negotiation L. Rev. 71 (1998).*

Kressel, Kenneth and Pruitt, Dean G. (ed.) *Mediation Research, The Process and Effectiveness of Third Pary Intervention, San Francisco,* 1989.

Kriesberg, Louis, *Constructtive Conflicts, From escalation to resolution*, Boston, 1998.

Kristensen, Marianne and Jørgen Bloch-Poulsen, *Dialog og dialogiske kompetencer – en ny form for magt?* (*Dialogue and competencies – a new kind of power*) in Alrø, H. and Kristensen, M. (eds). Dialog og magt i organisationer, Ålborg 2004.

Lang, Michael D. and Taylor, Alison, *The Making of a Mediator*, San Francisco, 2000.

Lax, David A. and Sibenius, James K., *The Manager as Negotiatior*, New York 1986.

Lederach, John Paul, *The Little book of Conflict Transformation*, Good Books, Intercourse, PA 2003.

Lederach, John Paul, Building Peace, *Sustainable Reconciliation in Divided Societies*, Washington 2000.

Lederach, John Paul, in David Augsburger: *Mediation across Cultures*, 1992.

Lewis Rasmussen, J., *Peacemaking in The Twenty-First Century*, in Peacemaking in International Conflict, Washington 1991.

Littlejohn, S.W and Deminici, K *Engaging Communication in Conflict*, 2000.

Love, Lela Porter, *Twenty-Five Years Later with Promises to Keep, Legal Education in Dispute Resolution and Training of Mediators*, Ohio State Journal on Dispute Resolution, vol. 17, 2002 no. 3, s. 597-607.

Løgstrup, K.E., *Den etiske Fordring (The ethical challenge)*, Copenhagen 1966.

Løgstrup, K.E., *System og Symbol (System and symbol)*, Copenhagen 1997, 2. udgave.

Løgstrup, KE., *Om spontane livsytringer i System og Symbol (Spontaneous Life-expressions in systems and symbols)*, Copenahgen 1997

Ludvigsen, Herluf, *En Berigtigelse*, in UfR 1947B, s. 280.

Ludvigsen, Herluf, *Effektiv Forligsmægling inden Retssag*, in UfR 1947B, s. 63.

Maggiolo, W., *Techniques of Mediation in Labor Disputes*, New York 1972.

Rosenberg, Marshall, *Ikke-voldelig kommunikation,»Giraf-sprog«. Brug din indfølingsevne og få både dine egne og andres behov tilgodeset*, (*Non-violent communicaation*), Borgen 1999.

Maslow, Abraham, *Motivation and Personality*, New York 1954.

Menkel-Meadow, Carrie, *Toward Another View on Negotiation, The Structure of Legal Problem Solving, 31 UCLA L. Rev. 1984 s 754ff*, 1984.

Metze, Erno and Nystrup, Jørgen, *Samtaletræning, Håndbog i præcis kommunikation, (Training dialogue – a Handbook in precise communication)*, Copenhagen, 1992.

Michael, David E., *Civil Litigation in 21. Century*, presentation at seminar arranged by Domstolsstyrelsen, Justitsministeriet og Det danske Advokatsamfund, Copenhagen, juli 2002.

Moffitt, M. *Ten ways to get sued: A Guide for Mediators*, 8 Harvard Negotiation Law Review, 81 (2003).

Monk, G. and Winslade, J., (ed.), *Narrative Therapy in Practice*, San Francisco 1996.

Monookin, Robert, *When Negotiations Fail, An Exploration of Barriers to the Resolution of Conflict*, The Ohio State Journal of Dispute Resolution, vol. 8 no. 2, s. 235-249, 1993.

Moore, Christopher W., *The Mediation Process, Practical Strategies for Resolving Conflict*, San Fransisco, 1996, sec. ed.

Mthembu-Salter, Gregory, *Mediation and Genocide, the case of Rwanda*, Center for Conflict Resolution, Cape Town 1999.

Munch-Petersen, *Den Danske Civilproces I Hovedtræk*, Copenhagen 1906.

Næss, Arne, *Gandhi and Group Conflict, An Exploration of Satyagraha, Theoretical Background*, Oslo 1974.

Neergaard, Preben, *Forligsmægling*, in UfR 1947B, s 94.

Odendaal, Andries, Modelling mediation. *Evolving approaches to mediation in South Africa*, Track Two 7:1 (April 1998), pp. 11-14.

Petterson, Knut, *Rettsmekling i Praksis (Mediation in Courts in Practice)*, Oslo 2001.

Raiffa, Howard, *The Art and Science of Negotiation*, Cambridge 1982.

Ramsbotham, O., Woodhouse, T. and Miall, H. *Contemporary Conflict Resolution*. Sec.ed., 2005.

Rasmussen, J. Lewis, *Peacemaking in the Twenty-First Century, in Peacemaking in International Conflict*, Washington 1991.

Riskin, Len., *Understanding Mediators' Orienttations, strategies and Techniques: A Grid for the Perplexed*, Harvard Law Review, vol. 1, 1996 s. 7-50.

Roehl, Janice A. and Cook, Royer F., *Mediation in Interpersonal Disputes, Effectiveness and Limitations, in Mediation Research, The Process and Effectiveness of Third Party Intervention 33*.

Rogers, Carl, *The Non-Directive Method as a Technique of Social Research*, American Journal of Sociology, 1974, 50(4).

Rosenberg, M, *Nonviolent Communication: A Language of Compassion*, Copenhagen 1999.

Rosenberg, M., *Resolving Disputes Differently, Adieu to Adversary Justice?* 21 Chreighton L. Rev. 1988 s. 801.

Ross, Alf, *Hvorfor Demokrati?*, Copenhagen 1946 *(English version, Why Democracy?, 1952)*.

Ross, Alf, *Om Ret og Retfærdighed (About Law and Justice)*, Copenhagen 1953.

Rothes, A.B., »*Memoire sur l'origine et l'organisation des Committés conciliateurs en Dannemarc*«, 1803.

Rubin, J., Pruitt, D. and Kim, D., *Social Conflict*, New York, 1896.

Rummel, R.J., *The conflict Helix, Principles and Practices of Interpersonal, Social and International Conflict and Cooperation*, New Brunswick 1991.

Rummel, R.J., *Understanding Conflict and War*, Vols. 1 & 2, New York 1976.

Sachs, ALbie, *The Strange Alchemy of Life and Law*, Oxford 2009

Salvesen, Paul Leer, *Menneske og Straff (Man ans punishement)*, Oslo 1991.

Salvesen, Paul Leer, *Tilgivelse (Forgiveness)*, Oslo 1999.

Salvesen, Paul Leer, *Forsoning etter krenkelser (Forgiveness – after serious assaults)*, Bergen 2009.

Sander, Frank EA, *Varieties of Dispute Processing*, oplæg på Pond Conference, 1976.
Schön, A. Donald, *The Reflective Practitioner*, San Fransisco 1987.
Schulz, www.campus-adr.org, Vol.3 No 2, February 2003.
Smith, Eva, *Civilproces*, 2. udg. 1991.
Smith, Eva, *Civilproces (Law of Civil Procedure)*, 4. udg. 2000.
Sousa Santos, Boaventura de, *The Politics of Informal Justice*, in Abel, R.(ed), The Contradiction of Informal Justice, New York 1982.
Stevens, C., *Strategy in Collective Bargaining Negotiations*, New York, 1963.
Stulberg, Joseph, *The Theory and Practice of Mediation, A Reply to Professor Suskind*, 6. Vermont Law Rev. 1981 B 6 (1) s. 85-117.
Suskind, L, *Enviromental Mediation and the Accountability Problem*, Vermont Law Rev. 1981 B 6 (1) s. 46-47.
Svedstrup, G., *Forligskommissionerne*, in UfR B, 1927 s.126.
Taksøe-Jensen, *Materiel Procesledelse*, Copenhagen 1976.
Tamm, Ditlev, *Den danske »Constitution« og den franske revolution*, in UfR 1989B s. 449-460.
Thesbjerg, J., »*Sagen henvist til Retten*«, in UfR 1947B s 95-96.
Tongeren, Paul von (eds), *People Building Peace II, Successful Stories of Civil Society*, Colorado 2005.
Touval, Saadia and Zartmann, I.W., (ed.), *The Man in the Middle, International Mediation in Theory and Practice*, Colorado 1985.
Tutu, Desmond, *No Future Withour Forgiveness*, London 1999.
Tutu, Desmond, *God has a Dream*, London 2004.
Umbreit, Marc, *Victim meets Offender, The impact of Restorative Justice and Mediation*, New York 1994.
Umbreit, Marc, *Humanistic Mediation: A Transformaqtive Journey of Peacemaking*, Mediation Quaterly 1997.
Vedfelt, Ole *Ubevidst Intelligens (Unconscious Intelligence)*, Copenhagen 2000.
Vedfelt, Ole, *Bevidsthed (Awareness)*, Copenhagen 1998.
Viemose, Søren, *Forhandlingsteknik (Negotiation Techniques)*, Copenhagen 1992.
Viemose, Søren, *Forhandlingsteknik – Nye muligheder gennem påvirkning og opbygning af tillid (Negotiation Techniques – New Possibilities through influence and building of trust)*, Copenhagen 2000.
Vindeløv, Vibeke, *Japan som med- og modspiller i civilretlige konflikter (Jaoan as co-and counterpart in civil law conflicts)*, TIR 1990 s. 889-906.
Vindeløv, Vibeke, *Retssikkerhed og konfliktløsning i civile sager*, Juristen nr. 9/10 1992 s. 397-404.
Vindeløv, Vibeke, *Ecology of Mind as a Decisive Basis in Conflict Resolution – A Preliminary Comparison between Japan and Denmark*, p. 66-77, Retfærd 1994.
Vindeløv, Vibeke, *Er mægling anvendelig i internationale børnebortførelsessager?(Is mediation possible in cases of international*

child abduction?), in Årbog for Forskningsenhed II, p. 121-135 University of Copenhagen, 2003.

Vindeløv, Vibeke, *Konflikt, Tvist og Mægling (Conflict, Dispute and Mediation (with English summary),* Copenhagen 1997.

Vindeløv, Vibeke, *Konfliktråd, tribunaler og sandhedskommissioner* (*Conflict counsels, tribunals and truth commissions*) in »Med lov ...«, Retsvidenskabelige betragtninger, Flemming Balvig and Jørn Vestergaard (red.), festskrift til Vagn Greve, Copenhagen 1998.

Vollmond, H., *Forligsmægling,* in von Eyben (red.): Proceduren, Copenhagen 1980.

von Eyben, W.E., *Dommertilkendegivelser*, Copenhagen 1987.

Wallensteen, Peter, *Från krig till fred, Om konfliktlösning i det globala systemet(From war to peace. About conflict resolution in the global system),* Eskilstuna 1994 (2008).

Watzlawick, P., *Change, Principles of Problem Formation and Problem Resolution,* New York 1974.

Weirsø, Bodil, *Girafsprog. Empatisk kommunikation i pædagogens arbejde,* Copenhagen, 2002.

White, R.K., *Fearful Warriors, A Psychological profile of U.S-Soviet relations,* New York 1984.

Whyte (ed.*), Industry and Society,* New York 1946.

Wilber, Ken, *Up from Eden, A transpersonal View of Human Evolution, Boston 19812.*

Williams, Gerald, *Legal Negotiation and Settlement, Minnesota,* 1983.

Wilmot, W. and Hocker, J., *Interpersonal Conflict*, McGraw-Hill, 6. ed. 2001.

Winslade and Monk, (ed.), *Narrative Therapy in Practice*, San Francisco 1996.

Wæver, Ole, *Securitization and Desecuritization,* in Ronnie D. Lipschutz (ed.) On security, New York 1995.

Winslade and Monk, *A New Approach to Conflict Resolution*, Jossey-Bass, 2000.

Young, O., *Intermediaries, Additional Thoughts on Third Parties,* Journal of Conflict Resolution, 1972 16(1).[1]

Zahle, Henrik, *Omsorg for Retfærdighed – Essays om Retlig Praksis (Caring for Justice – an Essay about Legal Practice),* Copenhagen 2003.

Zartman and Rasmussen (ed.), *Peacemaking in International Conflict,* Washington 1997.

Zartman, W., *Ripe for Resolution, Conflict and Intervention in Africa,* Oxford, 1989.

Zartman, W. and Touval, S. (ed.), *The Man in the Middle: International Mediation in Theory and Practice,* Colorado 1985.

Zehr, Howard, *The Little Book of Restorative Justice*, USA 2002.

Øberg, Jan and Ann-Sofi Jacobsson, *Konfliktløsning. En litteraturguide,* Lund 1994.

Index

A
a provision in contract *231*
a re-negotiation clause *322*
a structured process *53*
a zero sum *124*
accusation *256*
acknowledgement *117*
active listening *260*
advisers *247*
agenda *286*
aggression *64*
agreement *39*
agreement for a limited period *310*
agreement-focused model *41*
aids for the mediator *297*
Alrø, Helle *96*
amnesia *179*
an agreement is negotiated *56*
anxiety *74*
Arendt, Hannah *172*
atmosphere *245*
attorneys *132*
Aubert, V. *67*
Austbø, Anne *235, 325*
authority to take decisions *249*
avoidance *64*

B
Balvig, Flemming *200*
Barnard, C.I. *159*
Bateson, Gregory *64*
BATNA *137*
Bercovitch, Jacob *189*
Berkowitz, L. *74*
Berliner, Peter *61*
Best Alternative to a Negotiated Agreement *137*
bias *330*
blame *73*
Blechman, Frank *221*
Bloch-Poulsen, Jørgen *96*
Bono de *289*
Boserup, Hans *304*
Boulding, Kenneth *162*
Braiker, H.B. *58*
brain-storming *130*
breaks, focus on the future *299*
Brown, H. *135*
Buber, Martin *172*
build a bridge *118*
Burton, John *108*
Burton's application of needs to conflict resolution *108*
Bush, Baruch *20*
Butterfield, Herbert *188*
Buzan, Barry *193*

C
cartoons *70*
Center for Konfliktløsning *69*
Centre for Conflict Resolution (CCR) *151*
Centre for Effective Dispute Resolution (CEDR) *42*
Centre for the Study of Violence and Reconciliation in South Africa *173*
Christiansen, Lone Illum *318*
civil procedure *323*
clarification of roles *333*
clarifying questions *113*
Clausen, Steen *198*
Clausewitz, Claus von *188*
Cloke, Kenneth *92*
closed questions *113*
code of conduct *219*
co-existence *81*

cognitive barrier *140*
cognitive model *42*
Coleman, Peter T. *158*
co-mediation *241*
communication techniques *260*
community *37*
community values *45*
compromise *125*
concept of a 'party' *236*
concrete proposals *256*
condition of life *31*
confidentiality *53*
conflict ladder *79*
conflicting interests *296*
conflicts of interest *67, 337*
conflicts of values *67*
confrontational questions *115*
connected *39*
connection between facts and feelings *112*
consent to mediation *234*
contact facilitators *93*
continuing relationship *310*
Cook, Royer F. *321*
co-operation *135*
co-operative negotiator *125*
courage *198*
creating value *267*
creative options *128*
Creighton, J. *112*
cultural factors *107*
culture *98*
Curle, Adam *197*
cycle of conflict *65*

D
Danish Law *323*
deadlock *301*
decision-making authority *327*
declarations of intent *311*
de-escalation *83*
defendant *236*
definition of active listening *112*
definition of conflicts *60*
definition of contact *93*
definition of dialogue *96*
definition of empathy *95*
definition of mediation *52*
definition of negotiation *122*
definition of the problem area *56*
Demenici, Kathy *97*
democracy *14*
Deutsch, Morton *73, 135*
dialogue *31, 87*
Diamond, Louise *180*
different *151*
difficult situations *329*
dilemma of security *187*
dimensions of a conflict *66, 279*
disagreement *64*
dispute *62*
distributive justice *164*
dominance *25*
double acknowledgement *117*
draft agreement *304*
Druckman, David *66*
duty to be active *54*
duty to contradict *54*
Dworkin, Joan *92*

E
early evaluation *25*
ecology *38*
effective negotiation *132*
El Salvador *201*
empowerment *258*
Engebretsen, Geir *235, 325*
enlarging the pie *128*
escalation *57*
ethical dilemma *272*
Ethical Standards of Professional Responsibility *221*
ethics *205*
EU Member States *147*
evaluative mediation *208*
evaluative-broad *209*
evidence *147*
exchange information *255*
existential truth *90*
extent of confidentiality *144*

F
facial expression *255*
facilitated discussion *173*
facilitative-broad *209*
facilitative-narrow *209*
factual matters *304*
failed negotiations *138*
fairness *55*
fear *74*
Fisher, Roger *128*
Fisher, Simon *180, 187*
Fledelius, Karsten *177*
flip-chart *280*
Folger, Joe *20*
Follett, Mary Parker *159*
follow-up with the parties *317*
Fong, Larry *20*
Foreningen for Mediation og Konfliktmægling *220*
forgiveness *45*
formal requirements for an agreement *314*
freedom *25*
Freud *26*

G
Galtung, Johan *59, 180*
Gamborg, Helen *89*
Gammelgaard, Judy *95*
general amnesty *204*
generation of possible solutions *56*
genuine conflicts *61, 66*
Ghandi, Mahatma *267*
Gifford, D. *125*
giraffe language *84*
give and take *123*
global village *98*
Goleman, Daniel *95*
Gordon, T. *112*
group them by topic *297*
Grundtvig, N.F.S. *218*

H
Hammerich, Else *79*
Haynes, John and Gretchen L. *137*
headings *283*
Henderson, Valerie Land *95*
Henriksen, Claus Syberg *318*
Herz, John H. *188*
hidden agenda *260*
hierarchy of positions *105*
Hillel, Rabbi *172*
Hocker, J. *65*
hostile feelings *269*
hostility *81*
Hostrup, Hanne *93*
humanistic model *44*
Hume, Cameron R. *197*
Humle, Anne Suzette *113, 119*
humour *246*
hypothetical questions *292*

I
illusion about power *157*
imbalance of power *136*
impartiality *53, 149*
individual *39*
individual amnesty *204*
individualism *224*
individuality *31*
initiative for mediation *231*
injury *256*
injustice *266*
instrumental conflicts *67*
interdependent *39*
interpersonal conflicts *60*
intrapersonal conflicts *61*

J
Jacob, Lynn *92*
Sibenius *121*
joint meeting *302*
judge *26*
justice *163*
justice from above *168*
justice from below *168*
justified reaction *104*

K
Kaye, Judith S. *213*
keeping the problem and the person separate *79*
Keith, G. Allred *73*
Kelley, H.H. *58*
Kennedy, Gavin *124*
Keshavjee, Mohamed M. *101*
Kierkegaard, Søren *218*
Kim, S. *72*
Kimmel, Paul *100*
Kirschenbaum, Howard *95*
Kleiboer, Marieke *197*
Knoff, Roald *325*
Koch, Hal *218*
Kolb, Deborah *210*
Kovach, Kimberlee *205*
Kowach, Kimberlee *122*
Kressel, Kenneth *321*
Kriesberg, Louis *72*
Kristiansen, Marianne *96*

L
lack of motivation *326*
Lampen, John and Diane *78*
language of escalation *83*
lateral thinking *288*
lawyers *91*
Lax, David A. *121*, *123*, *138*, *191*
Lederach, John Paul *101*
legal concern *304*
legal consequence *304*
liability *205*, *226*
life cycle *65*
litigation *37*
Littlejohn, Stephen W. *97*
losing *59*
loss aversion *140*
Love, Lela P. *205*
Luskin, Frederic *20*, *45*
Løgstrup, K.E. *158*, *174*, *218*

M
Maggiolo, W. *269*
manager as mediator *155*
manipulation *272*
Marriott, A. *135*
Maslow, Abraham *107*
maximise gains *132*
McDonald, John *180*
meaningful life *224*
mediation and therapy *92*
mediation in groups *259*
mediation initiated by the parties' employer *234*
mediator *330*
Menkel-Meadow, Carrie *131*
mental preparations *240*
metaphor *22*
metatheory *25*
Metze, Erno *113*
miracle question *292*
misinterpretations *270*
misunderstandings *270*
moderating high expectations *302*
Mohammed *70*
Monk, Gerald *20*
Monookin, Robert *140*
monopoly of truth *39*
Moore, Christopher *42*
moral impartiality *152*
moral obligation *311*
morality *223*
Mthembu-Salter, Gregory *197*
multiparty mediation *242*
mutual dependence *57*
mutually satisfactory solution *31*

N
narrative model *44*
narrow mediation *206*
narrow-evaluative *209*
negative atmosphere *328*
negotiating strength *134*
negotiation 'minuet' *122*
neighbour dispute *309*
neutrality *53*, *149*

non-binding arbitration *25*
normative conflicts *68*
note taking *250*
Nystrup, Jørgen *113*
Næss, Arne *59*

O
objective criteria *128*
objective truth *39*
Odendaal, Andries *152*
offender *44*
open questions *113*
opening *56*
opponent *39, 124*
oral agreements *322*

P
Paradigms *37*
Pareto-optimality *268*
payment *237, 330*
perpetrators *179*
personal challenge *57*
phases *65*
philosophy *26*
physical needs *107*
physical preparations *239*
plaintiff *236*
point of despair *301*
polarisation *82*
positions *125*
post-mediation conduct *319*
potential of dialogue *97*
power *135*
prejudices *24*
preventing conflict *82*
prevention *204*
principle of confidentiality *54*
principle of equality *165*
principle of need *165*
principle of reasonableness *165*
principle of relativity *54*
principle of responsibility *54*
problem-solving *41*
problem-solving negotiator *127*
problem-solving strategy *127*
procedural justice *164*
procedural satisfaction *312*
professional activity *57*
professional brotherhood *338*
professional liability *238*
professional respect 338
professionally liability *238*
prophet *70*
prophet Mohammed *77*
Pruitt, Dean G. *72, 321*
pseudo conflicts *61*
psychological reaction *71*
psychological satisfaction *313*
punishment *204*

R
Raiffa, Howard *121*
Ramsbotham, Oliver *139*
Rasmussen, Lewis J. *185*
realists *192*
reality *31*
reality testing *300*
reconciliation *45*
reflection of feelings *115*
reflective practitioner *216*
reflective questions *292*
reframing *119*
relation *31*
relations *46*
rent-a-judge *25*
reparative/restorative justice *165*
repetition *115*
rephrasing *119*
representatives *327*
responsibility *332*
responsible relationship *224*
restate the roles *336*
restoration *55*
result *39*
retributive *165*
Richardt, Christian *168*
ripe moment *65, 138, 191*
risk aversion *139*
Riskin, Leonard *205*
risks and losses *139*
Roehl, Janice A. *321*
Rogers, Carl *84, 112*

role model *261*
Rosenberg, Marshall *84*
Ross, Alf *14*
Rubin, J. *72*
rules of conduct *248*
Rummel, R.J. *65, 72, 162*

S
Salvesen, Paul Leer *171*
sanctions *39*
Scandinavian non-model *21*
Schön, Donald A. *216*
Scott, Elisabeth *92*
secrecy *145*
security *107*
self-determination *44*
self-realisation *107*
self-respect *44, 107*
separate meeting *252*
share, dare and care *96*
Sibenius, James K. *123, 138, 191*
silence *114*
single text procedure *293*
social reality *59*
spiral of defence *74*
spiral of revenge *74*
Stevens, C. *268*
strength *135*
Stulberg, Joseph *212*
sub-headings *283*
substantial satisfaction *313*
substantive issue *46*
Sufi tradition *88*
summarising *114*
superficial arbitration *25*
supervision group *319*
Susskind, Lawrence *20*

T
technical impartiality *152*
terminating the mediation *265*
the agreement conditional *318*
the agreement is checked and approved *56*
the competitive negotiator *124*
the conflict ladder *279*
the Copenhagen school *193*
the good agreement *312*
the submissions of the parties and dialogue *56*
The Swedish Folke Bernadotte Academy *184*
threats *74*
timing *65*
to a joint meeting *278*
trade union representative *236*
transformative model *43*
transition *278*
TRC *202*
tribunals in Rwanda *200*
tribunals in The Hague *200*
trust *171*
truth *39, 87*
Truth Commission *201*
Tutu, Desmond *171*

U
Umbreit, Mark *20, 45*
unpopular agreements *328*
Ury *128*

V
validation *116*
value for money *326*
Vedfelt, Ole *95*
venting *257*
vertical thinking *130, 288*
Vestergaard, Bjarne *79*
Vestergaard, Jørn *200*
victims *44*
Viemose, Søren *121*
view of conflicts *58*
view of humanity *27*
voluntary participation *143*
voluntary principle *54*

W
Wallensteen, Peter *139, 185*
WATNA *137*
Watzlawick, P. *119*
weakness *125*
Weirsøe, Bodil *85*

Whatling, Tony *101*
White, R.K. *77*
Wilde, Jaap de *193*
Williams *125*
Williams, Gerald *133*
Wilmot, W. *65*
winning *59*
Winslade, John *20*
Worst Alternative to a Negotiated Agreement *137*
written contract *237*
Wæver, Ole *193*

Y

Young, O. *268*

Z

Zartman, I.W. *66*
Zartmann *139*
zero sum thinking *78*

Ø

Øberg, Jan *35*